T0358231

The Varieties of Economic Rationality

This book explores the central concept every economist or social thinker uses to describe how people behave in their economic relations. The concept of economic rationality commonly stipulates that every person behaves as a rational maximizer, calculating the gains and losses from every economic decision taken.

Applying the methods of the history of economic thought, with textual exegesis and as close as possible to the meaning of the original text, this historical account focuses on the work of those economists who have significantly contributed to the creation of a new concept of economic rationality. This book examines the contributions of Adam Smith, John Stuart Mill, Vilfredo Pareto, Lionel Robbins, Herbert Simon, and others.

The idea of a monolithic way of economic thinking is challenged and the reader will discover that economists used in the past, and continue to use, many different paths of thought about how economic agents behave. Furthermore, it is asserted that economics can no more pretend to explain economic reality unless it abandons the atomistic view of the rational individual choosing freely.

Michel S. Zouboulakis is Professor in the History and Methodology of Economics at the University of Thessaly, Greece.

Routledge studies in the history of economics

The Varieties of Economic Rationality

From Adam Smith to contemporary behavioural and evolutionary economics

Michel S. Zouboulakis

Routledge
Taylor & Francis Group

LONDON AND NEW YORK

First published 2014
by Routledge
2 Park Square, Milton Park, Abingdon, Oxon OX14 4RN

and by Routledge
711 Third Avenue, New York, NY 10017

Routledge is an imprint of the Taylor & Francis Group, an informa business

British Library Cataloguing in Publication Data
A catalogue record for this book is available from the British Library

Library of Congress Cataloging in Publication Data
Zouboulakis, Michel S.
The varieties of economic rationality : from Adam Smith to contemporary
behavioural and evolutionary economics / Michel S. Zouboulakis.
    pages cm
    1. Rational expectations (Economic theory)–History. 2. Rational choice
    theory–History. 3. Economics–History. I. Title.
    HB3731.Z68 2014
    330.15–dc23   2013030445

ISBN: 978-0-415-53084-2 (hbk)
ISBN: 978-1-315-81864-1 (ebk)

Typeset in Times
by Wearset Ltd, Boldon, Tyne and Wear

**To Martha, Tatiana and Andreas and to their
promising generation**

Contents

Preface and acknowledgements

This book is about the "hard-core" concept of rationality that underlies every explanation of the discipline of economics. My involvement with this concept started during my PhD studies in Paris in the mid-1980s, when I first read my supervisor's published PhD thesis *La formation d'une rationalité économique: A.A. Cournot* (Claude Ménard, 1978). I do not remember if I ever asked him directly "*pourquoi une?*", but I do remember quite well that this significant little word "*une*" had triggered a chain reaction in my mind: If there is "one kind of rationality" there must be some other kinds too! How many are they? Why are there so many? What are the implications for our discipline for having several "rationalities"? Is this not a scientific weakness for having so many? Briefly, I had found my own "*pierre philosophale*" and I felt so happy for it leads to immortality, according to the legend.

While undertaking my PhD work concerning the post-Ricardian epistemological tradition, I read few seminal texts by Sen (1977), Brochier (1981) and Arrow (1986) that acted as sources of inspiration and helped me to realize the depth of the problem. I feel indebted to them for the road they paved in my mind.

Many others have read, discussed and criticized various aspects of this book during conferences, seminars and courses. I should thank mostly the discussants and participants of various conferences for their suggestive remarks, and particularly Tony Aspromourgos and Philippe Fontaine (Strasbourg 2007), Sheila Dow (Stirling 2005), Wade Hands (Crete 2002), Daniel Hausman and Philippe Mongin (Paris 1997), Geoffrey Hodgson (Crete 2004), Uskali Mäki (Athens 2012), Peter Rosner and Eyup Ozveren (Paris 2003), Nathalie Sigot (Treviso 2004), Philippe Steiner (Valencia 1999) and of course several anonymous referees involved with the publications mentioned below.

During the last ten years, as a member of the scientific committee of the *European Summer School on the History of Economic Thought, Economic*

Philosophy and Economic History, I have significantly improved my views, discussing day and night with young (and less young) colleagues several aspects of this work and I feel obliged to recognize it publicly. I mostly thank André Lapidus, Richard Arena, Jose Luis Cardoso, Ragip Ege, Jean-Sebastien Lenfant, Jean-Pierre Potier, Annalisa Rosselli, Ramon Tortajada and Nathalie Sigot.

I am also grateful for all the help given by my friends and colleagues, the late Tassos Karayiannis, and Stavros Drakopoulos, Aris Hatzis, Christos Kollias, Nicholas Kyriazis, Dimitri Milonakis, Michalis Psalidopoulos, Iakovos Psarianos, Nicholas Theocharakis, Giorgos Stathakis, Ioannis Theodosiou, Lefteris Tsoulfidis and Yanis Varoufakis.

Pantelis Agianoglou has provided precious help, reading the entire manuscript and editing the English text.

Earlier versions of some parts of this book have appeared in print as separate articles or chapters in English, French and Greek language. I am grateful for permission to draw on material previously published in *History of Economic Ideas*, *Social Science Information*, *European Journal of the History of Economic Thought*, *Cahiers d'Economie Politique*, *Journal of Institutional Economics* and *Forum for Social Economics*.

Let the reader be aware that I remain solely responsible for any remaining errors and deficiencies.

Introduction

The role of the concept of economic rationality is essential to economics as a scientific discipline. It serves as the fundamental behavioural premise in every economic explanation, and in neoclassical economics it even guarantees the very existence of the discipline. The history of a concept goes far beyond its official definition by his or her founder. It often involves discovering implicit assumptions or mental representations in order to reveal particular expressions acting as indirect manifestations of an underlying conceptual development. This book is about the central concept that every economist or social thinker uses to describe how people behave in their economic relations. Still, the widespread idea about this concept, even between economists, is that it has a unique meaning universally accepted, from Adam Smith to the present. Thus, the concept of economic rationality commonly stipulates that every person is supposed to behave as a rational maximizer, which entails the calculation of the gains and losses from every economic decision that one takes. This is the widely portrayed image of the *homo oeconomicus*. Our purpose here is to establish that "economic rationality" is neither a unique nor a universal concept and has different, and often conflicting, interpretations in the evolution of the economic discourse. To achieve this, we will trace the historical evolution of the concept of economic rationality. It will be thus confirmed that this concept has many – no less than 12 – different meanings since the end of the eighteenth century. It is on the rich details of this conceptual transformation that we will focus in establishing the overall historical character of economic rationality.

Our objective is to tell a story about how the ideas of economists about rational economic man have evolved over the ages. To tell this story some fundamental questions will be asked: What is the purpose of an economic agent when making exchanges? How that person does choose? What makes one choice rational? What is the relation between rational choice and the psychology of the chooser? How do we know that a person acts rationally? What are the means of justification of the assumption of rationality? What is the range of validity of this assumption? What are the consequences for having a greater or smaller range of validity for the discipline of economics? In trying to answer these questions it is argued that "economic rationality" is far from being a universal concept with a unique meaning. Thus, the idea of a monolithic way of economic thinking is challenged and the reader will discover that economists held in the past, and continue to hold, many different trains of thought about how economic agents behave.

This is the work of a historian of economic thought, applying the methods of the field, with textual exegesis, as close as possible to the meaning of the original text. According to an old tradition, the aim of "the history of science consists in making perceptible – and for that reason intelligible – the complex, troubled, built-in and corrected edification of scientific knowledge" (Canguilhem 1968: 178, our translation). In doing so, one must discover behind the word rationality the true meaning of the concept employed by its author. Consequently, the history of the concept of rationality does not progress linearly, but, as just said, in a complex and contradictory way, following the historical evolution of the discipline. Thus, it will be proved that the words "rational" and "rationality" do not possess the same meaning from Adam Smith to Vernon Smith. Economic rationality can be characterized by self-interested goals or not. Behaving altruistically is not always equivalent to behaving irrationally. To many authors, rationality is mainly about the rational choice of means, whatever the goals are. In that sense, one can choose rationally to destroy someone else or even himself. Over and over again, rationality becomes only an instrumental concept, as for example in such different authors as Hume, Pareto and Nash. In the neoclassical mode of thinking, the economic is identical to the rational; while in some heterodox authors a great part of economic actions do not involve this kind of rationality at all.

The book is organized in 12 chapters. The chapters follow *grosso modo* the evolution of the 12 different varieties of rationality. For reasons that will be explained in the text, a choice of authors was made according to their significant contribution in the conceptual development of the concept: Authors are not chosen according to their overall significance to the discipline. This is not a book telling the story of the greatest economists of all times. Several economists of huge importance for the history of economic thought are missing (such as Ricardo, Fisher and Sraffa), while others are discussed very briefly (such as Cournot, Walras and Marshall). The main criterion to be part of our historical account was to have significantly contributed to the creation of a new concept of economic rationality.

Chapter 1 deals with the concept of rationality in Adam Smith. The great Scotsman had a unified view about human behaviour so as to subordinate his economic analysis to his moral philosophy. Economic behaviour in Smith is contained by moral sentiments. The demarcation from morals was established by John Stuart Mill, who has built upon the abstract method of David Ricardo, to justify the creation of a partial and limited science of political economy. As seen in Chapter 2, to sustain his deductive method of economic explanation, Mill recommends a principle of economic rationality that describes how a person, belonging to a particular geographical and historical context, behaves during his economic activities under the influence of the fundamental economic motive, namely the "desire of wealth".

Until the marginalist revolution, economic rationality was nothing but the fundamental behavioural assumption of economic explanation. In Chapter 3 we describe how this principle became the fundamental characteristic of the economic approach to the social phenomena. Jevons and the marginalists, following Cournot, introduced the principle of rationality (hereafter PR) as maximization in order to make possible the application of the differential calculus in economic analysis. This innovation was the result of a dramatic reduction of the scope of economics and of a radical separation from its social and historical preoccupations. But, the marginalist project was based upon a very strong commitment to utilitarianism. Many social thinkers believed that utilitarianism and utilitarianists' elementary psychology were excessively restrictive. Vilfredo Pareto made the first decisive step to liberate economics from hedonistic psychology, as it will be seen in Chapter 4. His significant contribution established the concept of instrumental rationality according to which economists have to care only for the objective results of rational choice, not for the motives and the aims of the choosing individuals. Pareto succeeded in cleaning out the relics of hedonistic subjectivism only by confining the field of economics to the study of "logical actions". Chapter 5 presents Robbins' masterful redefinition of the field thanks to the idea of scarcity. The most popular definition of economics ever, as the study of "human behaviour as a relationship between ends and scarce means which have alternative uses" asked for a new concept of rationality. Consistency becomes the alter ego of rationality for 50 years, and it is upon this concept that the general equilibrium model is constructed.

As with rationality as maximization, rationality as consistency faces many problems when confronted with reality. The 1930s was a decade full of criticism against the neoclassical research program and its fundamental assumptions. Many economists are aware of the bright contributions of Edward Chamberlin and Joan Robinson contesting the perfect competition hypothesis. Fewer economists know the harsh criticisms of Hutchison, Hall, Hitch and Lester against the validity of the rationality assumption, and Chapter 6 attempts to expose this important episode in the development of our discipline. Circumstances were aggravated after Keynes' theoretical contribution, and the insights of Hayek and Coase, all in the very same year, 1937, diminished the credibility of the neoclassical theory. Chapter 7 examines how these unconcerted attacks were eschewed by the neoclassicals by means of conventionalist arguments. The attempt to refute the irrefutable maximization hypothesis has failed, while the methodological arguments of Hayek and Hutchison remained unheard. Machlup used the ideal-type construction as an excuse to save rationality as maximization. Samuelson contributed to offer more reliability to Friedman, thanks to his methodological awkwardness, and the latter became the hero of neoclassical economists through his "surprising twist". Instead of offering counterevidence against the criticisms, he invented a methodological stratagem (the "as if" argument), overemphasizing the importance of prediction against explanation. As seen in Chapter 8, Popper advances a conventionalist argument of the same kind. His original "principle of complete rationality" was empirically false, and knowingly so.

The first serious attempt to construct an alternative PR dealing with the problems of risk and uncertainty and to apprehend theoretically the undisputed fact that people interact with other people when they make exchanges, was made in game theory. Chapter 9 presents John von Neumann, Oskar Morgenstern, John Nash and Leonard Savage and their effort to construct strategic rationality. Chapter 10 examines Herbert Simon's effort to downsize the claims of rationality as maximization, suggesting a PR that is less ambitious but more realistic. Bounded rationality is a general alternative to optimization and helps economists to explain real time economic choices. In fact, Simon takes again the road to psychology, focusing on the process of rational decision making. This road will be developed further by psychologists, not only to refute rationality as consistency, but also as a basis of new concept grounded on experimental data. This is the subject of Chapter 11. In Chapter 12, we examine two distinctive alternatives to build the rationality of the socially embedded individual. The last meaning of rationality is empirically sound (i.e. non-tautological and not false) and helps economists to overcome problems due the excessive distance from other social disciplines. Economics comes out less ambitious as to its generality, but more realistic and perhaps more useful.

In our conclusion, some lessons from this historical account of the evolution of the concept of rationality are drawn. Apart from establishing the existence of many varieties of economic rationality, which was our main concern, we suggest that economics can no longer pretend to explain economic reality unless it abandons the atomistic view of the rational individual choosing freely as if he or she was alone in this planet.

1 Adam Smith and the idea of morally constrained rationality

Economics is the scientific study of human activities aiming to produce and distribute wealth, explicitly goods and services that help people to survive and do well. The study of the phenomena of wealth was for a long time connected with the seeking of the best way of social governance and with the finding of solutions to the vital problems of every society. Historically, the development of social sciences is marked by the emancipation of the social endeavour from ethics, in the general movement of the Enlightenment. In that crucial period of the second half of the eighteenth century it was acknowledged that interfering in the evolution of societies was logically following the objective knowledge of social laws. Observation and explanation became an autonomous and self-sufficient goal for all social thinkers who wanted to deal scientifically with social problems. While, thus economic phenomena such as production and commerce in a monetized economy were present since at least the eighth century BC, political economy emerged as a scientific discipline only around 1750, after the stage of commercial capitalism was completed and the significance of economic processes became autonomous and widely visible. What is more significant from our point of view, is that political economy followed historically a great social transformation, as Karl Polanyi has emphasized long ago, "a change in the motive of action on the part of the members of society: for the motive of subsistence that of gain must be substituted" (Polanyi 1944: 41). Adam Smith's work arrives at the edge of the new era of the emancipated economic discourse.

Rationality enters first

The first abstract economic model was plainly established by David Ricardo in 1817. The "*Tableau Economique*", constructed by Francois Quesnay some 60 years later, was essentially a descriptive model not oriented to explain scientifically the workings of economic mechanisms.

Ricardo's non-formal corn model concerned the explanation of long-term evolution of the different shares of national income between the three classes – landowners, capitalists and workers – in such a way as to guarantee the continuous reproduction of the economic system itself. Without fracturing the social frame of economic activities, Ricardo is responsible for offering to political economists the priority to explain theoretically and objectively the mechanisms of the economic system, before any political and practical decision making.[1] In the pre-Ricardian era of political economy, economic thought was still a descriptive intellectual activity normatively oriented. Thus Adam Smith, in his battle against the fallacies of mercantilist policies was forced to explain how an economy would prosper if left to itself to function freely, without the visible hand of the sovereign ruler. To conclude, his brilliant theoretical insights were subordinated to his policy interests.

Yet, the idea of economic rationality – of how a thinker believes people rationally behave in economic activities – emerges long before the establishment of political economy as an autonomous scientific discourse. In David Hume's work (1739) for example there is a clear intention "to posit rationality as the basis of a theory of action" (Lagueux 2010: 50). Hume defines reason as the corollary of human volition, or will. Volition, together with other direct passions – such as joy, grief, hope, fear, desire, aversion – is the internal feeling that people have when they decide to act properly (Hume 1739: 207; cf. Diaye and Lapidus 2005). Yet, reason alone "can never be a motive to any action of the will". According to his famous dictum, "Reason is, and ought only to be the slave of the passions" (Hume 1739: 216). In other words, passions are the generic causes of any feeling of pain or pleasure, and among them it is desire and volition that are at work before any human action (Diaye and Lapidus 2012). But, desire can move a person without the interference of reason, which according to Hume exists to guide human actions through will: "The will exerts itself, when either good can be achieved or evil averted by some action of the mind or body" (Hume 1739: 227). Good and evil are externally given to reason. In that sense reason is only an instrument for achieving ends, and Sugden (1991: 753) rightly says that "Hume provides the most famous statement of the instrumental view of rationality". As seen extensively below, Hume's definition of rationality inaugurates the way the modern theory of rational choice deals with the subject.

Free exchange contained by mutual sympathy

From its very first steps, political economy was influenced from Newtonian celestial mechanics and economic thinkers were moved by the conscious effort to find the general causal laws of the "economic universe". In that sense, Adam Smith tried to establish the free – from state interference – market as the natural system of economic transaction, following the naturalist ideas of the French physiocrats. As will be shown below, in a society of free transactions, if everyone follows his/her natural motive of self-interest and insofar as he/she is guided by the moral rule of sympathy toward his/her fellow people, a general agreement is conceivable towards material welfare and social progress (Smith 1759: 9–13; 1776: 477).

Adam Smith's "Economic Man" so to speak, referred to a person belonging to a specific geographical and historical context and that during his/her real economic activities he/she "endeavours to produce the greatest possible value" (Smith 1776: vol. i, 477).[2] While people are supposed to act at their best personal interest, Smith explicitly condemned the egocentric view of the individual action. There are two major reasons supporting this judgment: the existence of many antagonistic motives governing human nature, and the human faculty of "sympathy".

Many different motives act concurrently upon individuals themselves, while "sympathy" connects individuals to one another. Smith believed that individuals are constantly under the influence of many antagonistic motives, whereas "sympathy" is the most important human faculty. In his *Theory of Moral Sentiments*, Smith did recognize that individuals are undeniably self-interested: "Every man is, no doubt, by nature first and principally recommended to his own care; and he is fitter to care of himself than of every other person" (1759: 82). Had he limited his analysis there, he would open the road to "utilitarian" calculativeness. But Smith insisted that although "self-love" is a natural impulse, it is not alone in governing and directing human action. There are many psychological motives that counteract the instinct of "self-love", such as the "desire for social esteem", "vanity", and the "desire for an easy life".[3] The first of these, the "desire for social esteem", means that people living in societies, besides seeking for "bettering their own conditions", seek also for the "approbation" of their fellow men (1759: 50). His very well-known figure of the "impartial spectator" is constantly present, "as a moral hector", looking over our shoulders to "scrutinize the propriety of our own conduct" (1759: 112).[4] The second motive, "vanity", comes into play when individuals acting in their "desire to be praised for what they themselves do not think praiseworthy" (1759: 64), promote "many respectable and amiable virtues", such as truth, integrity, sense of honour, cordial friendship, humanity, politeness, etc. (1759: 258).[5] As to the third motive, the "desire for an easy life", it stresses that the natural "interest of every man to live as much at his ease as he can", can be excessive when revenue predominates as a source of wealth leading to indolence and idleness, which definitely "corrupts the industry of those who ought to be maintained by the employment of capital" (1776: vol. i, 358). Consequently, Smith made systematic use of moral factors when he believed them relevant to his economic analysis: "Capitals are increased by parsimony, and diminished by prodigality and misconduct" (idem).

Moreover, the very idea of "civilized society" is founded upon the relationship of "mutual sympathy" connecting fellow human beings. For Smith, what distinguishes "civilized" from "savage" society, is not the fact that in the former most of the people are better off enjoying more goods, but principally that the greater part of the people also enjoy being "frugal and industrious" living under the rule of the law (Smith 1776, vol. i: 2). From the very first lines of the *Theory of Moral Sentiments*, it was clearly affirmed that

> How selfish so ever man may be supposed there are evidently some principles in his nature, which interests him in the fortune of others, and render their happiness necessary to him, though he derives nothing from it except the pleasure of seeing it.
>
> (Smith 1759: 9)

Smith's genetic concept of "sympathy" is a counter motive to "self-love", since it represents one's interest in the happiness of other people (Peil 1999: 59). Through "sympathy" one is imagining himself/herself in the situation of the other in order to share his/her feelings. In that sense it should not be confused with benevolence or altruism; neither should be treated as being opposed by self-interest.[6] It is rather a fundamental principle of human conduct that controls and complements the motive of "self-love" (Maitre 2000: 59). "Mutual sympathy", guarantees both the morality of human actions, together with social order and cohesion. Without it, as Evensky (2001: 515) has correctly observed, no ethical citizenry is possible.

Therefore, in Smith's sympathy perspective, individuals understand themselves as being always part of a social whole and act consequently, with "compassion for their fellowmen". When someone exchanges goods, he/she is acting reasonably, trying to get the best advantage of it without losing his/her predisposition to mutual sympathy. To obtain what one wants "mere self-love is not sufficient" because he or she has to consider unselfishly what the other party wants too. In a 1764 lecture, Smith made clear the insufficiency of self-love to conclude a commercial deal: "Man ... works on the self-love of his fellows, by setting them a sufficient temptation to get what he wants; the language of this disposition is, give me what I want, and you shall have what you want" (quoted in Kennedy

2005: 105). The very idea of socialized individuals is founded, according to Smith, upon this relationship of "mutual sympathy" with other human beings.[7]

Consequently, human behaviour and action are not to be considered as the result of rationalistic calculations of personal advantages and disadvantages alone. Individuals never act in isolation, but always within a society, that is in reference to the "moral sentiments" of other people. For that reason it was impossible for Smith to think that political economy is a fully autonomous and autarchic field founded solely on the principle of economic rationality. The "desire for more wealth", which explains why human beings produce more than their means of subsistence, is the fundamental motive in business relations. But it never works in isolation. As was rightly argued, "the idea of 'mutual sympathy' implies that an individual's personal identity, ambition and needs are not antecedent to the exchange, but are produced in the continuous processes of exchange in which the individual is engaged" (Peil 1999: 92). When someone exchanges, he/she endeavours to get the best advantage of it, always remaining committed to the prevailing social rules and values and continuing to "desire, not only to be loved, but to be lovely" (1759: 113). His legendary invisible hand mechanism (1759: 185, 1776 vol. i: 477) works only with morally constrained individuals who seek reasonably for their own interest and yet "with pity and compassion for their fellowmen". In modern terms, exchangers act "as having some idea about each other's preference patterns" (Fontaine 1997: 270; cf. Sen 1987a: 56).

Smith's social individuals

"Mutual sympathy" is the human faculty responsible for social morality. The pattern of behaviour founded upon it is formed out of a specific social context as a result of the socialization process. Smith explained repeatedly and extensively in his *Wealth of Nations* how informal social institutions, norms and values shape individual plans and behavior.[8] Most of the commercial transactions described in the book involve people who know each other belonging to a localized community of exchangers, thus making the importance of informal institutions greater. Whether all this is sufficient to qualify Smith as an early institutionalist is a question lengthily debated elsewhere.[9] What is significant from our point of view here is that on account of the concept of "sympathy", economic behaviour is rooted in the concrete social conditions of every particular society. Four examples suggesting social embeddedness of individual morality can be mentioned from the *Wealth of Nations*.

First, the quality of political institutions affects economic behaviour and subsequently the state of development of a country. To illustrate this, Smith bravely compares not only the despotic China and the democratic Great Britain, but also the two most important British colonies on the issue of the level of wages. He observes that in the constitutionally governed North American colony the "liberal reward of labour" is far greater than "that of the mercantile company which oppresses and domineers in the East Indies" (1776 vol. i: 82). The differences lie not in the fertility of land nor in the number of inhabitants, but mainly in the "genius of the British constitution which protects and governs America" (idem). Economic backwardness in China or even in British India, and consequently lower wages, are explained through the low quality of governance institutions.

A second example is his idea of "trust reposed in the workmen" as an essential quality of labour that should be taken into account when it comes to estimate its remuneration (1776 vol. i: 55). Smith even believed that trust was at the origin of one out of five significant exceptions to his general rule of equality of wages between different employments (1776 vol. i: 117). Using an earlier idea of Richard Cantillon and Hume, Smith explained that in the professions that require a high degree of trust from the employees "on account of the precious materials with which they are intrusted [*sic*]" – such as goldsmiths and jewellers – a higher wage should be granted. Similarly, the reward of liberal professions – such as physicians and lawyers – must be high enough to remunerate first, "the confidence" imbedded in them, second their "rank in the society which so important a trust requires" and third, their investment in time and money for their education (1776 vol. i: 118). This is customarily called trust in competence, meaning the ability of the trustee to perform something.

A third, and very significant, example is his idea of the coexistence of different systems of morality "in every civilized society", namely "the strict or austere [and] the liberal or ... the loose system" (1776 vol. ii: 315–316). Each moral system adopted by distinct social groups, leads to divergent patterns of behaviour as far as consumption, saving and investment are concerned. In that sense, he concludes, "in mercantile and manufacturing towns, where the inferior ranks of people are chiefly maintained by the employment of capital, they are in general industrious, sober and thriving" (1776 vol. i: 356).

Fourth, is the idea that the quality of the educational institutions (or culture in general) is the principal cause of the various talents observed between people. As he has thoughtfully remarked, "The difference between the most dissimilar characters, between a philosopher and a common street porter, seems to arise not so much from nature, as from habit, custom and education" (1776 vol. i: 19–20; cf. vol. ii, 282ff.). The last case is very important since it shows that while human nature is held to be constant, human character evolves along with proper social institutions (Elsner 1989: 203). Individuals, who have grown up in specific social conditions, are able in their turn to transform these conditions in intended and unintended ways, as Arrow (1994) would say. It was thus recognized that individuals are both constructive within and constructed through social institutions. Smith adopted methodological individualism without adhering to atomistic explanations. As in the whole tradition of classical economics, by aggregating the social individual's behaviour, Smith made "economic classes his preferred unit of analysis" (Davis 2003: 25).

There is more evidence that Smith viewed morality as a result of social embeddedness. Taking a significant example, although he explicitly says little about its emergence, it can be certainly assumed that trustworthiness in business activities arises because the exchangers have internalized moral values such as "fairness" and "justice". Smith believed them to be innate human traits:

> for one man to deprive another unjustly of anything, or unjustly to promote his own advantage by the loss or disadvantage of another, is more *contrary to nature*, than death, than poverty, than pain, than all the misfortunes which can affect him, either in his body, or in his external circumstances.
>
> (1759: 138, emphasis added)

In Smith's view, the market is not working, unless its participants respect the principles of justice (Bruni and Sugden 2008: 45). The idea that justice rules the exchange relation is explicitly stated also in the *Wealth of Nations*:

> Every man, as long as he does not violate the laws of justice, is left perfectly free to pursue his own interest in his own way, and to bring both his industry and capital into competition with those of any other man, or order of men.
>
> (Smith 1776, vol. ii: 208)

As long as economic agents follow the rules of justice, trustworthiness is at work in commercial exchange relations where "self-love" is the principal motive. People do make appeal to the "self-love" of others when they exchange, but they trust one another knowing by empathetic identification the intentions of the other; they believe that the other will restrain himself from hurting his interests.[10]

Smith's moral concerns are properly illustrated in the great confidence that he had upon the ethical merits of economic growth in the long run:

"The habits, besides, of order, economy and attention, to which mercantile business naturally forms a merchant, render him much fitter to execute, with profit and success, any project of improvement" (1776, vol. i: 433). Far from considering the economic process as an end in itself, he believed that wealth and accumulation are necessary steps to be made in the road to "civil society". He has thoughtfully remarked that the pleasures of "wealth and greatness are mere trinkets of frivolous utility" (1759: 181). What was more important to his view was to ensure the rule of reasonable institutions and "natural liberty" for citizens, which constitute the only final goals morally acceptable. Smith did recognize the deleterious moral effects of the extended division of labour on workers' character and intellectual ability (1776, vol. ii: 302), and he also deplored the alienating effects of rent-seeking upon human character.[11] This is why he insisted – as a therapy to alienation – upon the necessity of the systematic cultivation of ethical citizenry through education (Evensky 2001: 515). Overall, he had great faith in the civilizing force of economic development and subsequent social progress:

> commerce and manufactures gradually introduced order and good government, and with them, the liberty and security of individuals, among the inhabitants of the country, who had before lived in a continual state of war with their neighbours, and of servile dependency upon their superiors. This, though it has been least observed is by far the most important of all their effects.
>
> (Smith 1776, vol. i: 433)

To conclude, Smith does not limit his work *An Inquiry into the Nature and Causes of the Wealth of Nations* to the functional rationality of wealth production and distribution; he considers economic processes as an aspect of social relations. The *Wealth of Nations* contains an analysis of human action that avoids atomization because it is contained by their moral obligations. In a sense, Smith persists in the old Aristotelian view where acting rationally means "in accordance with good reasons". Thus, economic actors do not behave rationally as atoms in social vacuum conditions, i.e. as if other people were absent. Economic activities are instead, as some sociologists have recently pointed out, "embedded in concrete, ongoing systems of social relations" of industrial England in the late eighteenth century.[12] By the same token, his analysis is both general and historically specific: it is general because it uses some general concepts and leads to conclusions exceeding the narrow limits of the observation; it is historically specific since it is confined in particular socio-economic systems, in time and space.

The very idea that economic rationality is embedded in specific social context and has, therefore, very different meaning outside of it does not challenge Karl Polanyi's old argument (1944) about disembeddedness and the consequent autonomization of economic activities in capitalist societies. On the contrary, Smith, more than any other classical economist, shows how to deal with economic phenomena once capitalist societies have already emerged. What has been suggested here is that Adam Smith supported the idea that individuals act inside an institutional structure and are influenced by moral rules and social norms, although acting rationally for their own sake.

Notes

1 On Ricardo's epistemological break see Zouboulakis (1993: chap. 1).
2 Many ideas of the rest of the chapter draw from Zouboulakis (2005a) and (2010b).
3 Cf. Sen (1987) and (2005), Song (1995), Winch (1996: 103–108), Evensky (2001).
4 Cf. Raphael and Macfie's introduction to *Theory of Moral Sentiments*, Elsner (1989), Evensky (1992), Kennedy (2005: 52), and Ashraf *et al.* (2005), where Grampp's expression "the moral hector", is quoted.
5 On Smith's idea of "vanity" see Winch (1996: 73).
6 This confusion gave rise in the famous "Adam Smith problem" in nineteenth-century literature and beyond. For a clear-cut solution to this "problem" see Skinner (1987), Prasch (1991), Beraud (1992: 310ff.), Dupuy (1992:147ff.), Winch (1996: 105), Peil (1999: 58ff.).
7 Cf. Elsner (1989: 197), Peil (1999: 86), Kennedy (2005:103).
8 The distinction between formal/informal institutions is based on North (1990). Etzioni (1986) explores the effects of the internalization of moral obligations upon individual utility. Song (1995: 441) teases out the social origins of morality in Smith.
9 Cf. Elsner (1989), Song (1995), Peil (1999: 89ff.), Evensky (2001: 504). Song offers further bibliographical evidence.
10 On the idea of empathetic identification and its relevance in the *Wealth of Nations*, see Fontaine (1997).
11 For more on the moral effects of growth in Smith, see Hirschman (1976), Prasch (1991) and West (1996). Bowles (1998: 92) examines how markets do frame individual values since they "induce self-regarding behavior ... Markets affect 'nice traits' i.e. behaviors which in social interactions confer benefits on others". Moreover, Bowles (2008) reports evidence showing how public policies undermine ethical citizenry inducing people to adopt more self-interested behaviour.
12 Granovetter (1985: 487). Cf. Steiner (1999a: 39) and Zafirowski (2008).

2   John Stuart Mill and the concept of socially embedded rationality

Before Mill, economists offered little proof of the principle of economic behaviour other than introspective evidence.[1] Even if Adam Smith and David Ricardo, to take only the two greatest progenitors for example, were keen observers of economic life, they only mentioned introspection as a unique source of justification for the principle of economic behaviour. As a result, when Smith is writing about the "propensity in human nature to truck, barter and exchange", or when Ricardo is writing about the capitalist "envy for the most profitable investment", they were both exposed to the danger of subjectivist bias (Cf. Smith 1776: 17, Ricardo 1817, chap. iv). John Stuart Mill was the first to use a principle of economic behaviour as one of the fundamental premises of economic explanation with the ambition of an empirical generalization.

The method of social science

Mill's PR will be better understood once his idea of a "hierarchy of laws" between different social sciences is explained. In the sixth book of his *System of Logic*, Mill conceives a hierarchical structure of three levels in such a way that higher-level laws are the result of the combination of lower-level laws. At the first level of this structure we find the "empirical laws of the mind" established by psychology, or "the experimental science of human nature". These laws are inductive generalizations based on direct observation, with a very limited scope of validity (1843: 861). For this reason they have to be "connected deductively with the laws of nature from which they result". These ultimate laws, called "laws of mind", also established by psychology, differ from the empirical laws "not in kind but in their much greater degree of generality and exactitude" (Winch 1958: 69). At the second level Mill places the laws of human character formation, which constitute the subject matter of *ethology*, or "the theory of the causes which determine the type of character belonging to a people or to an age" (1843: 869, 905), the laws of which are deduced from the "laws of mind" supplied by assumptions about the physical, social and political environment. *Ethology* constitutes "the immediate foundation of Social Science", that is only able to produce causal laws resulting from the operation of the general laws of psychology on the circumstances of particular time and place.

> For every individual is surrounded by circumstances different from those of every other individual; every nation or generation of mankind from every other nation or generation; and none of these differences are without their influence in forming a different type of character.
>
> (Mill 1843: 864)

Therefore, the laws of ethology are "*axiomata media*" derived from the general laws of the mind. The social scientist aiming to explain social phenomena, must show how they follow from the "bridge laws" offered by the deductive science of ethology – not yet established – and ultimately from the lower-level psychological laws.[2] In that sense, ethology, a science that Mill was planning to develop – equivalent to modern cultural anthropology – provides "the intermediate links with the basic psychological laws of the human mind" treated in the first level.[3]

The third level consists of the laws of social science, the deductive science that deals with "the action of collective masses of mankind, and the various phenomena which constitute social life" (1843: 875). Political economy, together with political science, is an autonomous branch of this science. Just as ethology is founded on the laws of psychology, it also provides "the immediate foundation of social science" (1843: 907).

This hierarchy of laws presents social phenomena as the result of a composition of the laws of psychological phenomena. Mill writes: "Human beings in society have no properties but those which are derived from, and may be resolved into, the laws of the nature of individual man" (1843: 879). And later in the text, "the actions and the sentiments of human beings in the social state are, no doubt, entirely regulated by psychological and ethological laws" (1843: 896). Besides the fact that this hierarchy properly reflects Mill's methodological individualism, it shows convincingly the nature of the fundamental psychological premise of political economy that he had in mind. Mill's principle of economic behaviour, namely that every person desires as much wealth as possible, with as little sacrifice as possible, is supposed to be the result of a "long and accurate observation", an empirical generalization established by the science of psychology. The same observation applies to the rule of conduct he introduced, namely that everyone "is capable of judging of the comparative efficacy of means for obtaining that end" (1836: 321). For that reason, Mill believed that the principle of economic behaviour, together with the other three fundamental premises of political economy – namely the Malthusian principle of population, the principle of diminishing returns of land and the principle of non-decreasing productivity of capital and labour – are propositions ultimately true.[4]

Mill is trying to introduce here systematic psychological reasoning in economic theory, in order to establish the behavioural premise on a more objective source than introspection. Karl Popper raised serious objections against Mill's "methodological psychologism", saying that it leads to indeterminacy since "the human factor" is a source of uncertainty (Popper 1957: 158).[5] However, we dare to say, Popper oversimplified Mill's views. It is true that Mill wanted to introduce systematic psychological reasoning in economic theory in order to establish the behavioural principle on a more objective source than introspection. This is why he insisted that it is from psychology – "the experimental science of human nature" – that the economist should borrow the psychological premises of political economy, and try additionally to ground them on statistical or historical evidence (1843: 907).

The "ethology project", which planned to serve as a bridge between the science of society and the science of the individual, provides the second reason of not considering Mill as a "methodological psychologicalist [*sic*]". Mill had tried, early in his book *On the Logic of Social Sciences* to escape from the Scylla of free will and the Charybdis of social determinism. Eager to establish the causal laws of human behaviour, it was impossible for him to accept the idea of individuals acting inconsistently at their free will. But as a consequent individualist himself he could never adhere without qualifications to the "doctrine of necessity", as if human character was only a by-product of the social context. Thus by recognizing that social circumstances form human character, Mill definitely succeeded to break away from the Benthamite universalistic psychology of pain and pleasure. Still, by announcing the birth of *ethology* he wanted to explore also how human character affects social circumstances. As Persky (1995: 227), rightly remarked, Mill believed that "more or less rational choices made by one generation predispose the tastes of subsequent generations to reinforce similar choices".

Finally, Mill's behavioural principle is not psychologistic for a third reason. Reading his own words will save us from verbiage:

> By reasoning from that one law of human nature, *and from the principal outward circumstances* (whether universal or confined to particular states of society) which operate upon the human mind through

that law, we may be enabled to explain and predict this portion of the phenomena of society, *so far as they depend on that class of circumstances only*, overlooking the influence of every other of the circumstances of society.

(1843: 901, emphases added)

As it will be shown in more detail below, Mill keeps always in mind these "outward circumstances", i.e. the social context of individual action. Individual actors, such as consumers and producers, do not act in conditions of a social vacuum but inside a pre-existing and anticipated "particular state of society". His analysis does not suffer from the well-known "problem of infinite regress" similar to the puzzle of "which came first, the chicken or the egg", the society or the individual (Hodgson 1986: 219): obviously the society was there already when individuals started thinking about acting under the motive of the "desire of wealth", i.e. when the consumers felt the need of acquiring more wealth and the producers felt the need of producing more.

The justification of the rationality principle

Hollander (1985: 106, 112) noted that Mill was not always so clear in his will to break away from introspective evidence concerning economic behaviour. This is true only insofar as one refers exclusively to his early essay of 1836. In his *System of Logic*, he definitely affirmed that the psychological premises of political economy are established by psychology and should be furthermore grounded on statistical or historical evidence (1843: 907).[6] Unfortunately, Mill never knew any other psychology than the associationist psychology of David Hartley and James Mill, which is a discipline more philosophical than experimental. In reading chapter iv, of the sixth book of his *Logic*, one clearly understands that the psychology he is looking for was a science where causal connections between mental phenomena should be established according to the known experimental methods, and he especially mentions the method of agreement and the method of difference.[7]

Returning to the hierarchy of laws, it should be said that it shows also the interdependence between the branches of social science. As it was mentioned above, political economy is a separate, but not fully independent branch of social science. Mill explains that though social phenomena are complex and are produced by an "intermixture of causes", every class of human affairs depends on its own specific causes. Mill is using the mechanical analogy of the "composition of forces" in order to support his argument. He compares every "kind of cause", such as psychological, cultural or economic, with the components that are forming the resultant of forces. The social consensus is only decomposable by means of abstraction because, "different species of social facts are in the main depended immediately and in first resort on different kinds of causes" (1843: 900). Political economy is concerned only with that class of social phenomena, "in which the immediately determining causes are principally those which act through the desire of wealth; and in which the psychological law mainly concerned is the familiar one, that a greater gain is preferred to a smaller" (Mill 1843: 901).

What Mill is saying here is that economists are isolating by means of abstraction one specific range of social phenomena relative to production and distribution of wealth, leaving aside all non-economic aspects; they eliminate later every secondary economic "disturbing cause" that might influence the "desire of wealth". Mill labelled two such disturbing causes: the "aversion to labor" and the "desire of the present enjoyment of costly indulgences" (1836: 321). However, Mill is not saying, like Jevons did later on, that the autonomy of political economy is founded on the principle of economic behavior.[8] He rather grounds political economy on the fundamental cause of the "desire of wealth", which explains why human beings are producing means of subsistence. As Hausman (1981: 375) correctly pointed out "Mill is not claiming that people always prefer greater gains, but that this is one motivational 'force' which often predominates in relevant circumstances", i.e. when the determining cause in action is the desire of wealth. John Neville Keynes gave the definitive exposition of Mill's idea in this subject, saying that "neither the conception of the economic man nor any other abstraction can suffice as an adequate basis upon which to construct the whole science of economics" (Keynes 1891: 128).

The fact that political economy explains and predicts one portion only of the phenomena of society, implies that its deductions are strictly true only in the abstract. Mill's famous definition of economic man as a being "occupied solely in acquiring and consuming wealth", made in his essay of 1836, did lead many historians of economic thought (like Hutchison or Blaug) to a misconception about Mill's real meaning. Again, only if we read the sixth essay in the light of the sixth book of *Logic* can we understand that Mill was speaking about a partial and approximate science of political economy, the deductions of which need to be corrected not only after, but also before the explanation of economic phenomena by the results of other social sciences. Mill says that "this approximation is then to be corrected by making proper allowance for the effects of any impulses of a different description, which can be shown to interfere with the result in any particular case" (1843: 903).[9]

The main idea of social embeddedness of the economic motive was eloquently expressed in an often quoted line:

> In Political Economy ... empirical laws of human nature are tacitly assumed by English thinkers, which are calculated only for Great Britain and the United States.... Yet, those who know the habits of the Continent of Europe are aware of how apparently small a motive often outweighs the desire of money-getting, *even in the operations which have money-getting as their direct object.*
>
> (Mill 1843: 906, emphasis added)

The *Principles of Political Economy* contains many examples of correction of the behavioural premise *before* the explanation itself. We can mention two of them: first, his analysis of the national determinants of economic behaviour, and second his analysis of the sociological factors of productivity, namely the "degree of confidence of the laborers in society", and the "degree of security that society offers to its members" (1848, book i, chap. vii). In these cases economists need to correct their perspective, in order to take account of special social – i.e. non-economic conditions – or even some secondary economic "disturbing causes" that are modifying the action of the "desire of wealth".

The national determinants of economic behaviour were already mentioned in Senior's *Outline* in 1836 and continue to be so in Mill's *Principles*:[10]

> The efficiency of labor is connected with their [the Anglo-Americans] character; with their defects as well as with their good qualities. The majority of Englishmen and Americans have no life but in their work; that alone stands between them and ennui.
>
> (Mill 1848: 105 n.1)

What Mill observes clearly here is "the culture bound nature of Ricardian Economics" (Whitaker 1975: 1041). Notwithstanding its heuristic and explanatory power, political economy has according to Mill, a rather small domain of both theoretical and practical application, because its behavioural assumptions are "pertinent only to well-defined environmental conditions", as Hollander has rightly remarked (1985: 116). The scientific study of economic phenomena based on his PR provides therefore only a historically specific view of what was really going on in industrial societies of the mid-nineteenth century. Unlike the marginalists, Mill never suggested that there are behavioural principles of universal relevance. Quite the opposite, he claimed that "the human race does not have a universal character" (1843: 864).[11] This is the meaning of his warning to his fellow political economists not to extend their studies beyond the limits of industrial societies, unless they take account of the "national character", together with other significant local and temporal particularities. In the last case, economists need to modify their conclusions by means of verification, to embrace the "circumstances almost peculiar to the particular case or era" (1836: 333). Hence DeMarchi (1986: 91) concludes, "Mill's science was of very limited scope and potential. It dealt with one particular class of facts, the productions and uses of wealth insofar as these are affected by the [psychological] drive to pursue material advantage". In that sense, political economy is limited even inside industrial societies when individuals have other, non-economic motivations.

The second case is his treatment of social norms and values as an advantage of economic efficiency. Besides the traditional factors of "productiveness", such as the natural advantages and technical skill and knowledge, Mill includes many "qualitative determinants", as Hollander (1985: 200) has called them. There are intellectual qualities like "practical good sense", "quickness of perception", or "natural comprehension" that improve significantly labour productivity (1848: 108–109). But there is also, what Mill describes as "the moral qualities of the labourers", insisting particularly on trustworthiness: "The advantage of mankind of being able to trust one another, penetrates into every crevice and cranny of human life: the economical is perhaps the smallest part of it, yet even this is incalculable" (Mill 1848: 111). A pure optimization analysis, in terms of least pain or maximum pleasure, is unable to capture the significance, or even the existence, of social values affecting individual plans and behaviour. In contrast, Mill opens the field of economic analysis in order to embrace the social values that affect positively economic behaviour and performance. This was after all the source of his major difference with Bentham's utilitarianism: Mill believed that "some *kinds* of pleasure are more desirable and more valuable than others" (1861: 211, original emphasis), meaning that society decides about the higher or lower quality of a pleasure.[12]

The consequences of a limited and partial science of political economy

Mill's view of the approximate and partial character of political economy is much more significant as far as the theoretical application of its conclusions to particular cases exceeding the standard economic model is concerned. In cases where the institutional frame differs greatly Mill suggested that economic theory should be modified by means of verification in order to take account of national or social peculiarities.[13] Mill was aware of the fact that economic laws have a limited range of application, essentially because their premises are culturally bounded. For that reason he drew the economists' attention to a "common error", which consists of applying their analysis to other states of society "in which many elements are not the same" (1843: 903). Mill strongly emphasized this point: "the conclusions of political economy will so far fail of being applicable to the explanation or prediction of real events until they are modified by a correct allowance for a degree of influence exercised by the other cause" (Mill 1836: 323). When these conditions change, economists need to take them into consideration and modify their conclusions. In his *Principles of Political Economy* he proposed such modifications when he introduced his famous distinction between custom and competition (book ii, chap. iv). As Schumpeter (1954: 546) has justly observed, wherever custom is very influential "a general correction must be applied to all conclusions arrived at on the hypothesis of perfect competition". Mill admits, "English Political Economists ... exaggerate the effect of competition and take into little account the other and conflicting principle" (1848: 242). This is for Mill "partly intelligible [since] only through the principle of competition has Political Economy any pretension to the character of Science" (idem). For those who have understood Mill's methodology there is no puzzle in such a statement: the abstract laws of political economy are true only in the absence of significant disturbing causes. Yet, "our reasoning must, in general proceed as if the known and natural effects of competition were actually produced by it, in all cases in which it is not restrained by some positive obstacle" (1848: 247). The "positive obstacle" involved here is "custom", which is placed according to Ashley "side by side with competition as the other agency determining the division of produce under the rule of private property" Mill (1848: xix). The competitive case is the theoretical model under the *ceteris paribus* condition, just like Galileo's law of fall is valid in a friction-less world (1836: 330). When it comes to explain "the actual affairs of life [one should] consider not only what will happen supposing the maximum of competition, but how far the result will be affected if competition falls short of the maximum" (1848: 248).[14] Competition fails to be the regulator says Mill, for example, when the level of rents and prices is fixed by the customs of the country and not by the forces of supply and demand: in the "bookselling trade", in "professional remuneration" such as "the fees of the physicians, surgeons and barristers" (1848: 247). Custom corresponds here to a static, change-resisting factor, called by Mill "conformity". However, Mill identified elsewhere in his *Principles* a second kind of custom, capable of leading to an improvement of the human character and behaviour, that is "custom" in the sense of a system of shared habits, or "culture" (1848: 794).

Similarly, Mill has significantly modified the classical theory of distribution between three classes – landlords, capitalists and workers – in order to study the modes of distribution in continental Europe, where producers are at the same time also landowners (metayers and cottiers), or they cultivate their own fields themselves (peasant proprietors). After examining in one small chapter of four pages how the produce is distributed between three classes, Mill considers, in five chapters of more than 90 pages, other institutional arrangements prevailing outside the Anglo-American world (1848, book ii, chaps. vi to ix). In Switzerland, Norway, the Palatinate in Germany, and in the Flemish Belgium, where agricultural producers are at the same time landowners and cultivate their own fields themselves (peasant proprietors), the incentives to work and to accumulate differ from those of the capitalist mode of production. In the above cases, the private property and the small scale of production is beneficial not only to productivity but to social progress in general. On the contrary, French peasant proprietors or Irish cottiers (tenant farmers) proved themselves to be far less industrious, the former because their properties were too small and the latter because they were too divided from ownership.[15] Mill was very sensible to the "Irish Question" and devoted a long chapter, as well some 43 articles published in the *Morning Chronicle*, to suggest the "means of abolishing cottier tenancy" (1848, book ii, chap. x). The whole idea behind his project of reform of Irish agriculture, aimed to the creation of a new institutional organization of land property rights that would raise the productive capacity of the Irish farmers: "An excitable organization is precisely that in which, by adequate inducements it is easiest to kindle a spirit of animated exertion" (1848: 324).

Mill's attitude to modify the general principle of economic behaviour when it comes to be applied to different institutional settings is not a theoretical exegesis but reflects a fundamental objective of his system of political economy. By studying how the main behavioural principle works inside alternative real institutional settings, Mill wants to re-incorporate the complexity of social reality. As Joseph Persky has pointed out "Mill's central theoretical and empirical project was to use economic man, with his rudimentary but manageable psychology, to prove that institutions did matter" (Persky 1995: 224). To do this, he takes into account the influence of the significant "disturbing causes" omitted during the theoretical construction as a necessary step to the full explanation of economic phenomena.

Mill's conception of the principle of economic behaviour can be summarized as follows: (*i*) Mill's PR is not a heuristic fiction but a realistic construction with strong empirical content, based on long psychological observations of the economic activity. Mill's "economic man" describes how a person, belonging to a particular geographical and historical context, behaves during his economic activities under the influence of the "desire of wealth", insofar as these activities are "not modified by the pursuit of any other object"; (*ii*) The scientific study of economic phenomena based on this principle, provides only a partial view of what was going on in industrial societies of the mid-nineteenth century. Mill was adamant on the approximate character of economic explanation and on the necessity of close collaboration with other social sciences, as a consequence of their interdependence; (*iii*) No universal theory could be based on Mill's "economic man". If political economists wanted to extend their studies beyond the limits of capitalist economies, then Mill recognizes, as Schumpeter put it, "the necessity of studying actual economic behavior in all its local and temporal varieties" (1954: 452). In sum, Mill proposed a principle of economic rationality grounded on systematic observation, which leads to a partial, yet still realistic, study of the economic activity of a specific economic system.

Notes

1 This chapter expands on ideas published earlier in Zouboulakis (1997a, 2002, 2005a).
2 Kincaid (1996: 145ff.) offers some strong philosophical arguments against this possibility.
3 More about Mill's *Ethology* in Winch (1970: 25), Whitaker (1975: 1038), Hollander (1985: 135), Redman (1997: 332–333), Persky (1995: 226–228). Ekelund and Olsen (1973: 390), following Ashley's comment, have suggested that Mill proposed *Ethology* as a means to supplement Ricardian deductive economics with Comte's social speculations. Not all scholars agreed to assign to Mill's *Ethology* a role of "middle-level theory". For example, Ryan (1970:157) wrote: "*Ethology* tells us (only) how plausible are the assumptions about people's wants and wishes from which Economics starts".
4 Further analysis is made in Zouboulakis (1993: 91–102). On the nature of these assumptions see Whitaker (1975: 1042), Hirsch (1980: 105), Hollander (1983: 154), Meidinger (1994: 45).
5 Speaking of social progress, Popper wrote this: "Comte and Mill ... held that progress was an unconditional or absolute trend, which is *reducible to the laws of human nature*"; Mill, in particular, has tried to reduce "his law of progress to what he calls 'the progressiveness of human mind'" (Popper 1957: 152–153, original emphasis). "This doctrine [concludes Popper] arises from the false belief that this 'methodological psychologism' is a necessary corollary of a methodological individualism" (ibid. 157). See more in Zouboulakis (1997b) and below, Chapter 8.
6 His followers, J.E. Cairnes and J. Neville Keynes, were more clear than Mill in this point, affirming that it is from psychology that the economist borrows the premises of economic behaviour (Cairnes 1857: chap. iii §3; Keynes 1891: 88; cf. Hausman 1981: 377 and Hollander 1983: 154).

7 It should be noted that Mill, even though he remained unaware of the development of experimental psychology that took place in Germany after 1860, with
   Ernst Weber, Gustav Fechner and Wilhelm Wundt, explicitly rejected the idea
   of basing psychology on physiological laws. Cf. his *Logic* (book vi, chap. iv,
   3), where he expresses his reserves even for Alexander Bain's tentative attempt
   to integrate sensorimotor psychology to the psychology of association. See also
   White (1994: 217). The marriage between physiological psychology and economics was celebrated only in 1877, by F.Y. Edgeworth (Creedy 1984: 611).
8 Hollander (1985: 104–112), gives a different answer on this point.
9 DeMarchi (1986: 91–92) has rightly criticized Hausman (1981) on this point.
   For, Mill's political economy is better described as a science of very limited
   scope, rather as an inexact science. As DeMarchi said: "It is not correct to
   regard the tendencies of Mill's economic science as inexact laws. Rather, they
   are encompassing and wholly accurate as far as they go, but their domain is
   artificial and limited". More on this issue in Zouboulakis (2000).
10 Senior, speaking about national differences in the action of the "general desire
   of wealth", says that

   > the greatest and longest continued sacrifices will be made in those Coun-
   > tries in which property is most secure, and the road to social eminence is
   > the most open. The inhabitants of Holland and of Great Britain, and of the
   > countries that derived their institutions from Great Britain.
   >
   > (1836: 27)

11 On the local relevance of Mill's behavioural principle see Hollander (1985:
   145), Redman (1997: 347), Hollander and Peart (1999: 382) and Hodgson
   (2001: 67). For an opposite view see Hirsch (1992, 2000).
12 On Mill's differences with Benthamite utilitarianism see C. Smith (1973: 15),
   Quinton (1989: 43), Peart (1995b), Zouboulakis (2001). See also next chapter.
13 There is no consensus in the literature as to whether or not Mill suggested the
   possibility of improvement of economic theory by means of verification. Hollander (1985: 126), DeMarchi (1986: 94), Persky (1995: 225) and Hollander
   and Peart (1999: 375–376) hold that taking account of "disturbing causes",
   omitted during the theoretical construction, was necessary to the full explanation of economic phenomena. On the contrary, Hirsch (1992, 2000) and Peart
   (1995a), hold that this procedure of verification and correction refers exclusively to the application of economic theory for practical purposes.
14 About Mill's idea of custom: Winch (1970), Whitaker (1975), Hollander (1985:
   960), Redman (1997: 340–342).
15 In chapter viii, of the *Principles* Mill examines also the pros and cons of the
   system of "metayage", (sharecropping) prevailing in the southwest of France
   and northern Italy. In that system, the produce was divided between two
   classes, landowners and land-workers that live on the land and pay back to the
   owner a certain portion of the production, according to the established custom
   of the region.

3 William Stanley Jevons and the concept of rationality as maximization

The principle of constrained maximization of personal benefit was first introduced in economic theory by Antoine Augustin Cournot. But it was William Stanley Jevons that utilized it effectively as a fundamental component of a major theoretical shift called The "Marginalist Revolution".[1] This principle corresponds greatly to what Simon has defined as substantively rational behaviour, "appropriate to the achievement of given goals within the limits imposed by given conditions and constraints" (Simon 1976: 130).[2] In the *Recherches sur les principes mathématiques de la théorie des richesses* (1838) it appears as an axiom describing mutual gain maximization constrained by the law of demand. Cournot expressed for the first time in economics demand as a mathematical function of the market price $D=F(p)$, and represented it graphically as a negative slope curve. Nonetheless, he refused to connect his theory of demand with the theory of value, on top of denying any kind of subjectivist explanation of the individual motives. In truth, there is no agency theory in Cournot, and moreover his attempt to aggregate demand theory to the level of the national economy and to define a social optimum solution was unsuccessful (Ménard 1978: 144).[3]

In Jevons, the PR is associated with the application of differential calculus in economic theory and the consequent discovery of the concept of marginal utility. Both theoretical innovations have been possible thanks to the redefinition of the scope of economic analysis, from the social conditions of production, distribution and accumulation of wealth, to the subjective factors of exchange, or, in brief, from political economy to economics.[4] It is important to underline that behind all this stands the icon of physics. We can no longer understand the rise of the Marginalist School without recognizing the key role of the mechanical analogy, as was shown by some significant contributions.[5] Let us therefore examine briefly the consequences of the physical metaphor on the scope and nature of political economy, before dealing with the meaning of the PR.

The function of the mechanical analogy

Jevons had a mathematical perception of the laws of economic life, ever since he started reading political economy:[6]

> You will perceive that economy, scientifically speaking, is a very contracted science; it in fact a sort of vague mathematics which calculates the causes and effects of man's industry, and shows how it may best be applied. There are a multitude of allied branches of knowledge connected with man's condition; the relation of these to political economy is analogous to the connection of mechanics, astronomy, optics, sound heat, and every other branch more or less of physical science, with pure mathematics.
>
> (Letter to his sister Henrietta, 28 February 1858, quoted in Collison Black 1970: 12)

This mathematical perception of the economy was officially presented first in his *Notice on the Mathematical Theory of Political Economy* before the British Association for the Advancement of Science, in 1862.[7] Some nine years later, in the preface of the first edition of his *Theory of Political Economy*, he wrote:

> The theory of economy, thus treated, presents a close analogy to the Science of Statical Mechanics, and the Laws of Exchange are found to resemble to the Laws of Equilibrium of a lever as determined by the principle of virtual velocities. The nature of wealth and value is explained by the consideration of indefinitely small amounts of pleasure and pain, just as the theory of Statics is made to rest upon the equality of indefinitely small amounts of energy.
>
> (Jevons 1871: 44)

In this representation, economic activity is reduced to simple physical processes: the economic contractors represent antagonistic forces, the combination of which explains the exchange of goods. Jevons' originality lies in his novel theoretical approach to value and distribution using metaphors from mechanics. Jevons himself explained that his fundamental theory of exchange is a simple transcription of the equilibrium conditions of rational mechanics:

> Equilibrium of exchange of goods resembles in mathematical conditions of weights upon a lever of the first order. In the latter case one weight multiplied by its arm must exactly equal the other weight

multiplied by its arm. So, in an act of exchange the commodity given multiplied by its degree of utility must equal the quantity of commodity received multiplied by its degree of utility.

(Jevons 1876: 626)[8]

Not surprisingly, Léon Walras has independently made the very same discovery based on the analogy between economics and mechanics:

> Thanks to this mass, so defined, the mathematicians who elaborated celestial mechanics have been able to demonstrate that: "*the celestial bodies attract one another* in direct proportion to their mass and in inverse proportion to the square of their distance", and have explained astronomical phenomena and established mathematical astronomy. Thanks to *rareté*, defined in the same way, I have been able to demonstrate that: "goods tend to be exchanged one against the other in *inverse proportion to their rareté*" and have explained the principal economic phenomena and sketched out a pure mathematical political economy.

(Walras 1901)[9]

The new scope of economic analysis

The reduction of economic processes to physical ones reduced dramatically the scope of economic analysis. Jevons succeeded in defining the economic problem as one of exchanging goods through competitive market by assimilating the field of economic forces to the field of energy. In order to build a mathematical and homogeneous field of analysis, political economy had to be free from many social factors. What was, for Mill and other Ricardians, considered the social variables of production and distribution, now, with Jevons and Walras, became a parameter, external to economic analysis. This was unambiguously acknowledged: "Given, a certain population, with various needs and powers of production, in possession of certain lands and other sources of material: required, the mode of employing their labor which will maximize the utility of the produce" (Jevons 1871: 254, cf. Walras 1874: 277, §179). As exactly stated "for Jevons, the 'problem of economics' was to maximize the utility of the output obtained from a set of given resources" (Mosselmans 2007: 7).

According to this new vision, the market is capable of allocating efficiently scarce resources, either in production, distribution or exchange.[10] It was quite so in Walras' general equilibrium model. Given the initial distribution of resources and the individual utility functions, Walras describes an ideal auction market in which the auctioneer "cries" the prices until the gaps between supply and demand are adjusted to obtain a simultaneous equilibrium on all markets. Consequently, competition or the law of demand and supply is the only basis for price formation, assuming constant preferences, fixed supplies of the factors of production, and given technology. The exclusion of population theory, the abandon of a long run theory of value, the abolition of minimum rate of wages, as well as the underestimation of production theory, all these changes express the same attitude of building an autonomous and sufficient economic theory purified from social considerations.[11]

Narrowing the scope of political economy had another crucial consequence: it permitted the extension of its boundaries, or as Donald Winch (1972: 337) wrote so accurately, it "made it possible to be more ruthless in separating economic adjustment mechanisms from their integument, thereby strengthening claims to cross-cultural and intertemporal validity". For, if economic theory does not depend on any social, historical or cultural factors, as in classical political economy, its conclusions are applicable far beyond capitalist England of the mid-nineteenth century. Any human behaviour can thus be treated as economic as far as it concerns the maximization of a goal and Jevons was perfectly clear in his claim for generality: "the first principles of Political Economy are so widely true and applicable, that they may be considered universally true as regards human nature" (Jevons 1876: 624).[12]

It is precisely the shift of emphasis from the questions of production and distribution of wealth to the questions of exchange that gave to the principle of economic behaviour its crucial place in economic explanation. According to Jevons, specific assumptions about population growth, capital and labour productivity, and diminishing returns are obsolete, since they are all considered as given exogenously. The principle of maximizing behaviour is by itself a sufficient basis for explaining rational allocation of resources through competition, as well as their remuneration. By reducing economic phenomena to their psychological dimension, Jevons wanted to express "the feelings of pleasure and pain" in terms of a balance of forces, namely utility and disutility. He stated clearly that,

> it is the amount of these feelings which is continually prompting us to buying and selling, borrowing and lending, labouring and resting, producing and consuming; and it is from the quantitative effects of the feelings that we must estimate their comparative amounts.
>
> (Jevons 1871: 83)

Although he has strongly sided with Bentham and opposed Mill as to the idea that all types of pleasure might be reduced to quantities, Jevons was aware of the fact that it was impossible to establish a direct comparison of feelings between two different minds (White 1994: 217; Peart 1995b: 75). This is the reason why he wanted to make of the market prices, as it was correctly said, "the manifestation of internal balancing acts of the mind" (Schabas 1990: 86). Walras on the other side, helped by the analytical findings of Cournot, was able to derive demand curves directly from consumer's maximizing behaviour avoiding any recourse to utilitarianism.[13]

The nature of the assumption of rationality as maximization

A major question remains: what is the exact epistemological nature of the marginalist maximization principle? What's more, the maximization principle was assisted by the puzzling postulate of a "perfect market". In a perfect market, "all traders have perfect knowledge of the conditions of supply and demand and the consequent ratio of exchange" (Jevons 1871: 134).[14] Jevons explained his views on the nature of scientific hypotheses in his book *The Principles of Science* (edited in 1874). He developed the hypothetico-deductive model of explanation (already established by William Whewell in the 1830s), which is, in many respects, similar to the standard deductive nomological model.[15] According to this model, hypotheses are not propositions established by systematic observation, but mere suppositions about the nature of phenomena, we could say *conjectures* using the Popperian terminology. As Jevons explained, scientists are looking for "probable hypotheses" guided by their previous knowledge and imagination, or even by simple "coincidence" (Jevons 1874: 505). But when a plausible hypothesis is found, Jevons warns that its use in scientific explanation is justified only if the deductive consequences of this hypothesis agree with observation: "agreement with facts is the sole and sufficient test of a true hypothesis" (Jevons 1874: 510).

Unfortunately, Jevons never applied this process of "trial and error" of hypotheses to the case of maximization principle, despite the fact that he insisted that "the deductive science of Economics must be verified and rendered useful by the purely empirical science of Statistics" (1871: 90). Notwithstanding his pioneering applications of statistics to economics, Jevons referred erroneously to the notion of an average economic behaviour. He stated that "questions which appear, and perhaps are quite indeterminate as regards individuals, may be capable of exact investigation and solution as regard to great masses and wide averages" (1871: 86). Jevons' connection to the Belgian mathematician and astronomer Adolphe Quetelet and to his statistics is actually well known.[16] What is important to stress here is the crucial importance that Quetelet's notion of the "average man" had on

Jevons' exchange theory. The latter believed that it was possible to create a "representative individual" based on Quetelet's "arithmetical average". Still, Jevons also thought incorrectly that differences between individuals would cancel each other out, believing that, "the aggregate and the average are the same" (Mosselmans 2007: 37). He believed that in the average, all individual aspirations and special characteristics "balance", and therefore become insignificant. This error had important consequences for his definition of the "trading body" since it shaped his conception of exchange:

> Every trading body is either an individual or an aggregate of individuals, and the law [of exchange], in the case of the aggregate, must depend upon the fulfillment of law in the individuals.... Thus our laws of economics will be theoretically true in the case of individuals, and practically true in the case of large aggregates.
>
> (Jevons 1871: 135)

The explanation behind this view is to be found in his erroneous conception of the "fictitious mean" thus neutralizing the action of disturbing causes. Unlike Mill's analysis, where any persisting counterfact would possibly suggest the presence of a "disturbing cause" that has to be taken into account, Jevons paid no attention to the "whims of individuals" believing that such "noxious influences" do not count in the aggregate since they "balance" (Peart 1995a: 1202). The method of means believed to be capable of disentangling the multiplicity of causes and the intermixture of effects that were prohibiting, according to Mill and Cairnes any possibility of discovering an exact economic law with the aid of numerical data.[17]

It appears then that this erroneous methodological position created a major contradiction between Jevons' methodological rules expressed in his *Principles of Science* and their application to economic theory, concerning the establishment of scientific hypotheses. In the *Principles* it is maintained that experience is the only source of knowledge. Nevertheless, in his *Theory of Political Economy* it was recognized that "the Science of Economics is in some degree peculiar ... [because] *its ultimate laws are known to us by intuition*, or, at any rate they are furnished to us ready made by other mental or physical sciences" (1871: 88, emphasis added). As far as the maximization principle was concerned, Jevons seemed then to maintain that it was established without any other verification than the indirect one, through market prices: "there is no means of measuring pleasure and pain directly, but as those feelings govern sales and purchases, the prices of the market are those facts from which one may argue back to the intensity of the pleasure concerned" (Jevons 1872, in a letter to Cairnes, quoted in Schabas 1990: 87). For Jevons, the principle that all persons try to maximize their gain in every transaction has the character of an "obvious psychological law" (1871: 87).[18] The same applies to its corollary hypotheses as well:

> That every person will choose the greater apparent good; that human wants are more or less quickly satiated; that prolonged labor becomes more and more painful are a few of the simple inductions on which we can proceed to reason deductively with great confidence.
>
> (Jevons 1871: 88)

It is quite interesting that Jevons quotes Mill and Cairnes, who asked for "long and accurate observation" as a means to establish the premises of political economy, as seen above in the previous chapter. On the contrary, Jevons considers these premises as axioms, "known to us immediately by intuition" and ratified a posteriori, by comparison of the theoretical inferences with real facts. Not accidentally, he chooses the principle of free trade as an example of theoretical inference deducted from these premises, to conclude that "there is nothing in experience which in the least conflicts with our expectations" (Jevons 1871: 88).

The contrast becomes even more significant knowing Jevons' commitment to fallibilism. He stated clearly that "in Science and Philosophy nothing is sacred" (Jevons 1874: 276) and asked for "perfect readiness" to reject every theory inconsistent with facts: "readiness to reject a false theory may be combined with a peculiar pertinacity and courage in maintaining an hypothesis as long as its falsity is not actually apparent" (Jevons, 1874: 586). Even so, Jevons was particularly suspicious of eventual refutations of hypotheses, maintaining that it is only after multiple decisive experiments that we can decide on the falsity of a hypothesis (Jevons 1874: 516).[19] His reference to the statistical *homme moyen* testifies his erroneous conception in the use of statistics as a means of inductive validation. White (1989: 441) gives another example of Jevons' inaccurate use of statistics, examining his claim to validate the marginal utility theory through the King–D'Avenant Price–Quantity Table. White demonstrates that the original table "had to be both read and rewritten in marginalist terms before it could be used to illustrate [Jevons'] arguments". Kim (1995: 150) supports further this point about Jevons' attempt to "ascertain the law to which D'Avenant's figures conform": Jevons restated the original table as if the figures contained in it were statistical averages from a series of data, considering it as a "close approximation". And so, his final formula describing the relation between the price and the quantity of corn was a statistical inference "not far from the truth" (Jevons 1871: 182).

Why then is Jevons so confident in his maximization principle? The answer lies, in our view, in his determination to create a homogeneous and mathematical field of analysis by means of analogy. Having thus in mind that the "mechanical science is founded upon a few simple laws of motion", Jevons looked for analogous "universal principles of human nature". He took the principles of Bentham's utilitarianism and Alexander Bain's associationism as the psychological framework for his mathematical approach and accepted them as axioms "almost as self-evident as the Elements of Euclid". In order to build "the mechanics of utility and self-interest" (Jevons 1871: 90), he furthermore adopted Richard Jennings' principles of physiological psychology, explaining economic actions as "reflexes", as White (1994) has shown in a very convincing way. Jevons knew Jennings' *Natural Elements of Political Economy* (1855) since the early 1860s and quotes them abundantly in his *Theory of Political Economy* as a basis for the construction of his theory of exchange.

But the analogical reasoning shows clearly here its limits since, apart from helping us to represent the unknown "it also … creates similarities and differences where none existed before" (Ménard 1993).[20] As Schabas (1990: 96) wrote "like its counterpart in physics, the new system of economic mechanics would be reductionist, universal in scope, and above all, mathematical". In his search for universal principles that could be treated mathematically, Jevons evacuated the empirical content of the principle of maximizing behaviour, avoiding thus questions about the social determinants of economic rationality.[21]

Jevons' epistemological project can be clarified further if one looks closely to his idea about the science of logic, an aspect of the Jevonian system of thought generally neglected by economists. Mosselmans (2007: 38) emphasized that "Jevons' system is comprehensible only when interpreted in terms of extent of meaning". Anticipating the movement of logical positivism, Jevons believed that all terms should be transformed until they refer to one or more concrete objects. His ultimate goal was to develop a "natural classification" based on definitions in which "the meaning of all the words employed is made clear" (ibid.: 44). This would result in a system of unified science, in which logic is the foundation of mathematics, while all the empirical sciences like physics and economics were supposed to be mathematical sciences. Mosselmans (2007) argues convincingly that Jevons' project has failed because economic matters often require an interpretation in terms of intent of meaning thus involving a group of qualities. Jevons had tried to bridge the gap between extent and intent of meaning using the same erroneous conception of the "fictitious mean", which was assumed to equalize individual differences by the way of statistical normalization of observations.

We are now able to summarize Jevons' ideas on economic rationality in order to make easier the revolutionary mutation in the meaning of the concept: (*i*) the principle of maximization of pleasure (or profit) under constraint is, according to Jevons, a self-evident hypothesis or, in other words, an axiom of economic explanation introspectively founded, and verified only indirectly through market prices; (*ii*) the axiomatic nature of this principle makes possible the mathematical treatment of economic concepts such as "utility", "demand", "price", and also "rent", "capital", "production", etc.; (*iii*) Jevons' PR guarantees the universal application of the "economic approach" not only to any economic system but also to any field of human activity as far as it obeys a maximization of a goal under constraint. Thus, Jevons inaugurates the aggressive expansionism of economics to other fields that will flourish in the tradition of the so-called "economic approach to human behavior", where every human action is reducible to a utility maximization problem, whether it belongs into the economic sphere or not (Becker 1976: 7; Cf. Stigler and Becker 1977; Hirshleifer 1985).

In sum, Jevons constructed an axiomatic concept of economic rationality that "liberates" economic analysis from its social and historical boundaries to make possible the application of the differential calculus. Walras and Jevons' immediate followers, Edgeworth, Marshall and Wicksteed, will also adopt the idea of maximization under constraint as the behavioural premise of their economic analysis.

Notes

1 A much earlier version of this chapter was published in Zouboulakis (1997a).
2 This concept should not be confused with Polanyi's definition of "substantivist rationality", which concerns the activity of "materialist provisioning" of the pre-capitalist societies.
3 Ménard explores thoroughly the epistemological, ideological and theoretical conditions of Cournot's first mathematical model. He also explains convincingly the reasons of its late recognition by other economists. Walras wrote the first public review with a delay of 25 years, in 1863, Jevons recognized him as a precursor only in the second edition of his *Theory* in 1879, Edgeworth criticized him severely in 1881 and it was Marshall who finally made him famous in the preface of his *Principles* in 1890.
4 Many specialists saw in this episode a significant intellectual breakthrough in the history of economics. Cf. Collison-Black (1970), Coats (1972), Hutchison (1972), Jalladeau (1978), Birken (1988), Mirowski (1989). For the opposite – continuity – view see Stigler (1950), Blaug (1961), Hollander (1985).
5 Cf. Ménard (1978, 1993), Mirowski (1984, 1989), Schabas (1990), White (1994), Maas (2005) and Mosselmans (1997, 2007). Some other historians have also mentioned in the past the role of the physical metaphor in the rise of marginalism, without any further discussion. See Mays (1962: 237), MacLennan (1972: 66) and Deane (1978: 95).

6 Jevons studied chemistry, botany, mathematics and logic in UC London and worked for five years as a gold assayer in the Australian Mint to support his family, from 1854 to 1859. See Maas (2005, chap. 2). He first read Smith's *Wealth of Nations* in 1858, at the age of 23.

7 The *Notice* even though it contains the essential of his theoretical innovation, "had made no impact" according to Hutchison (1972: 450). Cf. Collison-Black (1970: 13), Schabas (1990: 24), White (1991: 154).

8 After reading passages like the above, one might not find excessive Mirowski's thesis, that "the progenitors of neoclassical economic theory boldly copied the reigning physical theories in the 1870s term for term and symbol for symbol, and said so" (1989: 3). Mirowski insists on the law competencies of the "progenitors" in physics and how this affected their comprehension of economic phenomena (1989: 254–261). However, this is not true for Jevons, Walras, Marshall, Pareto and Fisher, who had received solid scientific education.

9 Letter of 26 September 1901 to Henri Poincaré, quoted in Ingrao and Israel (1990: 157, original emphasis). Walras' conception of pure political economy as a "physicomathematical science" is presented in section 30, of the fourth lesson of his *Elements* (Walras 1874: 52).

10 Mosselmans (1999) argues that Jevons reasoned in terms of "a non-reproductive environment, in which scarcity is externally determined by objective societal mechanisms", and that this was due to his "loss of confidence in man's possibilities to alter the economic system".

11 For further development of this position see Hutchison (1972), Winch (1972), Jalladeau (1978), Garegnani (1984), Schabas (1990: 84–89) and White (1994: 199). Walras aspired to complete his "Pure theory of Economics" with a theory of "Social Economics" or national income distribution theory and a theory of "Applied Economics" or production economics, which were published in 1896 and 1898 respectively. See Ingrao and Israel (1990: 99).

12 Similarly, Walras (1874: 53) compares the "truths of pure political economy" to mathematical and geometrical truths as to their certainty and generality.

13 On the influence of Cournot upon Walras see Ménard (1978: 246), Ingrao and Israel (1990: 93).

14 White (1989: 439) explained that for Jevons, decision makers can make "accurate forecasts about the effects of variations in an exogenous variable over a number of harvest periods".

15 See apropos MacLennan (1972), Caldwell (1982: 28) and Schabas (1990: 71–72).

16 Cf. Voisin (1987), Schabas (1990), Peart (1995a) and Mosselmans (2007).

17 Cairnes, in the second edition of his *Character and Logical Method of Political Economy* (1875), responded directly to Jevons' attempt to obtain exact laws about economic relations, employing statistical methods. On the Jevons–Cairnes debate, see Kim (1995).

18 On the certainty of the psychological premises in Jevons see Mays (1962: 233) and MacLennan (1972: 67).

19 On Jevons' "critical fallibilism" see Hutchison (1982), Schabas (1990: 73–74).

20 Ménard (1993) makes a full case of the functions of analogical thinking in economic reasoning. The same issue was developed in his work (1978: 120, 244) regarding the model of Cournot.

21 Latsis (1976: 22) pointed out that one of the main advantages of the "situation determinist" approach is that it makes the application of mathematical techniques easier. This remark also applies in Jevons' case.

4 Vilfredo Pareto and the concept of instrumental rationality

Vilfredo Pareto's *Manual of Political Economy* (first edition in Italian 1906, second in French 1909) presented "the first complete formal exposition of the rational mechanics of *homo oeconomicus*" (Ingrao and Israel 1990: 131). In that sense it marks the ultimate step of the marginalist movement that aimed to build a new science of economics by focusing exclusively on the exchange of scarce resources through market mechanisms. In the lineage including Jevons–Walras–Edgeworth–Marshall–Fisher–Pareto, the latter makes the decisive theoretical advance that shaped the development of neoclassical demand theory for the first half of the twentieth century. As with real life, the evolution of concepts and ideas is never linear. This implies the existence of another distinct lineage going from Cournot, to Léon Walras and Pareto. As it is impossible to understand Pareto without reading Walras it is impossible to understand Walras' theoretical innovations without first understanding Cournot. Yet, from our point of view, Cournot and Walras shared the same concept of rationality with the English marginalists, that of maximization under constraint.

Disintegrating utilitarian rationality: Edgeworth, Marshall and Wicksteed

Despite Schumpeter's aphorism (1954: 831) about his detachment from utilitarianism, Edgeworth endorsed fully Bentham's calculus of pleasure and pain as well as Jevons' approach of economic rationality as a quantitative balance of utility between different pleasures.[1] His originality lies, as Marshall acknowledged immediately upon the publication of his *Mathematical Psychics*, in generalizing the application of mathematical methods "to the enquiry how work and wealth must be distributed so as to give the greatest possible happiness" at the level of society (Marshall 1881). Edgeworth used the "utilitarian principle" as a principle of arbitration in order to prove that a social optimum is located among different exchange positions along the "contract curve": "competition requires to be supplemented by arbitration, and the basis of arbitration between self-interested contractors is the greatest possible sum-total utility" (Edgeworth 1881: 56). Although he had a much more refined view than Jevons concerning the differences in the quality of pleasures and the individual differences in the "capacity for happiness", thanks to his knowledge of the latest developments in psychophysics,[2] both the individual objectives and the behavioural pattern remain fundamentally the same: every individual seeks to maximize its personal utility and acts purposively. A maximum social utility is only a matter of integration: "Greatest possible happiness is the greatest possible integral of the differential number of enjoyers × duration of enjoyment × degree thereof" (Edgeworth 1881: 57). To be able to portray social utility graphically, Edgeworth "devised indifference curves, or contour lines, to permit of a graphical analysis of utility in this case" (Stigler 1950: 103).

Marshall defined economics as "a study of mankind in the ordinary business of life" (1890: 1). Beyond his unrivalled theoretical novelty, he has consciously preserved many elements of the dynamic social approach of the pre-marginalist era. Part of his common heritage with the classical economists, and especially John Stuart Mill, so often disregarded in the secondary literature,[3] is his willingness to study economic phenomena in their social context: "economists, like other students of social science, are concerned with individuals chiefly as members of the social organism" (1890: 20). He believed that individual actions are integrated into a greater social whole, and consequently economists should not commit "the fault of claiming universality and necessity for their doctrines" (Marshall 1885: 18). As he concludes, "economists study the actions of individuals, but study them in relation to social rather than individual life" (1890: 21). And because individuals are social, their motives have more dimensions "besides that of pecuniary gain". This fact induces economics to open its perspectives beyond a strict economic calculation, especially to the "habits and customs" that influence "business conduct" (1890: 17).

Conversely, it is also true that Marshall, at least in his *Principles*, has shown "excessive reliance on subjective rationality" (Schumpeter 1984: 593). His maxim that economists "deal with man as he is; not with an abstract or 'economic man' but a man of flesh and blood" (1890: 22) was a polemical answer to the accusation of trying to "rehabilitate the abstract method of Ricardo", rather than a confession of adherence to the philosophy of empiricism.[4] Marshall's unmistakable commitment to utilitarianism and marginalist reasoning to individual behaviour proves that there was no significant conceptual advance in the idea of economic rationality. From Jevons to Edgeworth and Marshall one finds the same rational scheme to explain economic action on the basis of maximization of utility or profit under constraint, verified only through introspection. But, unlike Jevons and Edgeworth, Marshall shared with the classics the same belief in the complexity and temporal relativity of economic phenomena. That, together with his evolutionary inclination, explains his attitude against an excessive use of mathematics: "he feared that factors that could not easily be dealt with in mathematical form would be neglected" (Coase 1975: 31).

Philip Wicksteed (1910), an outsider to the economics profession, has tried to broaden the range of economic rationality by recognizing that individual choices are to be made inside a complex socio-economic reality composed of many rational and irrational elements alike, involving a "selection between alternatives" (Zafirowski 2008: 807). Yet, his "attempt to free marginalist economics from its hedonist basis was only partially successful" (Drakopoulos 2011: 463). Schumpeter has concluded that although

> the general complexion of his system is Jevonian ... he shook off so many corrections and developments – partly under Austrian influence – that he may be said to have worked out something that, though of course a revision of the marginal utility system, was his own.
>
> (1954: 832; cf. Schabas 1990: 122)

Most important was his consumer choice theory where he introduced the idea of "scale of preferences" and of the "transitivity of choices" in a way that portrayed the developments to be made in Robbins' essay (Blaug 1961: 576).

Pareto's trip away from psychology

Pareto shared with Mill the same desire for an objective source of knowledge concerning human behaviour as against any subjective or introspective methods similar to those employed by Bentham and Jevons. Nonetheless, unlike Mill, he refused to ground economic explanation to behavioural premises established by psychology and endorsed initially the maximization principle. On the one hand, he recognized that "all human conduct is psychological", and in that sense any "branch of human activity is a psychological study" (1917, quoted in Boland 1982: 27); but, he did emphasize on the other hand that "the principles of an economic psychology ... can be deduced only from facts", believing that experience is the only criterion of truth. In other words while he did subscribe to what Popper has called *psychological individualism* (cf. Boland 1982: 30; Gross and Tarascio 1998), he clearly wanted to circumscribe the field of economic analysis only to what is empirically observed through the results of individual action. As he emphatically said, "I am a believer in the efficiency of experimental methods to the exclusion of all others. For me there exist no valuable demonstrations except those that are based on facts" (Pareto 1897: 491).

It is evident from the above, that economic behaviour can be analysed in two parallel, yet different ways: either by reference to the feeling that the individuals obtain from their choices, following thus the utilitarian logic of pleasure and pain; or by reference to the act of choice alone without any allusion whatsoever to the hedonistic aspects of that choice (Meidinger 1994: 91–92). The hypothesis "all consumers maximize utility" is untestable because of the presence of the undefined term "utility", in the sentence (Caldwell 1983) and because of the indeterminacy of the process of maximization. Bluntly said, Pareto in the *Manual*, just like Cournot did in his *Recherches*, cares only for the objective results of rational choice, without worrying what is on a man's mind: "the real facts that we are able to observe are the sales of certain goods at certain prices" (quoted in Marchionatti and Gambino 1997).[5] Here lies the essence of his late departure from utilitarian psychology in order to build a logical theory of choice:[6]

> Let us suppose that we have a schedule of all possible choices indicating the order of preference. Once this schedule is available, *homo œconomicus* can leave the scene. We need no further characteristic of his.... The schedule or scheme which indicates his preferences is all that is needed.
>
> (Pareto quoted in Weber 2001: 554)

Hence, Paretian rationality is an objective, non-psychologistic quality of human action. The indefinite and subjective concepts of marginal utility and measurable satisfaction (Jevons, Edgeworth, Marshall) were at length replaced by the new concept of *"ophelimité"* as the basis of construction of indifference curves and relative demand functions. Although it is questionable whether Pareto has ever completely abandoned cardinal assumptions in his demand theory (Schumpeter 1954: 1063; Bruni and Guala 2001; Weber 2001), his proclaimed aim in the *Manuel* was to concentrate on the maximizing choices made by independent economic agents and no longer on the psychological motives that underlie those choices.

Pareto indicated two ways to derive the facts of choice, either experimentally, by asking individuals what their potential choices would be; or through market purchases, i.e. by observing real choices made in the marketplace (Gross and Tarascio 1998). Both ways lead to the empirical determination of indifference curves. From the observation of choices among different goods combined with budgetary constraint it was therefore possible to deduce the negative slope of demand curves (Stigler 1950: 122–123).[7] Rationality is, in this sense, only a matter of a reasoned choice of efficient means for serving any independently given objective and that is why is called "instrumental" (Sen 1987b: 70):

> In short, I am concerned with the fact that living beings (man, ass, or ant), placed between combinations *AB* and *CD*, cannot decide which to choose, and turn neither to the left nor to the right; placed between *CD* and *EF*, ditto; placed between *EF* and *GH*, ditto, and so on. I then say that *AB*, *CD*, *EF*, *GH* ... are combinations forming part of an indifference curve. Since all that we need to ascertain is whether the living being turns to the left or to the right, takes *AB* or *CD* or remains perplexed between the two, *there is no longer any psychological analysis. Even a machine can have indifference curves.*
>
> (Pareto 1909, chap. 3 §1. Engl. transl. by A. Schwier 1972, emphasis added)

There are two amazing things in this quotation. First, it shows clearly how Pareto focused on the logic of choices to establish his indifference curves, distancing himself from psychology; given that the number of indifference curves is unlimited, so are knowledge and the computational capacities of the rational subjects. Second, Pareto extended his concept of rational choice to every living organism. Not only does Pareto not confine rational choice to political economy exclusively, but he explicitly suggests that "logical actions" can be found everywhere in social life, even in the life of social animals: "Most of actions in the arts, the industry, the commerce, the arts of war and politics are of this kind [experimental and logical]" (Pareto 1898, quoted in Steiner 2003: 231, our translation).

In his definitive exposition on the subject of social action, Pareto (1917) distinguished logical from non-logical actions. *Logical* actions – with which only political economy deals, though not exclusively – are those actions within which the subjective aim of the actor is reasonably connected to the action's objective goal. These actions are then logical both subjectively and objectively, that is they "logically conjoin means to ends not only from the standpoint of the subject performing them, but from the standpoint of other persons who have a more extensive knowledge" (Pareto 1917: §150). It should be stated that the actor knows then all the necessary means to achieve his goal and is also capable of calculating correctly and judging of the comparative efficacy of those means (Steiner 2003: 231).

However, logical actions are far from predominating social life. *Non-logical* actions form the greater part of social conduct and are principally the subject matter of sociology. In those cases the subjective aim does not correspond to the effect produced by the action itself, regardless of what the actor believes. In Pareto's own words:

> Non-logical actions originate chiefly in definite psychic states, sentiments, subconscious feelings, and the like. It is the province of psychology to investigate such psychic states. Here [in sociology] we start with them as data of fact, without going beyond that.
>
> (Pareto 1917: §167)

Pareto has suggested four types of non-logical actions (NLA): (*i*) NLA of the first type when they are deprived of both subjective and objective rationality, and the individual acts without knowing the reason (e.g. I put always the knife on the right side and the fork on the left side of the plate); (*ii*) NLA of the second type, when they are deprived only from objective rationality (e.g. I pray for the rain to come); (*iii*) NLA of the third type, when they are deprived only from subjective rationality and the individual acts following a customary rule (e.g. I always eat turkeys on Christmas day); and (*iv*) NLA of the fourth type, when the logical action has an unintended consequence that differs from the individual goal (e.g. I drop my own sell prices to get more demand, and I get less because every other competitor does the same). Except the last case, the only one with an economic interest, insofar as the actors behave following their sentiments (love, faith, superstition, etc.) or some traditional values and social customs, then they act in a *non-logical* manner; that is they are not looking for the objectively and subjectively best way to achieve the goal they are looking for (Steiner 1999a: 21–22; Legris and Ragni 2005). As he has explained in his earlier work, non-logical action does not necessary mean irrational action, but only action following a non-logical process of deliberation (Pareto 1909: 41).

Yet, by recognizing the fact that people act in real life mostly on the basis of non-logical motives (called *residues*) and invent self-justifications for them afterwards, Pareto wanted to build a much more general theory of action, far beyond the strict boundaries of rational economic action, comparable only to Max Weber, his illustrious colleague. Instead of expanding rational behaviour analysis to explain social actions (*à la mode* of the rational choice theorists, Allen, Hicks, Robbins and the like) he took the opposite way; he reduced the domain of pure economic theory based on the rationality assumption to the status of "a first approximation to the full theory of economic phenomena", just like John Stuart Mill has suggested before him. He was in fact criticized for that by early neoclassicals, namely Wicksteed and Robbins (Steiner 1999b; Bruni and Sugden 2007: 157). As he emphasized: "economists ... do not know and will never know the concrete phenomena in all their details" (Pareto 1897: 490). The study of *homo oeconomicus* has therefore to be complemented with the study of *homo moralis, homo religiosus, homo eroticus* and so on, in turn to say something relevant about real men (Schumpeter 1984: 593). This is why, at the end of his academic career, he has tried to build a unified social science to understand fully the concrete reality of social life (Aspers 2001; Bruni 2002: chap. 4).

Pareto, Weber and the split from utilitarianism

Max Weber regarded economics as the example of a science having the features of his "ideal-type analysis".[8] He has explicitly recognized that his definition of the "ideal-type", as "one sided emphasis and intensification of one or several aspects of a given event", is borrowed from economics. Although he did not bring to light his direct sources, it is commonly admitted that he had in mind the members of the German speaking "Marginalist School", when he was referring to the "abstract economic theory" (Weber 1904: 90).[9] Weber's strong involvement in the *Methodenstreit* offers more evidence to this position. Nevertheless, the construction of ideal types reminds in many aspects the definition of economic rationality made by John Stuart Mill. As seen above, Mill tried to delimitate the field of economics by isolating by means of abstraction one specific range of social phenomena relative to the production and distribution of wealth, inside which a particular type of economic behaviour was dominant. Both Mill and Weber did use their theoretical constructions, as theoretical models which enable the social scientist to explain in individualistic terms the real world in a given historical and geographical context.

Weber created his concept of "ideal-type" as a means of incorporating the chaotic multiplicity of social phenomena into an "ideal" reconstruction of events. The term "ideal" should be understood, as he explicitly suggested, in the sense of Galileo's "absolute vacuum", i.e. like a theoretical "model" (Weber 1922: 20) and not in the normative sense (Hausman 1992: 80). Weber made clear that his concept was not a pure "hypothesis" since it derives from reality, and yet it is not a "description of reality". As he asserted "action takes exactly this course only in unusual cases, as sometimes in the stock exchange" (Weber 1922: 9). Following Mill, he constructed a generic concept which, from a collection of attributes, extracts the more typical elements in a pattern of action. Such a mental construction, obtained by means of abstraction "possess only essential and lack non-essential properties" as Schumpeter wrote (1954: 819). In the case of economic action, this double movement of simplification and exaggeration is obtained by "excluding the influence of political and other extra-economic factors" (1917: 420). This is, as we have seen above, a methodological device originated in Mill's sixth essay (Steiner 1998: 51). Moreover, like Smith and Mill, Weber wanted to explain the nature of social phenomena in terms of socialized individuals who have internalized in their plans the sentiments of their fellowmen (1922: 13).[10]

However, unlike Mill and similar to Pareto, he emphasized "how erroneous it is to regard any kind of psychology as the ultimate foundation of the sociological interpretation of action" (Weber 1922: 19) This is why he vigorously criticized Lujo Brentano's effort to ground the marginalist theory of subjective evaluation on Gustav Fechner's psychophysical laws.[11] Weber's main objective was to suggest a method of explaining historical events beyond the particular and the contingent yet without espousing the Humean model of causal explanation. His prominent idea of "interpretative explanation" linking subjective understanding with objective causality, is perfectly reflected in the concept of "ideal type".[12] Weber's ideal-type analysis helps one to understand historical phenomena from the viewpoint of their cultural significance, without the fear of being accused of historical determinism. Still, Weber did not envisage the concept of ideal type in a unitary way. Raymond Aron (1967) has identified three distinct meanings of the concept: "Historical ideal types", which correspond to a particular historical context (e.g. "capitalism", "western-city"), "sociological ideal types", which focus on the perpetual elements of historical reality (e.g. "bureaucracy", "feudalism") and finally a third kind which can be called "theoretical ideal types" like those used in economic theory (Hausman 1992: 80; Hollis 1994: 150). Weber's renowned four ideal types of social action (instrumentally rational, value rational, emotional and traditional) are thus "theoretical", meaning both general and historically embedded. They are general in the sense that they can be significant beyond a specific society, yet without being universal, i.e. pertinent to all times and places (Weber 1922: 24–25).[13] Pareto's "logical action" fits perfectly to a sub-type of Weber's goal oriented action called "accurate rationality" (*Richtigkeitsrationalität*) (cf. Steiner 2003).

It should be emphasized that Weber does not associate to the concept of *Zweckrational* neither the meaning of the "historical ideal type" nor the meaning of the "sociological ideal type". The meaning of "instrumentally rational", profit oriented economic action relates to the third kind of theoretical "ideal type", that is closer to Mill's "principle of economic behaviour" and to Pareto's "logical action". As Weber himself points out (1922: 339) not all instrumentally rational actions are economic, but all economic actions are necessarily instrumentally rational. Weber's meaning is at distance with Menger's "purely fictional agent". As he wrote, "the empirical forms here under discussion, e.g. absolute pure oxygen, pure alcohol, pure gold, a person pursuing only economic aims, etc., exists in part only in our ideas" (Menger 1883: 61). Menger's idealization refers to "what people do in very unusual, perhaps impossible circumstances when they are engaged in economy". For that reason he did not recognize any historical preconditions for the maximization of economic interests. Menger, together with Jevons and Böhm-Bawerk, believed that his concepts were "universally true as regards to human nature" (Jevons 1876: 624; cf. Böhm-Bawerk 1890: 264). On the contrary, Weber aimed to construct theoretical models historically confined, rather than applicable to all times and places (Hodsgon 2001: 121). The example of the generalization he uses in order to make his intentions clear is very characteristic in terms of its historical peculiarity: "the generalisation called Gresham's law is a rationally clear interpretation of human action under certain conditions and under the assumption that it will follow a purely rational course" (1922: 10).

Weber's choice to idealize an empirical generalization relative to a particular historical context, testifies his willingness to create theoretical propositions that explain *what would necessarily occur if* human actions were indeed "unequivocally directed to a single end" (1922: 9). As correctly said economic rationality is "a social structural phenomenon and not simply an expression of the human capacity for accurate computation" (Ingham 1996: 256). This theoretical model, "to which actual action is more or less closely approximated" (Weber 1922: 26), needs to be readjusted in order to take account of "the observed deviations". These deviations could be the result of factors such as "misinformation, strategical errors, logical fallacies, personal temperament, or considerations outside the realm of strategy" (1922: 21).[14] Consequently, Weber's ideal type of "instrumental rationality" is a general concept that captures partially the reality by idealizing the goal-oriented (profit maximization) rational behaviour characteristic of the historical and cultural context of the Western European capitalism (cf. 1904: 92). Thus, Weber bridged the gap between the historicists and the marginalists by keeping an equal distance between them.

Measuring the distance from rationality as maximization

We can evaluate now the differences in the meaning and content between Jevons' maximization principle and Pareto's concept of instrumental rationality. Jevons built his mathematical economic theory based on the hypothesis of constrained maximization of utility. For that reason he centred his attention to subjective motives as a necessary explanation of economic behaviour. Moreover, Jevons' PR guarantees the universal application of economic reasoning not only to any economic system but also to any field of human activity, as far as it obeys a maximization of a goal under some external constraint, as Becker (1962, 1976) has claimed (cf. Stigler and Becker 1977; Vriend 1996: 266).[15]

Pareto on the other hand focused mostly, not on the map of tastes, but rather in the acts of choice that are directed towards the acquisition of goods. Changing from his initial marginalist positions, he has eliminated psychology from the pure theory of economics (Bruni and Guala 2001). It was he, who inaugurated the "consistency approach" that equates rationality with consistent choices (Giocoli 2003: 41). So, he unwillingly paved the way first to Hicks' ordinalist consumer theory then, to the "complete preordering" axiom of general equilibrium theory, and to Samuelson's "theory of revealed preference". The distance made from utilitarianism to the *Manual* is substantial. In his later sociological work, Pareto opened the gap wildly by shrinking the limits of the domain of economics to a tiny portion of human action. This is probably a sufficient explanation why the neoclassical historiography insisted upon reducing Paretian theory of human action to pure logical actions only, underestimating his thorough study of non-logical actions.

Notes

1 Cf. Sen (1977: 89); Creedy (1984: 616); Voisin (1987: 104) and Zafirowski (2008: 802).
2 Edgeworth was well aware of the developments in experimental psychology and used them to establish the law of decreasing marginal utility. He has also collaborated with Francis Galton, the founder of psychometrics in his effort to construct a "hedonimeter" (cf. Creedy 1984; Voisin 1987: 142–143; Bruni and Sugden 2007: 151, Colander 2007).
3 On the intellectual links between Marshall and Mill see Keynes (1924: 328); Hollander (1985: 930); Zouboulakis (1993: 175ff.); Groenewegen (1995: 145–149); Hodgson (2001: 72–74); Whitaker *et al.* in Raffaelli *et al.* (2006: 38, 149, 120).
4 The accusation was made by W.J. Ashley (1891), the first academic economic historian. About Marshall's position vis-à-vis the classical, the historical and the marginalist competing schools in the late 1870s and 1880s see analytically Zouboulakis (1993: 175–183); Hodgson (2001: 97–110).
5 Pareto's conception of social action has significantly evolved from his earlier purely substantive view held in his *Cours d'Economie Politique* (1897), to his formal views defended in his *Manual*. More on this in Steiner (1999b).
6 On Pareto's departure from psychology see Ingrao and Israel (1990: 124); Bruni (2002: 132) and Gioccoli (2003: 67).

7 It should be reminded that Cournot in 1838 made the first attempt to extract the negative slope demand curve from observed quantities (Ménard 1978: 19–20).

8 This section draws from an earlier version published in Zouboulakis (2001).

9 Weber refers explicitly to Gossen and Menger. Moreover, he was aware of the latest developments in Austrian economics of his age, and mentions also von Böhm Bawerk, and von Mises for their theories on marginal utility, money and capital. See Weber (1922: 69, 78, 107); cf. Machlup (1967); Smelser and Swedberg (1994: 10); Zafirovski (1998: 84–86); Hodgson (2001: 122–123).

10 On Weber's methodological individualism see Gordon (1991: 470–472); Hollis (1994: 147–151); Hodgson (2001: 118–119).

11 See Freund (1965: 95); Gislain and Steiner (1995: 26); Zafirovski (1998: 85); Maas (2009: 509).

12 There is a dispute about the origin of the term "ideal type" between those who say that Weber borrowed this term from his colleague in Heidelberg, Georg Jellinek (Freund 1965: 443, n.23; Hodgson 2001: 121) and those who say that he attached to the term of ideal type, the meaning he must have found in Simmel's *Philosophy of Money* (1900) (cf. Klant 1988: 101 and Terlexis 1999: i 190).

13 On the meaning of the four types of social action see Hamilton (1994: 191), Gislain and Steiner (1995: 94–96), Trigilia (1998: 63).

14 Despite the fact that Weber clearly shows how "the observed deviations" can be taken into account, it is rightly pointed out that he "fails to indicate what it is in social reality that might kick against the ideal types the social scientist attempts to impose on them" (Eidlin 1990: 11).

15 As Stigler and Becker ambitiously assert, "we are proposing the hypothesis that widespread and/or persistent human behaviour can be explained by a generalized calculus of utility-maximization behaviour" (1977: 76).

5 Lionel Robbins and consistency of choices under scarcity

According to Lord Robbins' illustrious definition, "Economics is the science which studies human behaviour as a relationship between ends and scarce means which have alternative uses" (1932: 16). Robbins continues, two decades after Pareto, in developing economic analysis based on a concept of rationality free of hedonistic elements but, as we shall see, with a fundamentally different ambition: Pareto shrinks the limits of the domain of economics to that of logical actions, while Robbins expands its boundaries to every act of choice "conditioned by scarcity". Furthermore, Robbins holds that economic rationality is an obvious proposition, "the stuff of our everyday experience", verified simply by the means of introspection. Conversely, he cares to bind the idea of rationality as consistency of preferences with the ability of perfect foresight. The great theoreticians of the general equilibrium model (Hicks 1939, Debreu 1959, Arrow and Hahn 1971) will use the same concept of perfect rationality without any reference to psychology whatsoever – not even of the trivial introspective kind – and yet without any concern for its empirical relevance.[1]

The suspended step of economics away from psychology

"By the end of 1920s it was already clear that the more ambitious efforts to infuse psychology into economics, or to reconstruct basic economic theory in terms compatible with the new psychologies, had manifestly failed" (Coats 1976: 52). As will be seen below, in Chapter 11, psychology will be brought back to economics progressively after 1960, with the movement of behavioural economics. But in 1932, the year of the first edition of his essay aiming to bring to a close "the 40-year methodological vacuum", according to Hutchison (2009: 299), Robbins will start from redefining the field: "Economics is essentially a series of relationships – relationships between ends conceived as the possible objectives of conduct, on the one hand, and the technical and social environment on the other" (1932: 38).[2] To distance himself from "psychological hedonism" of wants and desires, he explicitly used Max Weber's analysis of means–ends rationality: "Economics ... is concerned with that aspect of behavior which arises from the scarcity of means to achieve given ends" (Robbins 1932: 24; cf. Maas 2009: 511). Nonetheless, the foundation of his anti-hedonistic argument is unreservedly Paretian: "All that we need to assume as econo-mists is the obvious fact that different possibilities offer different incen-tives, and that these incentives can be *arranged* in order of their intensity" (1932: 86). The idea of ordering preferences is derived directly from the conception of scarcity of means, assuming "for each individual, goods can be ranged in order of their significance for conduct; and that, in the sense it will be preferred, we can say that one use of a good is more important than another" (1932: 138).

To clarify the nature of the "assumption of completely rational conduct", Robbins will do more than to decline the idea of measurement of subjective valuation; he aims to defend the ethical neutrality of eco-nomic theory and expel, among other things, the prospect of interpersonal comparisons of utility outside the realm of positive science.[3] Following Pareto, he believes that it is sufficient to observe, "individuals can arrange their preferences in an order, and in fact they do so" (1932: 78–79). As he explains, individuals do make "rational disposal of goods" in a consistent manner (ibid.: 91), but their respective rankings are only a matter of "normative valuation" (ibid.: 139). Because this kind of purposive beha-viour depends on the expectations of consumers and producers about actual and future opportunities, a subsidiary assumption about "perfect foresight" is – as he says – "convenient to postulate" (1932: 94). Robbins recognizes that individual choices in reality are not always consistent, since "exchange, production, fluctuation – all take place in a world in which people do not know the full implications of what they are doing" (1932: 92). This is why it is assumed that people act purposively, in a per-fectly rational manner, by knowing everything they need to know in order to take the right decision. These assumptions are made "to enable us to study, in isolation, tendencies which, in the world of reality, operate only in conjunction with many others" (1932: 94). This argument is in fact a century old, stated explicitly by Mill and Senior in 1836, as already seen above. Robbins thus appeals to a behavioural assumption as "an exposi-tory device – a first approximation used very cautiously at one stage in the development of arguments" (1932: 97).[4]

Yet, the justification of the assumption of rationality differs signifi-cantly from the one that was made in classical political economy. It is no more the result of a "long and accurate observation", an empirical general-ization established by the science of psychology, but an obvious and self-evident proposition based on introspection in the pure marginalist tradition: "We do not need controlled experiments to establish their validity: they are so much the stuff of our everyday experience that they have only to be stated to be recognized as obvious" (Robbins 1932: 79). By pushing so hard his willingness to deny "any connection with psychological hedonism", Robbins refused any assistance from experimental psychology, on ·the basis of an anti-naturalistic argument: "the procedure of the social sciences which deal with conduct, which is in some sense purposive, can never be completely assimilated to the procedures of the physical sciences" (Robbins 1932: 89).[5] Even so, he does not endorse Pareto's definitive divorce from psychology either, recognizing that the very structure of means–ends rationality is "psychical not physical".

Let us explain why there is no discrepancy here: challenging Pareto's views, he affirms that "it is really not possible to understand the concepts of choice, of the relationship of means and ends, the central concepts of our science, in terms of external data" (Robbins 1932: 89–90). The assumption of completely rational conduct is after all a psychological assumption showing how people behave in situations of scarcity. The problem is that psychology has failed, according to Robbins, to measure empirically "the scales of relative valuation" of individual feelings. We can only feel an individual's subjective valuation process without being able to observe it as a fact (1932: 87; Caldwell 1982: 101). Economists should therefore abandon this Sisyphean task which finally leaves the door open to subjective, i.e. normative judgments. What Robbins is saying, is briefly this: Mill's psychological assumption is obsolete; Jevons and Edgeworth have driven the economists to a dead end; Pareto is claiming too much, denying any relation to psychology and Weber's instrumental rationality is historically specific.[6] What is left is the old philosophical mode of introspective evidence as a support of the elementary psychology of rational conduct.

Hence, Robbins "minimized the importance of psychology to the simple and indisputable facts of experience" (Maas 2009: 513) in order to understand economizing behaviour under scarcity. His behavioural assumption is only suitable to his definition of the domain of economics, as "a study of the disposal of scarce commodities" (1932: 38). As skilfully pointed out, "economics is thus about starting with the definition and working out what it implies" (Backhouse and Medema 2009: 493). By making a most narrow definition, leaving aside the social context of production and consumption, Robbins has circumscribed economic theory to the acts of rational choice following from the relationship "between ends and scarce means with alternative uses". By the same token, this narrow definition of economics is easily expandable to any act of choice under scarcity conditions.

Robbins was more than aware of that opportunity. He was even proud of it: "all conduct under the influence of scarcity has its economic aspect" (1932: 28). Economics is therefore good to explain every conduct under scarcity conditions. And, from the moment "we have been turned out of Paradise.... Scarcity of means to satisfy ends of varying importance is an almost ubiquitous condition of human behavior" (1932: 15). Let us compare Pareto and Robbins on this point: while they both focus on the act of choice as the key element of economic rationality, the former minimizes the limits of the domain of economics to the tiny portion of logical actions, while the latter maximizes its boundaries to embrace every purposive act involving time and scarce means (Steiner 1999b).[7] In brief, Pareto maximizes the distance from psychology to minimize the field of economics, while Robbins minimizes the influence of psychology to maximize the boundaries of economic science. In both cases, the upper and lower limits are never attained.

The Austrian connection

Robbins was not alone in the way he defined the nature and character of the assumption of economic rationality. Frank Knight, Ludwig von Mises and Friedrich von Hayek have also underlined the obviousness and certainty of the principle of rational action. In the preface of the first edition of his essay Robbins "acknowledged [his] especial indebtedness to the works of Professor Ludwig von Mises", and throughout his text, citations of Austrian contributions abound. In the fourth chapter of his essay, in the very section where he discusses the nature of the "assumption of completely rational conduct", he refers to von Mises' definition of rational conduct to clarify the purposive character of rationality, as opposed to "irrational conduct in the sense of *inconsistent*" (1932: 93, original emphasis). Furthermore, Robbins has used the mode of deductive reasoning from a series of postulates "in a manner reminiscent of Mises" (Backhouse and Medema 2009: 488). The use of a deductive-nomological model in economic explanation was a Ricardian achievement, fully established by N.W. Senior (1836: 26–86) and J.S. Mill (1836, 1843: book vi, chap. ix). Having said that, both the justification and the nature of the four main assumptions used as premises of deductive explanation in classical political economy differ significantly, as seen above. The principle of economic behaviour, together with the Malthusian principle of population, the principle of diminishing returns of the land and the principle of non-decreasing productivity of capital and labour were meant to be true propositions, scientifically established. In contrast, Robbins – *à la* von Mises – considers the three general propositions of economic theory as "simple and indisputable facts of experience":

The main postulate of the theory of value is the fact that individuals can arrange their preferences in an order, and in fact do so. The main postulate of the theory of production is the fact that there are more than one factor of production. The main postulate of the theory of dynamics is the fact that we are not certain regarding future scarcities. These are not postulates the existence of whose counterpart in reality admits of extensive dispute once their nature is fully realized.

(Robbins 1932: 78–79)

This axiomatic exposition follows logically from his analytical definition of economics as the study of the implications of choice under conditions of scarcity and was only a prelude to the formal axiomatization of the late 1940s and 1950s.

Robbins of course, was not an Austrian economist.[8] He would never accept that economics is a sub-discipline of "praxeology" the science of human action, which is a strictly logical science, neither would accept Mises' radical apriorism, albeit he will be blamed as an apriorist, as seen in the next chapter.[9] Mises claimed that all the fundamental assumptions of economics are synthetic propositions that are a priori true: "a proposition of an aprioristic theory can never be refuted by experience" (Mises 1960: 30; cf. Caldwell 1982: 104; Lagueux 2010: 92). Robbins, in his effort to banish value judgments from "pure theory", opts for a norm of behaviour that has some, though very weak, empirical basis. It was correctly alleged that "the postulate itself is directly confirmed by introspection" and can be additionally subjected "to intersubjective tests" (Papandreou 1950: 718).

On the other hand, and despite his selective methodological dualism he was opposed to Hayek as to the possibility of establishing causal explanations of economic phenomena. On no account would Robbins approve the anti-naturalistic spirit of Hayek and his subjectivist-hermeneutic method. We will have the opportunity to discuss this method in the next chapter. Here we have to underline that one of the main elements of Hayek's anti-naturalistic methodology was his strong thesis about the "pretence of knowledge" and the limited human computational capacity to manipulate all available information (1952: 60–61). Although he agreed with Mises and Robbins on the obviousness of the rationality principle, he distanced himself from both as to the perfect knowledge assumption, following Knight. Hayek's paper of 1937 marked a significant transformation of his original views about information and knowledge and thus "found himself in the most profound disagreement with Mises".[10] In the next chapter we will see how Hayek, a year before Hutchison's enduring attack, advocated that propositions about economic rationality are mere tautologies unless someone is able to fill them "with definite statements about how knowledge is acquired and communicated" (1937: 33). Precisely that was missing from Robbins' idea of rationality as consistency of choices under scarcity conditions.

Making rational choices free from psychology

Robbins' effort to immunize marginalist economic theory from subjective elements coincides with the most systematic reaction against the assumptions of neoclassical economics ever, as will be examined in the next chapter. It will need more than 20 years to become the official doctrine of neoclassical orthodoxy, after the adoption of Robbins' formal definition of economics from the leading figures of general equilibrium modeling.[11] Although Robbins was not supporting the axiomatic method as it is commonly understood, post-war mathematical economists of all kinds – general equilibrium theorists, game-theorists and behaviourists – used his definition because it fitted perfectly with their vision of economics (Backhouse and Medema 2009). The road opened by Robbins was leading to a bifurcation point, already signalled before the war, by two highly innovative articles, Hicks and Allen (1934) and Samuelson (1938), each one leading to a different destination. From Robbins' point of departure one could either follow the road ahead leading to rational choice as consistency free from any psychological reference, or the road turning towards behaviourism. Let us follow these two trails, starting from the second.

Samuelson's "weak axiom of revealed preference" (WARP) was another major step on the way to ground demand theory directly to observable data rather than to subjective elements such as utility functions. The WARP postulates that "if an individual selects batch one over batch two, he does not at the same time select two over one" (Samuelson 1938: 65). Consumers reveal thus their preferences by choosing, in a consistent manner, one bundle of goods over another when both bundles are affordable, regardless of income and prices. What is implicitly assumed here is, so to speak, a congruence of choice and self-interest: The chosen alternative is always the preferred one that coincides with the best one (Sen 1987b: 69). Starting from this axiom, one could construct a set of indifference curves for two bundles of goods and then, under some additional restrictive conditions, generalize this axiom to an infinite number of goods and consumers.[12] Demand functions were therefore theoretically derived from observable behaviour, instead of non-observable subjective evaluations, although this observation is only "empirically determinable under ideal conditions" (Samuelson 1938: 62). Pointing directly to Hicks and Allen's contribution, Samuelson (1938: 62) has explicitly tempted to "drop off the last vestiges of the utility analysis". Still, from our perspective, his

WARP theory was a move forward to a behaviourist justification of economic rationality, and therefore a step away from Robbins' project to free economics from the chains of psychology (cf. Hausman 1992: 157–158).

But, in the immediate post-depression era, as it was dramatically put, "Robbins needed introspection and the profession needed Robbins' solution" (Hands 2009: 837). By the "profession" here is meant the hard core of neoclassical economics, i.e. microeconomics and general equilibrium theory. Hicks and Allen's 1934 article fully recognized the "immeasurability of utility" and advanced Pareto's ordinal analysis significantly through the concept of "marginal rate of substitution" (MRS).[13] Samuelson (1938) observed that this new "entity" appeared to be "to say the least, ambiguous" in the sense that it was breaking only artificially with utilitarianism.

However, Hicks and Allen reestablished the axiomatic mode of explanation that is deduction from a set of propositions granted for true. The first and most important axiom was the rationality principle, which implies that every individual has a complete scale of preferences and makes consistent choices in order to maximize his utility function. In opposition to Pareto, Hicks and Allen did not assume that the consumer is able to identify indifferent bundles for large changes in the quantity of goods, but only marginal changes between two goods at the consumption point, the so-called MRS. As Hands (2006: 155–156) emphasizes, this is an important difference about "what is exactly observational", the entire indifference curve representing different combinations of two bundles of goods (Pareto) or the local consumption point of a specific rate of exchange between them (Hicks and Allen)? Later on, in his major book, Hicks set himself the impossible task of introducing the dimension of time in a mainly static analysis framework, and to "study the interrelations of markets" starting from the generalization of partial equilibrium situations (1939). To do so Hicks described the dynamic adjustment process as a sequence of "temporary equilibria", a concept he has invented (Ingrao and Israel: 239). The whole project required the necessary condition of perfect foresight: "men must always act in such a way that the prices [present and future] on which they base their actions, should actually be realized. Disequilibrium is the disappointment of expectations".[14]

What is more, to assure the possibility for an aggregate and integrable demand function, additional restrictions will be imposed upon individual ordinal ranking of preferences: completeness, transitivity, continuity and convexity. To close the movement towards the axiomatization of economic theory initiated by Cournot and Walras long ago, it was necessary to introduce these formal hypotheses with no reference to the interpretative values of the concepts implied.[15] *Complete* are the preferences when they include a choice for every bundle of goods: individuals must choose if they prefer

A from B, or B from A, or if they are indifferent between A and B. *Transitive* are the preferences, for all options A, B and C, if the individual prefers A to B and B to C, then he/she prefers A to C; and if he/she is indifferent between A and B, as well as between B and C, then he/she is indifferent between A and C. Transitivity is necessary to secure the consistency of choices. *Continuous* preferences mean that for any bundle of goods there is at least another bundle of the same goods in different proportions preferred by the individual. In plain English, continuity means that sudden preference reversal never occurs, although its purpose is mainly a mathematical one, as Samuelson first recognized (1938: 63).[16] Finally, *convexity* of the indifference curves means that they have this particular curvature "parallel" to the intersection point, which translates a diminishing MRS. In economic terms it is assumed that consumers prefer to make a weighted average of the two bundles and are never satisfied by excluding completely one bundle of good for another.[17] The axioms of completeness, transitivity, continuity and convexity guarantee the existence of "complete preordering of preferences" for every individual, which are necessary yet not sufficient conditions for the existence of a general economic equilibrium.

The evolution of the brilliant mathematical achievements that were made after the Second World War until the early 1970s to support the general equilibrium theory is a very long story that exceeds our aims here. Arrow and Debreu, separately or in collaboration in the early 1950s, Malinvaud in 1953, McKenzie in 1954, Arrow and Hurvicz in 1958, Debreu in 1959, and also Arrow and Hahn in 1971, Sonnenschein in 1972 and 1973 and Mantel in 1974, have tried to demonstrate the existence and the conditions of uniqueness and stability of general equilibrium solution.[18] To achieve a mathematically relevant solution, numerous heroic assumptions were adopted concerning – among other things such as "perfect competition"[19] – the existence of the so-called "contingent markets" suggesting that individuals are able to make plans about their actual as well as their future needs for every possible "state of the world" and to calculate its eventual outcomes. Beyond the fact that rational agents are considered to possess given indifference maps and comparable initial endowments, it is furthermore suggested that they actually act, according to Patinkin's famous allegory, as "utility computers into whom we 'feed' a sequence of market prices and from whom we obtain a corresponding sequence of 'solutions' in the form of specified optimum positions" (Patinkin 1965, quoted in Velupillai 1995: 261). As accurately stated "they are demands that economists impose upon themselves, perhaps in the mistaken belief that the achievement of definiteness, precision and internal consistency in the theory requires the imputation of the same traits to the subject matter"

(Nelson and Winter 1982: 59).[20] In any case, and despite the tremendous intellectual energy spent, the final outcome was unsuccessful as to the uniqueness and stability of general equilibrium solutions.

To conclude, one of the objectives of Pareto, Robbins and Hicks was to construct an aggregate – i.e. societal – welfare function from the individual sets of preferences, once the incompatibility of interpersonal utility functions was taken for granted. Yet, as is nowadays well known, Arrow has logically, as early as 1950, proved that the possibility of constructing a social welfare function from that departure is not feasible, and that "the only methods of passing from individual tastes to social preferences which will be satisfactory and which will be defined for a wide range of sets of individual orderings are either imposed or dictatorial" (Arrow 1950: 342). The old utilitarian project of measuring the social utility of a policy measure was simply leading to a blind alley. Arrow has conclusively revealed that the whole project was doomed *ab initio*: "The failure of purely individualistic assumptions to lead to a well-defined social welfare function means, in effect, that there must be a divergence between social and private benefits if we are to be able to discuss a social optimum" (Arrow 1950: 343).

In 1934, Hicks and Allen were proudly announcing that they were following the path initiated in the early 1870s, aiming to provide general explanations of social phenomena that result from purposive behaviour: "By transforming the subjective theory of value into a general logic of choice, they extend its applicability over wide fields of human conduct" (Hicks and Allen 1934: 54). This path went from Bentham, to Jevons, to Walras, to Edgeworth, to Pareto, to Robbins and arrived at the mathematical achievements of the general equilibrium theorists, which eliminated the human individual from economics (Davis 2003: 31). In the meanwhile, serious doubts about whatever was left behind in the process of abstraction to continue on this path were about to be spotted. In the late 1930s the neoclassical program would face the heaviest and most substantial critique ever, which it would successfully overcome with a glorious retreat from its empirical claims.

Notes

1 Giocoli (2003) made a detailed and documented study about the project of transforming economics from psychological to a rational choice discipline.

2 We refer to the third edition (1984) of Robbins' essay, which is a reprint of the second revised edition (1932) with a new introduction, originally published in 1981 at the author's Richard T. Ely Lecture.

3 On the aims of Robbins' essay see Backhouse and Medema (2009), Collander (2009), Hands (2009), Maas (2009).

4 Cf. Blaug (1980: 74), Caldwell (1982: 101), Karayiannis (2001a: 240).

5 Robbins will stand by his anti-behaviourist/anti-naturalistic positions until the end of his life, as his 1981 Ely lecture demonstrates:

> the methods and problems of economic science are very substantially different from those of the so-called natural sciences. This springs from the fundamental circumstance that the subject-matter is an aspect of human action and therefore must be conceived as including purpose.
>
> (1932: xiv)

6 Robbins firmly condemned the idea that "the generalizations of Economics are essentially 'historic-relative' in character [as] a dangerous misapprehension" (1932: 80).

7 In a demonstration of his authentic style Robbins writes this: "The distribution of time between prayer and good works has its economic aspect equally with the distribution of time between orgies and slumber. *The 'pig-philosophy'* [to use Calrlyle's contemptuous epithet] *turns out to be all-embracing*" (1932: 26, emphasis added).

8 Susan Howson (2004) offered some textual evidence about Robbins' originality of thought vis-à-vis his Austrian contemporaries. She claims that "by the end of 1928 Robbins had found his definition on the subject matter of economics.... It owed most to Wicksteed and there was nothing particularly 'Austrian' about it" (2004: 426).

9 "There can be no theory other than an aprioristic and universally valid theory (i.e. a theory claiming validity independent of place, time, nationality, race, and the like), because human reasoning is unable to derive theoretical propositions from historical experience", von Mises (1960, preface to the original German edition of 1933).

10 According to Hutchison (2009: 308) Hayek described von Mises as "the person from whom I have probably learnt more than any other man". Yet, he has also acknowledged that von Mises was personally involved with the three major intellectual crimes, namely "false individualism", "the fatal conceit" and the "pretence of knowledge".

11 This is also illustrated by the delay in reception of consumer theory (Drakopoulos and Karayiannis 1999).

12 On the formal conditions relative to the "integrability question" of the demand functions see Mongin (2000), Chipman and Lenfant (2002), Hands (2006) and Varian (2006). Samuelson's position seriously evolved between 1938 and 1950, partly because of Houthakker's definition of the so-called "strong axiom of revealed preference", which generalizes the conditions of integrability in order to construct aggregate demand functions. Some commentators (Wong 1978, Schmidt 1985) have thus spoken about a discontinuity in Samuelson's work. Mongin (2000) makes a detailed analysis of this evolution.

13 Hicks and Allen (1934) have also rediscovered "Slutsky's effect" dating from 1915, that is the differentiation of the effect of a price change into two distinct results, the "income effect" and the "substitution effect". On the details of their collaboration see Fernandez-Grela (2006). On Slutsky's important contribution see Stigler (1950: 127–128), Chipman and Lenfant (2002).

14 This is a quotation from an unpublished draft of 1932, published later by Hicks in 1973. See Ingrao and Israel (1990: 421).

15 In the early 1930s, independently from Hicks, Allen and Samuelson, a group of German speaking mathematicians formed a "new cradle for general economic

equilibrium theory" following the example of Gustav Cassel: Karl Schlesinger, Heinrich von Stackelberg, Karl Menger, Abraham Wald and John von Neumann. See Weintraub (1983), Ingrao and Israel (1990: 188–210), Velupillai (1996).

16 Continuity in the demand function was an explicit formal prerequisite already in Cournot's *Recherches* of 1838. See Ménard (1978: 23).

17 For the definition of these axioms cf. Hausman (1992), Jehle and Reny (2001: 13).

18 With the exception of the first one, the main contributions were published in *Econometrica:* Arrow, "An extension of the basic theorems of classical welfare economics" (1951); Debreu, "The coefficient of resource utilization" (1951); Arrow and Debreu, "Existence of an equilibrium for a competitive economy" (1954); Malinvaud, "Capital accumulation and efficient allocation of resources" (1953); McKenzie, "On equilibrium in Graham's model of world trade and other competitive systems"; Arrow and Hurvicz, "On the stability of the competitive equilibrium i" (1958); Arrow *et al.* "On the stability of the competitive equilibrium ii" (1959); Sonnenschein, "Market excess demand functions" (1972); Sonnenschein, "Do Walras identity and continuity characterize the class of community excess demand functions?" (1973); Mantel, "On the characterization of aggregate excess demand" *JET* (1974). Of course, there were two landmark publications in book form: Debreu's *Theory of Value* (1959) and Arrow and Hahn's *General Competitive Analysis* (1971). For a detailed historical analysis see Weintraub (1983), Ingrao and Israel (1990, chaps. 10–12) and Screpanti and Zamagni (1993, chap. 10).

19 As every economist has learned during his undergraduate studies "perfect competition" is a state of market where is assumed (*i*) an infinite number of buyers and sellers, (*ii*) free entry and exit from the industry, (*iii*) product homogeneity, and (*iv*) perfect (i.e. full, instant and costless) information about input prices, production technology and selling prices.

20 This is known as "the fallacy of misplaced concreteness", consisting of mistaking the abstract for the concrete. It was first formulated by A.N. Whitehead in his book *Process and Reality* (1929), to explain that a concrete physical object cannot be located without reference to its relations to other concrete objects. Hayek argued that to treat an abstract idea as a fact is a "realistic naiveté" (Hayek 1952: 83).

6 Neoclassical rationality under fire

Theoretical, methodological and empirical critique in the late 1930s

From 1937 to 1939 both the concepts of rationality as consistency and that of maximization under constraint were severely criticized from every possible point of view: theoretical, methodological and empirical. In 1937, a year after the publication of his masterpiece, Keynes contested the assumption of certain knowledge, just as Hayek did in the same month, from his own angle. In the very same year, a young scholar, Ronald Coase (aged 27) in his pioneering article criticized the neoclassical theory of the firm and particularly the lack of definite statements about the costs of acquiring all relevant information. In 1938, another young scholar, Terence Hutchison (aged 26) attacked the methodological foundations of neoclassical theory by introducing the Popperian criterion of testability in economics. He skilfully demonstrated that the assumption of maximizing behaviour is unworkable without the secondary but restrictive assumption of "perfect expectation" that guarantees that this behaviour will indeed result in a situation whereby the economic agent will attain a maximum. Last but not least, Robert Hall and Charles Hitch (1939) claimed that entrepreneurs never care to maximize profits in the sense of the neoclassical theory. In their empirical work they have confirmed that entrepreneurs set their prices by comparing not the marginal cost to the marginal revenue, but simply matching up to a rough notion of total cost – called "full-cost" – the market price. This line of criticism was also defended by Richard Lester seven years later, who also contested the empirical relevance of the marginalist principle. The neoclassical orthodoxy will overcome this fundamental critique only through a methodological stratagem, by emptying the empirical substance of the maximization principle.

1937: the year of uncertainty

The theoretical dispute over the main economic assumptions has a long history that goes back to the older German Historical School (Schmoller,

Hildenbrand and Knies) and the first tenants of the American institutional-ism (Veblen, Commons and Mitchell). Still, the hard core of neoclassical economics was never endangered, not until the early 1930s when Chamberlin, Hotteling and Robinson constructed alternative models to challenge the assumptions of full competition and economic rationality. The decisive strike came of course with the publication of Keynes' *General Theory*. Among other things, Keynes contested openly the idea that entrepreneurs can make sound "long-term expectations" in order to be able to calculate their future profits. After condemning the "foolishness" of being confident about the future, he contested the possibility of knowing it: "The outstanding fact is the extreme precariousness of the basis of knowledge on which our estimates of prospective yield have to be made" (Keynes 1936: 149).

A year later, answering to the American reviewers of his book (Viner, Taussig, Robertson and Leontief), he underlined the novelty of this "discovery". All the writers before him took for granted that "the amount of the factors employed was given and the other relevant facts were known more or less for certain". Briefly, in economic thinking prior to Keynes, as he says, "facts and expectations were assumed to be given in a definite and calculable form" (1937: 212–213). But since "our knowledge of the future is fluctuating, vague and uncertain", Keynes believed that the method-ological and theoretical tools of the so-called "classical school" are com-pletely unsuitable. Therefore, he accused economists for using "polite techniques" to sustain the principle that people behave in the marketplace as if they know everything about the future. What people in fact do, according to Keynes, is to extrapolate from past experience, making only "correct summing up of future prospects" and imitating the action of others, believing that they are "perhaps better informed": "I accuse the classical economic theory of being itself one of these pretty, polite tech-niques which tries to deal with the present by abstracting from the fact that we know very little about the future" (1937: 215). The whole Keynesian theory of the rate of interest is based precisely on the idea that people are rewarded for risking not "to hoard their money". In a neoclassical world of certainty, "why should anyone outside a lunatic asylum wish to use money as a store of wealth?" (ibid.: 216).

Hayek in 1937, in a significant publication that, according to Hutchison (2009: 308), "marked a turning point of fundamental importance in Hayek's intellectual biography", meaning his views on the merits of market vs. planned economies. The main concern in this article was to strengthen the scientific status of economics. The only way to transform the tautologies of formal equilibrium analysis into propositions about the real world is to establish how "knowledge is acquired and communicated" (1937: 33). In Hayek's view the state of equilibrium is logically deduced from a series of a priori valid propositions about the human faculty of rationally combining the knowledge of "given data" in order to follow a certain "plan": "actions of a person can be said to be in equilibrium insofar as they can be understood as part of one plan" (ibid.: 36). As he explains, apart from individual tastes, "some of the 'data' on which any one person will base his plans, will be the expectation that other people will act in a particular way" (ibid.: 38). The equilibrium exists insofar as individual anticipations prove themselves correct, suggesting that individuals possess all the relevant knowledge to make the right choices. Assuming that one knows what is necessary, the objectives are always attained, unless one makes mistakes: "It seems that that skeleton in our cupboard, the 'economic man', whom we have exorcised with prayer and fasting, has returned through the back door in the form of a quasi-omniscient individual" (1937: 45). So, the crucial element, the one that transforms the propositions of the "Pure Logic of Choice" to empirical ones, is the process describing how people acquire and communicate the "relevant knowledge" to decide properly.

To speak about equilibrium at the level of a whole society, Hayek recognizes that an additional empirical condition has to be satisfied, apart from the logical one concerning the "inter-compatibility of the individual plans", that is, the "tendency towards equilibrium" (1937: 47). This is how Hayek introduces his genuine idea of "spontaneous interaction between of a number of people, each possessing only bits of knowledge" (ibid. 49). The problem of knowledge which "different individuals must possess in order that [general] equilibrium may prevail" is not a matter of a "social mind", i.e. of a planner that would perform the role of an "omniscient dictator" (ibid.: 51). In order to avoid both the fiction of the "quasi-omniscient individual" and the spectre of the collectivist planner, Hayek appeals to the problematic condition of "the tendency towards equilibrium which we have reason to believe to exist on empirical grounds" (ibid.: 53), as a means to guarantee the efficiency of a decentralized market mechanism.[1] In his future work, he will be devoted to defend the superiority of the spontaneous order resulting from the actions of independent individuals as against the "collectivist prejudice" of centralized allocation of resources (1952: 52). The concern remains the same, it is the problem of the acquisition and utilization of knowledge: decentralized market mechanisms do a better job because they incorporate indirectly through signals like prices, every piece of dispersed individual information.[2]

Coase in 1937 was the first neoclassical economist to ask "why is there any firm?" In his celebrated answer he explained that firms exists mainly for two reasons, first because a firm reduces "the cost of using the price mechanism" and second because, having a durable business organization reduces the danger of uncertainty. In the general equilibrium model and in Hayek as well, resources are allocated by means of the price mechanism to produce commodities that are also distributed to the consumers through the very same mechanism. The entrepreneur decides how and how much of one or more commodity will be produced, transforming inputs into outputs, and gains the profit (or bears the loss) that results from his decision. In that sense no business firms are really needed. Whenever an entrepreneur foresees a profit in a particular industry, he/she gathers instantaneously and without any cost the best available resources to produce what the consumer needs. Moreover, entrepreneurs are supposed to have unlimited cognitive capacities not only about the present quality and price of inputs but also about the future of consumer preferences and market characteristics. Thus, neoclassical entrepreneurs live in a world without uncertainty, as Keynes and Hayek have also indicated.

Coase criticized the unrealisticness of this view and pointed out that in the real world there are important costs of organizing production, such as costs for "discovering what the relevant prices are", "costs of negotiating and concluding a separate contract for each exchange transaction", costs to manage and "obey the directions of an entrepreneur" and finally costs of making long-term contracts to minimize the risks of an uncertain future (Coase 1937: 390–391). These costs have come to be known (after Arrow in 1969) as "transaction costs",[3] and because they form an important part of the business world, durable profit-seeking organizations do exist to minimize their burden. As Keynes and Hayek, Coase subscribes to the view, initially expressed by Frank Knight, that uncertainty and imperfect knowledge are fundamental elements of rational economic behaviour (1937: 399).

Hutchison brings Popper into economic methodology

Terence Hutchison (1938) advanced the most significant methodological critique of Lionel Robbins' effort to defend the foundations of neoclassical economics. In doing so, Hutchison has introduced brand new ideas on refutability from Karl Popper in economic methodology, only four years after their publication in German and many years before making a major impact among physicists (Blaug 1980: 81).[4] According to this new criterion of demarcation of science from pseudo-science, "all propositions with scientific sense, then, are either conceivably falsifiable by empirical observation or not, and none can be both" (1938: 27). Hutchison will apply this criterion to evaluate the empirical validity of the propositions of economic theory. He starts from establishing a dichotomy between the propositions of "pure theory" (which are "independent of all facts" and their validity

depends only upon their logical consistency) and the empirical propositions. The latter ought to have some empirical meaning, i.e. they have to
be testable by empirical evidence. More specifically, "propositions obtain
their empirical content so far as, if true, they *exclude, restrict,* or *forbid*
something" (ibid.: 26, original emphasis). This is the meaning of being
"conceivably falsifiable",[5] to point out some possibility of being somehow
tested by facts. When is it possible to refute a theoretical conclusion in
economics? John Elliott Cairnes has argued long ago that a theoretical
conclusion "if questioned, can be *refuted* only by showing, either that the
principles and conditions assumed do not exist, or that the tendency which
the law affirms does not follow as a necessary consequence from this
assumption" (1857: 62, italics added).

Hutchison makes the next logical step and explains further the nature of
Cairnes' "hypothetical method of Economics". While subscribing to the
right of the economist to investigate in isolation the "problems of the
world as it is" by the means of "simplified cases and examples" (1938:
36), Hutchison requires all propositions intended to play the role of an
assumption in a hypothetical analysis to be "asserted as facts" (ibid.: 39).
Unless the assumptions are able to say something about facts, they are not
capable of being "conceivably falsifiable". Here again Hutchison follows
Cairnes as to the proper use of the *ceteris paribus* clause. In his *Character
and Logical Method of Political Economy*, Cairnes (answering to Senior's
objections about the dangers of a hypothetical science based on "arbitrarily
assumed premises") clarifies that the premises of political economy are
"true, and yet incomplete – true so far as the facts which they assert go,
and yet not including all the conditions which affect the actual course of
events" (1857: 38). These conditions correspond to the "disturbing causes"
that are neutralized with the help of the *ceteris paribus* clause, just as in
every other empirical science. Like Hutchison, Cairnes was not unaware
of the distinctive way this clause was used in economic explanation.
Contrary to astronomy, where the interfering factors are few and less
complex, or chemistry where they can be isolated by experimental means,
political economy uses abstraction as a "substitute for experiment" without
being able to calculate or even enumerate "the agencies in operation at any
given time in any given society".[6] In Hutchison's terms, "the *cetera* in the
natural sciences themselves act in accordance with known laws", while in
economics the same clause "sweeps all the unknowns together under one
portmanteau assumption for a logical solution" (1938: 42).

Hutchison devotes a whole chapter to the PR or "the fundamental
maximum assumption" as he calls it. Since the assumption of maximizing
behaviour is a scientific proposition, it has to have a testable empirical
content. Nevertheless, all the definitions of the "fundamental assumption",

from Bentham to Ricardo, to Mill, to Joan Robinson, "appear further to postulate, and only are applicable if the further postulate is made, that all expectations are perfectly correct" (1938: 85). Leaving aside the strange amalgamation of such different authors, Hutchison is right in emphasizing that most economic thinkers did not bother to explain "*how* one is to maximize one's returns". With the possible exceptions of Mill and Hayek, economists were not preoccupied before Simon with the rationality of "the process of arriving at the expectations", but only with the result of this process (ibid.: 87).[7] The explanation that Hutchison gives is that economics theorists think in a world without uncertainty. Thus consumers and producers are assumed to know for certain all the relative conditions of the market and are in a position to anticipate all their future preferences, as well as the technological innovations to come and the evolution of future prices and incomes. If the assumption of perfect expectations is not fulfilled, maximizing behaviour will never really result in the agent attaining a maximum. To sum up, whenever there is uncertainty, economic agents are not in a position to acknowledge that they have obtained the maximum of their advantage.

If by "perfect expectation we mean practically omniscience about the future" (1938: 101), the fundamental assumption becomes empirically empty since "people become more or less automata" (ibid.: 88). Quoting Knight, he recognizes that in a world without uncertainty and risk, economic calculation is mechanical and choices are pointless.[8] Hutchison comes to the conclusion, that the postulate of "perfect expectation" turns the fundamental assumption to be an analytical proposition equivalent to the propositions of logic and mathematics and therefore totally inappropriate as a foundation of an empirical science. In order to attain some empirical meaning, "you have to fill in all the assumptions" with real information as to how people behave in conditions containing uncertainty and imperfect knowledge.[9] Only then, one can evaluate its empirical validity, under specific circumstances and market conditions (Latsis 1972). Significantly, Hutchison follows Knight in order to specify the nature of economic behaviour containing risk and uncertainty, and also Keynes to explain investment decision making depending on the "prospective yield of capital".

Nevertheless, Frank Knight received his young colleague's book very disapprovingly. In his 32-pages long book review he concluded that "in the present writer's opinion, all this is fundamentally misleading and wrong, if not actual nonsense" (1940: 5). Hutchison's methodological prescriptions about the testability of economic propositions were "particularly irritating to the reviewer". According to Knight, Hutchison is asking too much from economists who, unlike natural scientists, are dealing with a subject matter with no definite criteria for testing their theories: "The fundamental propositions and definitions of economics are neither observed nor inferred from observation in anything like the sense of the generalizations of the positive natural sciences, or of mathematics, and yet they are in no real sense arbitrary" (1940: 5). The subject matter of economics is human conduct motivated by interests and Knight is quite certain about its a priori validity: "If anyone denies that men have interests or that 'we' have a considerable amount of valid knowledge about them, economics and all its works will simply be to such a person what the world of colour is to the blind man" (ibid.: 12). Knight accuses Hutchison of "positivism" as he is denying introspection as a valid source of founding economic behaviour and pretends that "knowledge of people's minds" should be grounded on "observation of their physical behavior". In Knight's view economics is a science of human action that is concerned with motives, values and errors, and not a positive science dealing with causes and regularities (Hausman 1992: 155).

The most astonishing point about this response is not that Knight exaggerates Hutchison's positivism, as Hart (2010) rightly shows, but that his criticism pays no attention to the substantial contribution of Pareto, to free economics from its subjectivist elements.[10] Knight's line of defence is a full move back to the older "psychological method" of the marginalist school, quoting Gossen and Wieser, and to its subjectivist means: "the first of these postulates is the reality of economizing, or economic behaviour, the general meaning of which is known to any possible participant in any economic discussion – intuitively" (1940: 15). As will be seen below in Chapter 9, intuition had for Knight a major role to play in helping individuals to make judgments and take decisions about the future containing risk and uncertainty. In his response, Hutchison (1941: 746) criticizes Knight's "intuitions unverifiable by any empirical procedure" to be insignificant to the explanation of "any concrete economic problem". For the young scholar educated in the aftermath of the Great Depression and living in Nazi Germany, not having a solid criterion for distinguishing scientific facts from ideological propaganda was intolerable.[11]

Empirically testing profit maximization

In 1939, Robert L. Hall and Charles J. Hitch published the results of an empirical survey aiming to investigate "the way in which business men decide what price to charge for their products and what output to produce" (1939: 12). Using the questionnaire method they collected a non-representative sample of 38 businessmen interviews and found that the greater part of these firm leaders set their prices by comparing not the marginal cost to the marginal revenue, not even the average cost to the average revenue, but simply by comparing a rough notion of total cost – called "full-cost" – to the market price. Their analysis suggested that this pricing mechanism was only a "rule of thumb" alien to the maximization principle; thus, the first round of the marginalist controversy, known as the "full cost pricing controversy" was initiated.[12] According to this pricing rule the firm equates the price of its product to the average cost of production, at full utilization of its productive capacity, plus a percentage margin, a "mark-up" of a relatively stable size.[13] So, "maximum profits, if they result at all from the application of this rule, do so as an accidental (or possibly evolutionary) by-product" (Hall and Hitch 1939: 18–19). What is more, in this pricing rule there is no concern about consumer demand: "all discussion of demand curves is meaningless in the business world" (Tsoulfidis 2010: 241). Entrepreneurs really don't care whether the demand curve for their product is elastic or not: most businessmen "were vague about anything so precise as [demand] elasticity" (1939: 18). This is why, according to the survey, they do not respond to demand changes through prices, but only by adjusting their productive capacity.

Despite this forceful anti-marginalist critique, Hall and Hitch failed to convince their contemporaries. Partly because of the methodological mistakes and partly because of the theoretical contradictions, the marginalist maximization hypothesis survived this attack. Methodologically, the survey was based upon a small, non-representative sample of mainly industrial firms and failed to provide a conclusive test of the marginalist theory. Mongin (1986: 116) has argued that a conclusive test necessitates an unequivocal definition of the initial conditions of the market. But, as is reported, the firms surveyed belonged to very diverse market conditions, from monopoly to oligopoly to monopolistic competition (1939: 26, table 6). Theoretically, Hall and Hitch tried to develop an alternative theory to explain the behaviour of the firm based on Chamberlin's ideas of monopolistic competition and the concept of "kinked demand": every entrepreneur "fears" that his competitor will follow only when the price is decreased; in the opposite case of price increase, the entrepreneur believes that few competitors will follow.[14] Therefore, every firm anticipates that the demand curve has a considerably different elasticity below one point because the demand to the firm exhibits a kink at the prevailing market price (1939: 23). This conclusion directly contradicts their previous claim, which is based on their empirical observations, and according to which it seems that "producers cannot know their demand or marginal revenue curves" (1939: 22).

Empirical testing of the marginalist theory of profit maximization was also undertaken by Richard Lester in 1946, who initiated the second round of the marginalist controversy, this time throughout the pages of the

American Economic Review.[15] Lester agreed that the previous empirical tests were not conclusive in refuting the marginalist theory of the firm. So he undertook a large case study to verify the existence of a marginalist behaviour in southern entrepreneurs. Lester used the method of mailed questionnaires to study the hypothetical behaviour of a non-representative sample of 58 southern businessmen.[16] To test directly their maximizing pattern of behaviour he asked them a series of questions with preselected answers. One of them concerned whether they "tend to think in terms of marginal variable cost". From 1937 to 1941, many states of the American South legislated a minimum wage. As a result, labour employment together with the cost of labour grew dramatically, eliminating the wage differential with the same branches of industry in the North (1946: 76). Lester asked them the following question:

> assuming no other change in your costs and no decline in the nation's demand for the type of products you manufacture, how would your firm be likely to adjust to such a permanent 50 percent reduction in the North–South wage differential?
>
> (1946: 77)

The executives were requested to give percentage ratings for relative importance of six alternative adjustments to this wage differential. "Contrary to the presuppositions of conventional marginalism" only four businessmen put the marginalist type of adjustment first, i.e. to "reduce production by deliberate curtailment of output", to minimize higher production costs (Lester 1946: 79). Instead, 35 of them preferred mostly to "improve efficiency through better production methods, organization, supervision, [work] incentives, etc." meaning that their plant was not already producing under its maximum capacity. Instead of reducing production to face increased variable costs, business leaders were concerned to increase production and "keep sales up when profits begin to be squeezed". Based on this empirical evidence Lester concluded that "unlike economists, business executives tend to think of costs and profits as dependent upon the rate of output, rather than the reverse" (1946: 81).

Machlup responded immediately and extensively to Lester's challenge. Only his criticism of Lester's article will be discussed here, as we will have the opportunity to examine his overall position on the meaning of rationality in the very next chapter. As he summarized his response, "the alleged 'inapplicability' of marginal analysis is often due to a failure to understand it, to faulty techniques, or to mistaken interpretations of 'findings'" (1946: 148). First, Machlup objected that Lester's method of mailed questionnaire without supporting interviews was "hopelessly inadequate for empirical studies of business conduct" (ibid.: 183–184). This is how Machlup explains the very low number of "usable replies" and so contests the credibility of the answers collected: "psychologists will readily confirm that statements by interviewed individuals about the motives and reasons for their actions are unreliable or at least incomplete" (ibid.: 170). Second, Machlup believed that Lester failed to interpret correctly his findings: "where competition is not pure ... output adjustments to higher production costs take place by way of changes in selling prices" (ibid.: 189). Hence, Lester does not prove his case, thereof he is not able to interpret the conditions of the market inside which industries are operating.

As to the so-called "failure to understand marginal analysis", Machlup adopts a rather loose concept of rational behaviour to overcome the criticisms by Lester, Hall and Hitch. Instead of reaffirming the relevance of maximization under constraint he turns to conventionalist arguments: "businessmen do not always 'calculate' before they make decisions, and they do not always 'decide' before the act" (1946: 154). And a few pages later:

> The business man who equates marginal net revenue productivity and marginal factor cost when he decides how many to employ need not to engage in higher mathematics, geometry, or clairvoyance.... On the basis of hundreds of previous experiences of a similar nature *the business man would "just know" in a vague and rough way*, whether or not it would pay him to hire more men.
>
> (Machlup 1946: 167–168, emphasis added)

Lester has tried, certainly in a clumsy way, to verify empirically how entrepreneurs know what to do facing realistic yet imaginary cases. And Machlup answered to this challenge "they just know it".

The "marginalist controversy" would continue for the next seven years and Lester would write two more articles in the *American Economic Review*. He was to be supported only by Eiteman and they would both receive the bitter replies of Machlup, Stigler, Kaplan and others. The debate closed only in 1953, totally surmounted by Friedman's landmark paper (to be examined in the next chapter) and the escape would be achieved through the "irrealistincness" of the maximization principle, as suggested by Mongin (1986). The marginalist principle of behaviour survived its empiricist attacks, initiated by Hutchison in 1938 and continued after the war. One of the supporting actors of this story, Andreas Papandreou plainly described the cul-de-sac situation, while the controversy was still alive:

The only basis, in fact, for rejecting the postulate would consist in the discovery that human behavior is a) strictly or primarily random, b) "irrational" in the sense that is inconsistent, c) instinctive, d) strictly traditional. In so far as the presence of "deliberative process" can be confirmed, the essence of the rationality of the maximization postulate must be accepted.

(Papandreou 1950: 718)

Notes

1 Hutchison (1938) explicitly criticizes this additional assumption as being equally non-testable as the assumption of perfect knowledge: "The assumption of a tendency towards equilibrium implies, on the usual definition, the assumption of a tendency towards perfect expectations, competitive conditions and the disappearance of money" (1938: 107).
2 In his 1945 article "The Use of Knowledge in Society" Hayek advances further on this direction. Cf. Hayek (1952: 161) and Longuet (1998: 111).
3 Although the concept is definitely established by Coase, the term TC was coined by Arrow in a US Congress committee paper in 1969, as Williamson (1985: 18) reports. For a detailed analysis of the concept see Furubotn and Richter (1998: 47–76). Cf. below, Chapter 10.
4 Hutchison, at the early age of 23, after a first degree in Economics at Cambridge, obtained a teaching post as a Lector of English in Bonn from 1935 to 1938. Being very much interested in logical positivism as a student (Wittgestein and Carnap in particular), he was immediately influenced by Popper's book upon its publication in 1935 (Caldwell 1982: 106). Although extremely important, Popper's achievement to resolve the two most controversial issues in philosophy of science – the problem of induction and the problem of demarcation – it remained mostly inside the community of German speaking philosophic community. The first English edition appeared in 1959, and the French one only in 1973. In Hart (2002) Hutchison reports that Popper acknowledged him "to have some responsibility for this 'strange event' [of being knighted] because you [Hutchison] were first to quote me in English". Nevertheless, Hayek (1937: 33) was the first to quote Popper, without any further discussion.
5 The term "refutable" is nowadays commonly preferred to the term "falsifiable" to avoid the negative connotations of the latter.
6 Cairnes made the following claim:

> But in the moral and political sciences, in which we have to deal with human interests and passions, the agencies in operation at any given time in any given society are numerous, while, being in this case precluded from experiment, we are unable to prepare the conditions beforehand with a view to preserving the necessary *ceteris paribus*.

> (Cairnes 1857: 141)

More on the use of this clause in post-Ricardian political economy, in Zouboulakis (1993: 118–124).
7 Mill was the first to suggest, if only very succinctly, the rule of rational conduct, namely that everyone "is capable of judging of the comparative

efficacy of means for obtaining that end" (1836: 321). See above, Chapter 2. About Simon's "procedural rationality", see below, Chapter 10.

8 This was also Morgenstern's point in 1928, that the rationality of economic acts is so perfect that there are no more acts of choice or decisions (Leonard 1995: 741). Hutchison has read Morgenstern.

9 In his conversation with Hart (2002: 363), Hutchison quotes a sarcastic comment to sum up Robbins' methodology: "If we had some bacon, we could have some bacon and eggs, if we had some eggs. Well I mean that is it – you have to fill in all the assumptions". Caldwell (1982: 115) criticizes Hutchison for having failed to establish the analyticity of the fundamental generalizations of economic theory.

10 Although he refers to Edgeworth's indifference curves and to Hicks and Allen paper, Knight refuses to recognize their theoretical novelty: "in the absence of any technique of measurement, there is no clear differentiation between a subjective state and an objective quality, and the reference of an experience to the external world or to the mind is shifting and largely arbitrary" (1940: 19).

11 As Hutchison wrote:

> Against the sufferer from delirium tremens not much is necessary, but against the crank, the propagandist, and the coloured-shirted champion of some persecuting mass creed (by whom I was surrounded when I wrote my book), if the scientist can ever struggle at all, it is only by the firm, persistent appeal to testing by the facts.
>
> (1941: 739; cf. Hart 2010: 369)

12 From the rich secondary literature about the "Full-cost pricing controversy" we have consulted Lee (1984), Mongin (1986), Hausman (1988) and Tsoulfidis (2010: 241–242).

13 This procedure is summarized as follows: "prime (or 'direct') cost per unit is taken as the base, a percentage addition is made to cover overheads (or 'oncost', or 'indirect' cost), and a further conventional addition (frequently 10 percent.) is made for profit" Hall and Hitch (1939: 19).

14 Hall and Hitch were directly inspired from Chamberlin's *Theory of Monopolistic Competition* (1933). They were not aware of Paul Sweezy's famous paper on "kinked demand curve", published many weeks later in the *Journal of Political Economy*.

15 From 1946 to 1953, 22 articles were published in the *American Economic Review* on that same question involving a number of American economists such as Machlup, Stigler, Blum, Eiteman, Oliver, Apel, Bishop, R.A. Gordon, Haines, Reynolds, Bronfenbrenner, Kaplan and Ritter. The full list of articles is provided by Mongin (1986: 149).

16 Lester sent his questionnaire to "the presidents or executive officers of 430 Southern manufacturing firms in industries known to have a significant North–South wage differential". Only 68 replies were received, and ten of them only to say they were unable to answer.

7 Three conventionalist responses

Machlup, Samuelson and Friedman

From the early 1930s to the late 1940s one can readily admit that "Marginalism faced a scientific credibility problem" (Hands 2009: 840). This chapter maintains that the disconcerting anti-marginalist attack was effectively overcome thanks to the combined methodological stratagems of the most prominent priests of neoclassical orthodoxy of the post-war period, namely Fritz Machlup, Paul Samuelson and Milton Friedman. Machlup (1946, 1955) first attempted to eschew the empiricist critique by claiming that the fundamental assumptions of economics are not directly testable and cannot be refuted by empirical investigation, reintroducing thus conventionalism to economic methodology (Latsis 1976). Samuelson in 1947 gave a comparable response: a neoclassical theory based upon economic rationality produces "operationally meaningful theorems", that is, "hypotheses about empirical data which could conceivably be refuted if only under ideal conditions". His "Revealed Preference" theory is a thorough application of this methodological point of view. But the most celebrated conventionalist response to the empiricist critique is undoubtedly Friedman's celebrated essay of 1953. According to Friedman "theories are good for predictions only". Therefore, it is useless to criticize the unrealistic nature of economic assumptions like economic rationality, since the aim of any assumption is only to provide the basis for successful predictions. This is the meaning of his famous F-twist: "the more significant the theory, the more unrealistic the assumptions".[1]

Rational behaviour as an ideal-type

Machlup has tried, as seen above, to surmount the difficulties raised by the empiricist critique and to defend the correct nature of the fundamental behavioural principle of neoclassical economics. He answered to Lester's empirical controls of the marginalist theory of the firm and concluded that they were insufficient to "discard" the theory. A few years later he fully admitted the necessity of empirical testing and defended a version of the Popperian refutability: "testing an empirical hypothesis results either in its disconfirmation or its non-disconfirmation, never in its definitive confirmation" Machlup (1955: 4). In his article, Machlup claims that contrary to "specific hypotheses" (like those referring to particular consumption habits) and the "low level" hypotheses (related for example to the elasticity of demand of a good), "fundamental assumptions are not directly testable and cannot be refuted by empirical investigation" (Machlup 1955: 11). Such a hypothesis is the one that refers to rational behaviour. It is not a synthetic proposition, since it would not survive empirical testing, nor is an analytic proposition since it partly describes the reality. As an empiricist, Machlup would neither accept Ludvig von Mises' idea of a priori valid rationality: any action whatsoever, by the very fact it is a purposeful human action, is rational (Latsis 1976: 3, Lagueux 2010: 92). The maximization principle belongs to a "middle category" of propositions that "remain accepted as long as they have heuristic value, but will be rejected in favor of other rules (assumptions) which seem to serve their explanatory functions more successfully" (Machlup 1955: 16). For that reason, the "assumed type of action" of the rational agent is an idealized type of behaviour that is used in the abstract economic model and helps the "understandability" of economic actions.

Hutchison (1956) criticized this position, saying it avoids empirical testing: "not knowing how it can be tested, one cannot tell at all precisely what can be deduced from it", that is assuming that people act rationally or not (1956: 482). In his famous "rejoinder to a reluctant empiricist" he persists in claiming that "the heuristic postulates and idealized assumptions in abstract models ... are neither 'true or false' nor empirically meaningless" (1956: 486). At the end, Machlup clarifies plainly his views by endorsing openly the Weberian notion of "ideal-type" to characterize the role of the rational behaviour hypothesis. After admitting that no real observation of the ideal type is possible, he concludes that "homo œconomicus" is a logical construction "that helps us to understand the observations of the list of data, such as price relations, returns, employment, profits that are obviously, the results of human actions" (Machlup 1967: 130, our translation). As an ideal-type construction it is not confirmable but only replaceable by another that explains better economic phenomena. Nonetheless, this solution only eschews the empirical control of theoretical results and evades the problem of the content of the rationality principle, leaving its empirical meaning still uncertain (Latsis 1976: 11). Machlup's position will be discussed further at the end of this chapter, for he was a leading figure of the methodological controversy of the early 1960s between Friedman, Samuelson and others, on the realisticness of economic assumptions.

Samuelson's operationalism

Samuelson, although a well trained economist and statistician, was directly influenced by the interwar theoretical explosion in physics.[2] The influence of Willard Gibbs and Percy Bridgman was particularly obvious in Samuelson's idea about the form and content of the theoretical propositions of economic theory. Briefly put, Samuelson believed that the aim of science is to search for relations between observable variables and to draw from them testable conclusions: "Good science discerns regularities and simplicities that are there in reality [*sic*]" (1963: 236). This conviction is utterly reflected in two particular matters of great interest to us here, his operationalist view of economics as a science and his empiricist view about the nature economic theory. The latter concerns his debate with Friedman on the realism of economic assumptions, and will be discussed in the last section of this chapter. Samuelson's operationalism comes first.

Meaningful theorems

Samuelson follows Bridgman's operationalism as a method of scientific analysis to establish the idea about observable variables that lead to theoretically testable conclusions. Bridgman believed that scientific concepts acquire their empirical meaning through the functions or operations "that are necessary to verify their application or measurement" (Christodoulides 1979: 156). The aim of science is to establish the "principles of correspondence" of the theoretical concepts (such as length, velocity, density) to the experimental operations of the natural phenomenon described by each particular concept. Similarly, Samuelson in his influential *Foundations of Economic Analysis* (1947) aimed at determining the variations of unknown variables that result from the rise and fall of known parameters: "our theory is meaningless in the operational sense unless it does imply some restrictions upon empirically observable quantities, by which it could conceivably be refuted" (1947: 7). Thus he introduced the idea of an "operationally meaningful theorem" that is to say a "hypothesis about empirical data which could conceivably be refuted if only under ideal conditions. A meaningful theorem may be false" (1947: 4).[3]

His *Foundations* rest upon two fundamental theorems. The first is about the equivalence between equilibrium and the maximization (or minimization) of a magnitude (1947: 5). The consumer or the producer reaches equilibrium when they maximize their gains, or minimize their losses under specific constraints. The second theorem concerns the general stability of the economic system that is gifted with the internal quality to return naturally to equilibrium after every perturbation. The first chapters of the *Foundations* are precisely devoted to the mathematical techniques that are necessary to economists to be able to prove the conditions of equilibrium and stability (Backhouse 2002: 311).

His theory of "revealed preferences", as seen above in Chapter 5, was a considerable effort to eliminate any utilitarian residue left in consumer theory that was discouraging any inter-subjective control of the theoretical results. Samuelson succeeded to ground his theory only to observable data related to consumer behaviour, such as the consumer's preferences about different goods revealed before price changes. In that sense, his theory was a direct application of "operationalism" since it was determining a functional relation between two independent observable variables, namely market prices (p_i) and demand quantities (x_i): $\Sigma p_i \Delta x_i \leq 0$ implies $\Sigma (p_i + \Delta p_i) \Delta x_i < 0$. With his usual self-confidence, Samuelson proudly recognized that,

> the importance of this result can hardly be overemphasized. In this simple formula are contained almost all the meaningful empirical implications of the whole pure theory of consumer choice. Moreover, these are expressed in the form which is most suitable for empirical verification.
>
> (Samuelson 1947: 111)

Nevertheless, this theory, too, had some serious methodological deficiencies, since it was built upon two auxiliary hypotheses, very hard to be tested as Samuelson would hope for. The first refers to the internal consistency of consumer preferences. Its control would require strict laboratory conditions since by definition this hypothesis excludes the tendency to diversification of choices and characterizes as inconsistent any behaviour that reflects changes in the consumers' tastes in the long-run.[4] The second is relative to the influence of the so-called "income effect" upon the behaviour of the consumer. If this effect is not prevailed over each time the price of a good is changed by the "substitution effect" then it will be impossible not only to check out what a consumer will do, but also to be able to construct properly his negative slope demand curve (Wong 1978; Blaug 1980: 140–141). Yet, the empirical control of these two auxiliary hypotheses has never been feasible, eliminating thus every attempt to build the empirical implications of the revealed preferences theory.[5] As with Pareto's theory of indifference curves, Samuelson's theory proved to be irrefutable, despite the requirements of operationalism. His theory remained untestable, as long as the ideal conditions that will permit its control and eventual refutation are inaccessible.[6] As Papandreou quite early remarked, "empirical meaningfulness in the Samuelson sense constitutes a program of research rather than an accomplished fact" (1958: 11).

Non-meaningful methodology

Beyond these methodological contradictions, Samuelson is responsible for a more problematic attitude, as far as his theoretical practice is concerned. On the one hand he firmly believed that his only aspiration was to reproduce faithfully the external reality, a reality that is simple and visible to every observer: "in some areas at least, Nature seems to show an inexplicable simplicity" (1964: 739).[7] Machlup (1964: 734) immediately indicated this inconsistency between Samuelson's methodological rhetoric and theoretical practice, taking as an example his theory of international trade. Samuelson builds his theory on no less than eight auxiliary hypotheses that reconstruct the reality of international transactions and eliminate the influence of some fundamental factors upon it.

Conversely, he had this peculiar idea of the instrumental use of mathematics. Undoubtedly, this was Samuelson's greatest achievement in economics: the general acceptance of mathematical techniques as a tool of economic analysis and teaching. As Baumol (2005: 22) has nicely put it, before Samuelson's *Foundations*, anyone willing to use an equation in an economic publication had to apologize first that this was made only for the sake of clarity and precision, and second to acknowledge that human psychology was too complex to be apprehended that way. Due to Samuelson, the use of mathematics became the standard mode of presentation of economic thinking, and no one asks apologies from the reader for expressing his ideas mathematically.

Yet, Samuelson believed throughout his life that "Mathematics is a language", just like English or Greek (1952: 56), and therefore that "mathematical symbolism can be replaced by words" (1952: 58). He was always so confident as to declare:

> I should hate to put six monkeys in the British Museum and wait until they had typed out in words the equivalent of the mathematical formulas involved in Whitehead and Russell's *Mathematical Principia*. But if we were to wait long enough, it could be done.
>
> (Samuelson 1952: 58)

Surprisingly, Samuelson, one the greatest theoretical economists of the twentieth century, seemed to ignore that there are things said in words which cannot be described in mathematical symbols. He also seems to overlook, that the use of mathematics was based upon a great reconstruction of the field of economic analysis, consequently to expel from it an important number of social variables, as seen above in Chapter 3. He equally seems to disregard the fact that the use of mathematics requires the reduction of complex economic processes to a homogeneous field of counterbalancing forces that equilibrate into a certain point. All that in order to explain economic processes through the market mechanism, by keeping a balance between costs and benefits, and by neutralizing the interaction of any other "external" influence. He finally, seems to have underestimated that many notions, such as "demand elasticity", or "marginal productivity", would never exist if they had not been discovered, by the use of differential calculus. The same applies to many of his own theoretical discoveries, like the "accelerator model" and the "model of equivalence of the international prices of productive factors". Reading again one of his last interviews (in Suzumura 2005), one is surprised by Samuelson's methodological innocence concerning the self-image of what an economist of his rank, was thinking of what he was really doing.

Friedman and the realisticness of assumptions

In writing his 1953 essay Friedman aimed to offer a definitive answer to the critics of neoclassical theory, demonstrating that their effort is condemned to failure since the validity of a theory has nothing to do with the truth of its assumptions, but only with the correctness of its predictions. Although it was rightfully characterized as an example of philosophical mess, the discussion which his essay created is of great interest for many reasons. First, because it involved many eminent economists of the time such as Baumol, Boulding, Koopmans, Machlup, Samuelson, Simon *et al.* Second, because for the first time ever, an economic issue attracted some of the leading philosophers of science of the late twentieth century: Nagel, Popper, Watkins and Musgrave, who have directly or indirectly participated to the debate thus contributing to the clarification of the issues involved.

Realistic assumptions: advantage or disadvantage?

The epistemic status of the assumptions used by economists as premises of the explanation of economic phenomena is always a very crucial matter. It is obvious, at the first sight, that not all assumptions have the same epistemic status. For example, the hypothesis of perfect competition is of a different nature than the assumptions about the social and natural determinants of production, such as the law of diminishing returns and the law of increasing cost. The latter refer directly to the social and natural environment of production so they are directly testable by everyday experience. On the contrary, the hypothesis of perfect competition and the principle of rational behaviour as well, are the results of a rational reconstruction of reality, and consequently they are not directly testable by it.

For these hypotheses, which result from a high level of abstraction, many questions arise as far as their empirical relevance is concerned. For, if they are to be considered as true propositions, they have apparently to be left aside after their refutation. If they are just good approximations to the truth, the question is how to choose a good one? If they are just realistic reconstructions of reality,[8] how can anyone be sure that they are describing the essence of reality and not just the appearance of it? If, finally, they have an axiomatic basis, like the axioms of Euclidean geometry, is there a way to decide which is the best?

Friedman apparently knew the blind alley of the inductive process and the philosophical discussions in the positivist circles of the early 1950s, although he never refers to a single philosopher of science.[9] He simply points out that a hypothesis can never be sufficiently confirmed in reality by inductive means. The problem with Friedman is that he never suggests any criterion of empirical control of economic hypotheses, but tries to avoid the problem by denying it exists. Friedman (1953: 7) has made his point as clear as possible: "the ultimate goal of a positive science is the development of a 'theory' or 'hypothesis' that yields valid and meaningful (i.e., not truistic) predictions about phenomena not yet observed". The only safe way to control the validity of a hypothesis, says Friedman (1953: 9–10), "is the comparison of its predictions with experience". As to the question of how to choose between hypotheses that are equally valid, his answer is to prefer "the simpler" and "the more fruitful".

As said repeatedly above, because of the nature of the subject matter, economists rationally reconstruct economic reality, to reveal the real causes of economic phenomena and go beyond the occasional and the accidental. Friedman (1953: 24, 32, 40) also recognizes that a hypothesis "consists of an assertion that certain forces are, and by implication others are not important for a particular class of phenomena and a specification of the manner of action of the forces it asserts to be important". By definition then, economic assumptions are not meant to describe the reality as it is, in every detail, but only that part of reality isolated by means of abstraction, where economic forces are working without any "external" interference. Yet, Friedman – with an indeed "surprising twist" (Hollis 1994: 54) – concludes that it has consequently no meaning to persist to control the relation of economic assumptions to reality, because it is already known that they are, by definition, far from it. What is important, to his opinion, is to make good predictions starting from these assumptions. Even worse, the relation of assumptions to reality is, according to Friedman, almost the opposite suggested by the view under criticism. Truly important and significant hypotheses will be found to have "assumptions" that are wildly inaccurate descriptions of reality, and, in general, *the more significant the theory, the more unrealistic the assumptions* (in this sense).

(1953: 14, emphasis added)

Friedman believed that his position was the consequence of the abstract method: a theory is important "if it abstracts from the common and crucial elements from the mass of complex and detailed circumstances surrounding the phenomena to be explained and permits valid predictions on the basis of them alone" (ibid.: 14). And because it makes an abstraction of these circumstances, Friedman concludes, that it does not reflect reality and then is false. Bluntly put, "to be important therefore, a hypothesis must be *descriptively false in its assumptions*" (ibid.: 14, emphasis added). And since, all theories or assumptions are "inaccurate descriptions of reality", the best thing to do is to consider them temporarily "as if" they were true and choose the ones that predict better.

Friedman's way to close the discussion about the lack of realism of economic assumptions, such as maximizing behaviour, originated a voluminous literature and occupied economic methodology for three decades. Most of the critics have focused on the vagueness and logical inconsistencies of the essay, although not always successfully (Boland 1979, 1982: 148–150). An effort will be made to codify Friedman's flaws in the spirit of this book.

The variety and the role of economic assumptions

Friedman speaks about assumptions in two different ways. By the term "*hypothesis*" he refers to the theoretical constructions of economics and for that reason he explicitly identifies "hypothesis" with "theory" (1953: 7, 14, 24, 40). By the term "*assumption*" he refers to the premises of economic theories. The vagueness is created from the moment when he reserves far too many different meanings to the term "*assumption*". He speaks thus about "approximations" (1953: 15, 33), or about "axioms" of the "as if type" (1953: 25–26), and also about "ideal-type constructions" (1953: 34–36). The whole problem about the realisticness of his assumptions is seriously affected by this lack of precision, and philosophers like Nagel and Musgrave have spent much time in clarifying Friedman's confusion.

Musgrave (1981: 378) distinguished three kinds of assumptions:

a   "negligibility assumptions" assuming that "some factor F which might be expected to affect that phenomenon actually has no effect upon it".

A classic example of this kind, quoted by Friedman, as well by Nagel (1963) is Galileo's law of free fall. Just as Galileo's law is valid "as if" the bodies were falling in vacuum conditions, the law of demand, claims Friedman, is also valid "as if" consumers were moved by monetary motives alone.

b "domain assumptions" that testify that a "theory will only work if factor F is absent and restrict its applicability to cases of this kind" (Musgrave 1981: 381). An example of this type is the assumption of full competition that is valid only when there is no state interference. Musgrave says that an abstract assumption can be transformed into a domain assumption after the rejection of the former. The full competition assumption, valid when there is no state interference, can be transformed into a field assumption by excluding the cases where the state is active.

c "heuristic assumptions" that intentionally simplify a situation in order to build a theory, by assuming that a factor effective in the situation does not interfere. At a second stage, the neglected factor is taken into account "and says what difference it makes to its results" (ibid.: 383). An assumption of this kind would be of the form "let us assume for a moment that there is no state interference". In the next step, the state action is included to approximate real conditions. This is the meaning that Friedman adopts when he writes about "assumptions ... [which are] a far less economical presentation of the hypothesis" (1953: 24), comparing perfect competition with frictionless movement in physics.

Alan Musgrave's main argument is that Friedman is not capable of distinguishing between these three kinds of assumptions and for that reason he arrives at the wrong conclusion "the more significant the theory, the more unrealistic the assumptions". Even if his typology is not free from problems (Mingat *et al.* 1985: 286ff.), it shows convincingly that in any case, economic assumptions cannot be in opposition to reality.[10]

Realistic assumptions: the debate Friedman–Samuelson–Machlup

It has been already said that since Ricardo, economists are isolating, by means of abstraction, one specific range of social phenomena relative to production and distribution of wealth, leaving aside all non-economic aspects. For that reason they make use of assumptions as premises of economic explanation. Apart from his terminological vagueness, was Friedman right to claim that any economic theory, because of an original abstraction, is "descriptively false in its assumptions"?

Friedman's notion of "realistic assumption" can have many different definitions, ranging from "descriptively accurate", to "empirically tested", or even to "true propositions" (Caldwell 1982: 177). Mongin (1988) identifies no less than 13 different theses of assumptions emanating from the notion "realistic assumption" in Friedman's text. At a first glance, Friedman would disagree with Koopmans and Clower about their requirement to accept only true assumptions that have been adequately tested by experience (Koopmans 1957: 140; Clower 1994). This was put forward by Ricardo and his school. The four main assumptions of economic explanation – namely diminishing returns of land, Malthusian principle of population, increasing productivity of capital and labour and rational behaviour – were propositions established inductively and/or borrowed from the sciences of agriculture, engineering and psychology (Zouboulakis 1993, chap. 3). Friedman was sufficiently aware of the problem of induction to decline this requirement.

Furthermore, Friedman would never admit that he had an obligation to ground an economic explanation to "true propositions" only. Since assumptions, like "full competition" are often refuted, his clear-cut position that "the more significant the theory, the more unrealistic the assumptions" would then mean that he would build a theory on renowned false propositions. In that case, if we can explain and predict phenomena based on false propositions, any charlatan can make predictions and hope for an accidental confirmation.[11] But even in that intolerable case, it is still necessary to know how far from reality the assumptions are, so we can first choose between two "theories" that make correct predictions every now and then to improve these predictions.[12]

It is clear from the above that Friedman meant by "realistic assumptions" those which are "descriptively accurate", describing thus economic reality in every detail. However, as Nagel (1963: 218) remarked, every attempt to reproduce reality in its details leads no further than simple empirical generalities. It is therefore trivial to say that scientific theories are not exact descriptions of reality (Blaug 1980: 89). Yet, this trivial thesis provided the opportunity for a bitter discussion between Samuelson and Machlup. The former has maintained, as seen above, that theories should rest on "hypotheses about empirical data that could conceivably be refuted if only under ideal conditions". Samuelson thus believed that every theory or assumption should correspond, at least partially to the reality it refers to. Consequently, Friedman's position, that "a theory cannot be tested by comparing its assumptions directly with reality" (1953: 41), is untenable. For that reason Samuelson has coined the expression "the F-twist" to discredit Friedman's position.

But Samuelson advanced too far his criticism, claiming that theories are logically deducted only from true premises (1963: 232). He gave an example of the hypothetico-deductive model of explanation as follows:

symbolizing by (A) the hypotheses, by (B) the theories and by (C) the predictions based on the theory, then we must always have $A \equiv B \equiv C$. In other words, hypotheses identify themselves with theories, which in their turn can be identified with predictions. If the hypotheses are false, so are the theories and predictions as well, except those predictions proven to be accidentally true (Caldwell 1982: 193). In this way, Samuelson believed that he was demolishing Friedman's main argument, "a theory works [if] it yields sufficiently accurate predictions" (1953: 15).

Machlup (1964: 733) responded without delay to Samuelson, emphasizing that "a theory, by definition, is much wider than any of the consequences deduced". When it is said that $A \equiv B \equiv C$, what really happens is that any attempt of theorizing is denied, since a theory becomes nothing more than the reality it describes. As Machlup remarked, a theorist does not deduce a consequence only from a theory, but also from a combination of the relations explained by the theory with the occurrence of a variation or specific condition. Surprisingly, instead of agreeing with this obviously right position, Samuelson makes an epistemological slip willing to defend the full correspondence between theory and reality:

> Scientists never "explain" any behavior, by theory or by any other hook. Every description that is superseded by a "deeper explanation" turns out upon careful examination to have been replaced by still another description, albeit possibly a more useful description that covers and illuminates a wider area.
>
> (Samuelson 1964: 737)

Thus, according to Samuelson, science cannot explain reality; it can only make a description of it! As he wrote elsewhere, "All sciences have the common task of describing and summarizing empirical reality. Economics is no exception" (1952: 61).[13]

Samuelson's position is wrong for many reasons. First, the very identity he uses to attack Friedman ($A \equiv B \equiv C$) is just a tautology, true by definition and no empirical testing can be made of it (Wong 1973: 322). Second, he abandons very easily the ability of science to establish causal explanations. Either because he had an Aristotelian ideal of explanation in mind, to reveal the inner essence of things, or because he simply confused explanation with description, Samuelson seems to deny that explanation and scientific laws go beyond observation (Caldwell 1982: 194). As precisely written, while scientific explanation tries to explain the known by the unknown, description is the explanation of the known by something already known (Boland 1989: 121). Third, he confuses the lack of meaning of a proposition with the lack of realisticness of that proposition. Ignoring the blind alleys of logical positivism,

Samuelson continues to distinguish between "theoretical statements", supposed to contain only theoretical terms, and "observational statements" formed by observational terms.[14] This confusion leads him to look pointlessly to find the "correspondence rules" between every theoretical proposition and the observational terms (Mariyani-Squire 2009). However, most of the "theoretical terms" that he uses himself, such as "Pareto optimum", "social welfare function", etc. although they do have some logical meaning, they lack the possibility of being observables. Moreover, every observable magnitude is always linked to some theory and has a different meaning when attached to some other theory. For example, the terms "value", "surplus", "income" have different meaning in classical theory, in neoclassical theory and in Marxist theory. His overall conviction that he is "primarily a theoretician, but my first and last allegiance is to the facts" (quoted in Szenberg *et al.* 2005: 332) seems to be naive!

Summarizing the discussion so far, by the term "nonrealistic assumptions", Friedman meant those assumptions that are descriptively inaccurate, since no theory reflects reality as it is. So, because all theories are unrealistic, they should be treated "as if they were true", by their capacity to make good predictions. Using an example from Botany, Friedman says that we can predict the position of the leaves of a tree if we assume that they are oriented towards the sun, "as if they were willing to maximize their exposure to the sun". It does not matter that the leaves do not "think" that way. What matters is that this assumption "has great plausibility because of the conformity of its implications with observations" (1953: 20). Obviously, Friedman misunderstood the function of the abstract method. A rational reconstruction based on the abstraction of some non-essential parts of reality, cannot be an imaginary, or even worse, a false reality. This would overthrow a scientific tradition of more than three centuries. Since Newton's famous dictum "hypotheses non fingo" (*Principia Mathematica* 1687), science admits that it cannot rely on arbitrary and empirically invalid assumptions (Losee 1980: 90). The realisticness of its hypotheses is therefore the precondition for every theory aiming to explain reality.

Prediction, explanation and the meaning of science

A last philosophical issue remains open from the discussion above: can prediction be the ultimate aim of science? Friedman has identified that the aim of science is "the prediction of unknown phenomena", in order to bypass any discussion about the realisticness of the assumptions of neoclassical theory. If theories were only instruments of prediction, as Friedman claimed, it is useless to worry whether they are true or not. "The decisive test is whether the hypothesis works for the phenomena it purports to explain" Friedman (1953: 30; cf. 15, 18, 26, 33). A theory works, if it yields sufficiently accurate predictions. In a few words, if a theory predicts correctly, its truth status does not matter at all. Wong (1973) and Boland (1979, 1982, 1989), interpreted Friedman's methodology as "instrumentalist", and Friedman has accepted this label (Boland 1982: 151).[15] In our view, we can read Friedman's instrumentalism as a soft version of the philosophical school of Pragmatism, created by Charles Peirce, William James and John Dewey. Pragmatism adopted as the ultimate criterion of truth of every scientific theory its practical usefulness or applicability. In contrast to Pragmatism, Friedman was not looking for an alternative criterion of truth. His only care was the ability of theories to produce sound predictions and for that reason it is "futile" criticizing Friedman for adopting untrue propositions to serve as premises of economic reasoning (Boland 1981, 1982). For, Friedman limits himself only to economic theories that are suitable for useful matters.

There are two serious reasons for declining Friedman's instrumentalist position about "prediction as the ultimate aim of every positive science". First, no science can predict accurately without explaining first. If scientific activity is not reduced to an "arbitrary guesswork", as Hausman (1989: 121) remarked, then we must base our predictions on accurate generalizations about economic life. After all, explanation is not an inverted prediction. The symmetry thesis between explanation and prediction is logically false and philosophically untenable (Wong 1973; Blaug 1980: 96). It is actually broadly recognized in philosophy of science that explanation should logically precede prediction and should be independent from it (Drakopoulos 1994).[16]

Second, by adopting instrumentalism we desert the search for truth. Saying that we only really care about making sound predictions means to abandon the *raison d'être* of scientific activity. This is why Popper rejected instrumentalism, because it forces scientists to limit themselves only to empirical generalizations, disregarding whether they are true or not.[17] Despite the fact that Popper never referred to Friedman explicitly, instrumentalism is not acceptable even if one reduces its authority to issues of practical policy science, as Boland has suggested. Instrumentalism is philosophically indefensible if economics aims to explain social phenomena and make correct predictions based on sound assumptions, like the one relative to economic rationality.[18]

Notes

1 The rest of the chapter readapts parts of the book chapters published in Greek, in Zouboulakis (2007) and (2010a).
2 Samuelson studied economics in Chicago and statistics in Harvard under Edward Wilson, who was a student and research associate to Willard Gibbs, the father of chemical thermodynamics (Backhouse 2002: 310). As Mirowski

(1989: 378–386) has shown extensively, Samuelson was very much amused in imitating the rhetorical novelties of physics, without really using the content of physical theories. Part of this exegesis were the titles he used in his articles: "A quantum theory model of economics", "The law of conservation of the capital-output ratio", "Two laws of conservation in theoretical economics" etc.

3 See Blaug (1980: 85–86), Caldwell (1982: 190), Boland (1989: 10). Many of Samuelson's contemporaries were very enthusiastic, as Papandreou (1958: 7) testified: "the introduction of operationalism in economics has been viewed by many as the coming of age of the science".

4 Cf. Sen (1977: 1987), Kolm (1986: 90–1), Mirowski (1989: 364) and Lagueux (2010: 48). In their famous paper Stigler and Becker (1977: 76) assert as a fact that "tastes neither change capriciously nor differ importantly between people".

5 See Wong (1978), Blaug (1980, chap. 6), Caldwell (1982: 150–154) and Hausman (1992: 157).

6 Schmidt (1985: 140–146) measures convincingly the distance between Samuelson's operationalism and Popper's methodology.

7 Characteristic of what Samuelson believed he was doing is the following: "all economic regularities that have no common-sense core that you can explain to your wife will soon fail" (1963: 235). He humbly called his position the "Samuelson's razor which unlike Occam's which is purely aesthetic, is based on a lifetime of sad experience [*sic*]"!

8 It is more appropriate to speak about the "realisticness" of assumptions – i.e. their empirical meaning – instead of their "realism", which refers to a series of ontological and semantic concession (Mäki 1989).

9 See Caldwell (1982: 176). Karayiannis (2001a: 263), Boumans and Davis (2010: 80) report that Friedman had met Popper in person in 1947 and that he was greatly influenced by him. Blaug (1976) considers that Friedman simply misunderstood Popper and incorrectly applied his ideas to economics.

10 About the typologies of Archibald, Melitz and Machlup see Blaug (1980: 91–92).

11 Cf. Blaug (1980: 99), Caldwell (1982: 182), Gordon (1991: 41). Mongin (1988: 287) suggests considering Friedman's thesis in the light of the so-called "partial interpretation view": A hypothesis can be false and yet true inside a particular domain.

12 See Hausman (1988: 99), Mayer (1995: 70), Lagueux (2010: 137).

13 More on the subject in Blaug (1980: 96ff.), Karayiannis (2001a: 269–275).

14 For a detailed analysis of the so-called dichotomy between theory and observation see Chalmers (1976: 28–34), Christodoulides (1979: 179–226), Losee (1980: 184–185).

15 The interpretation of Friedman as instrumentalist is also endorsed by Mongin (1988: 285), Hausman (1998: 192) and Mariyani-Squire (2009).

16 Cf. Blaug (1980: 96), Caldwell (1982: 179).

17 Popper (1965: 107–114); cf. Karantonis (1980: 134), Caldwell (1982: 52 and 180).

18 Mingat *et al.* (1985: 409), discuss the dangers of adopting Friedman's instrumentalism for the economics profession. Lagueux (2010: 143–149) re-assesses the whole question about Friedman's real meaning and proposes a "middle position" between ontological realism and pure instrumentalism.

8 Popper's retreat and the "principle of rationality"

Karl Popper's research program for social sciences, inspired from the neo-classical economic analysis, was founded on the "analysis of the individual situation".[1] In two seminal papers (Popper 1961, 1967) he introduced his so-called "principle of complete rationality": Individuals act rationally when they act appropriately to their situation. As he insisted this proposition has no psychological, subjective, or hermeneutical basis. It is a universal proposition that is "not only false, but also nearly empty". One would say, it is metaphysical. This serious retreat from his own refutability principle was for Popper the only way to save the empirical status of economics, by considering rationality as an "animating principle" that plays a role in situational analysis similar to that of Newton's laws in the explanation of motions in the solar system.

Popper has defended, as early as 1945, a strict methodological individualistic thesis, mainly for political reasons, in his combat against totalitarianism:

> All social phenomena, and especially the functioning of all social institutions, should always be understood as resulting from the decisions, actions, attitudes etc., of human individuals, and that we should never be satisfied by an explanation in terms of so-called "collectives" (states, nations, races etc.).
>
> (Popper 1945: 298–299)

To make explicit his main thesis, Popper has introduced his "situational logic", which according to his own terms was "an attempt to generalize of economic theory (of the marginalist kind in particular) in a manner to be applicable to other social sciences" (1974: 162, our translation). His method of situational analysis was founded upon the assumption that individuals act in a rational way, "making the optimal use of all available information for the attainment of whatever ends they may have" (Popper

1957: 140). Popper's authority as a philosopher of science imbued economic methodologists with a kind of duty to refer persistently to "situational logic" and to its corollary "principle of complete rationality", either to support or to criticize his contradictions. Thus, in the early 1990s, a significant debate took place, questioning not only Popper's thesis, but also the limits of methodological individualism itself.[2]

Popper's principle and neoclassical economics

Methodological individualism does not imply by definition any particular kind of individual behaviour. An individual can act selfishly or altruistically, rationally or traditionally, as a maximizer or not. An individualistic starting point to explain social phenomena is thus compatible with any hypothesis about economic behaviour (Arrow 1986, Brochier 1994). The PR, which lies at the core of what has been rightly characterized by Köertge (1975) as "Popper's metaphysical program for the social sciences", is just Popper's way to explain individual behaviour.

The PR says that individuals act rationally "when they act appropriately to their situation" (Popper 1967: 145). Popper assumes that individuals do possess somehow all available information concerning their situation as they understand it in order to make the best combination between their goals and feasible means. Not accidentally, he considers the PR as equivalent to Newton laws that "animate the model of the solar system": the PR is the universal law that helps us to build "typical social situations" in order to explain social phenomena (1967: 143). We could say that the PR plays the role of the fundamental law of the deductive-nomological model of explanation in social sciences. Noretta Köertge (1975: 440) has accurately schematized Popper's situational analysis as follows:

TABLE A

Description of the situation:	Agent A is in situation C
Analysis of the situation:	In situation C, the appropriate act is X
Principle of rationality:	Agents act appropriately to their situation
Explanandum:	*Agent A will do X*

Spiro Latsis (1972, 1976, 1983) in his so-called "single-exit model", has provided the most well-known application of situational analysis in economics, which characterizes the neoclassical theory of the firm. The way a firm behaves is rational in Popper's sense because it takes into consideration all the elements of the situation, such as the prices of inputs and outputs, the available technology and the conditions of the market, and aims to maximize its profits using all available means. According to Latsis, the PR lies at the heart of "situational determinism whose central characteristic is the autonomy of economic decision making and the deliberate exclusion of the decision makers' inner environment from explanations of economic behavior" (Latsis 1976: 17).[3] Therefore, situational determinism is the philosophical basis of the neoclassical theory of the firm in many market structures, including large competition, monopoly or monopolistic competition. On the contrary, in oligopoly or duopoly, decisions are made in a state of "multiple exit situations", because they are influenced by psychological and sociological factors, by learning procedures and by information gathering procedures (Latsis 1972: 214; 1976: 16).

The PR describes only to a degree the main behavioural hypothesis of neoclassical economics since, as said above, rationality does not necessary imply maximization or even optimization (Mongin 1994). Nobody can replace the PR by the maximization principle without serious consequences regarding the validity of neoclassical theory. Even though, there are many questions arising about the empirical meaning and epistemic nature of the PR. If it has no psychological meaning, as Popper himself insisted tirelessly, is it possible to conceive rationality subjectively, as the individual perceives the situation? If this is not the case, how can anyone comprehend the subjective perception of the situation by the agents themselves? What about its epistemic nature then? If it has the status of a universal proposition, as it should be, to be able to serve as a premise to any causal explanation, what happens when it is frequently refuted by experience? Is there not then a serious retreat of the empiricist Popperian methodology to conventionalist tracks? In our effort to offer some answers to these pending questions, we will examine the three dimensions of Popper's methodological individualism.

The three dimensions of Popper's methodological individualism

The questions asked above can lead to fundamentally divergent interpretations of the "Popperian research program for social sciences". To make our task easier, we will group our own answers under three main theses. In our view, Popper's individualistic methodology is better understood as having three dimensions, namely anti-psychological, anti-subjectivist and anti-hermeneutic.

Anti-psychological individualism

In his famous book *The Poverty of Historicism* (1957), Popper gives a definition of what he calls "the postulate of methodological individualism" on the basis of which "the task of social theory is to construct and to analyse our sociological models carefully in descriptive or nominalist terms, that is to say, *in terms of individuals*, of their attitudes, expectations, relations etc." (Popper 1957: 136, original emphasis). "Psychologism" characterizes a particular form of individualism that claims to explain every social phenomenon, as a result of individual action motivated by psychological motives. Popper's opposition to psychological interpretations of human actions is one of the main characteristics of his social philosophy. "Methodological psychologism" leads to indeterminacy, since "the human factor is *the* ultimately uncertain and wayward element in social life and in all social institutions" (Popper 1957: 158, original emphasis). We have seen above in Chapter 2, how critical, yet unfair, he was to J.S. Mill, who was willing to establish social explanations to psychological premises. Popper attacks, in fact, only the most simplistic version of "psychologism", according to which humans live in a pre-social state of society and act separately, in isolation of other human beings (Koniavitis 1993: 383–384; cf. Blaug 1980: 45). This "Robinson Crusoe" situation was definitely not Mill's, nor any other classical economist's vision of social explanation.

Popper, the fervent opponent to holistic explanation, does not hesitate to identify himself to Karl Marx in his refusal to reduce "the social laws to the psychological laws of human nature" (Popper 1945: 289). Chapter 14 of his *Open Society*, containing his main individualistic thesis, quoted in the beginning of this chapter, is dedicated to the "autonomy of sociology" in relation to psychology, the latter being only a branch of social sciences, and not even a fundamental one.[4] Popper holds that social phenomena are the "non-intentional and often involuntary" result of human activity, and therefore cannot be explained through psychological motives. The social situation that individuals are confronted with, is not reducible to the psychological situation of every individual alone. On the contrary, the social situation is perfectly reducible to the individual situations that compose them. In his situational analysis, Popper emphasizes that "we replace the concrete psychological experiences by abstract and typical situational elements such as 'goals' and 'information'" (Popper 1967: 144, our translation from the original French text).

Anti-subjectivist individualism

An individualistic explanation that is not of a psychological nature can eventually be subjectivist. Indeed, some parts of Popper's article are open to this plausible interpretation of the PR as "a minimum principle that supposes the adaptation of our acts to our problem situations – *as we perceive them*" (Popper 1967: 149, emphasis added). Here the accent is put on the subjective perception of the situation by the individual, and commentators like Watkins (1970) have described it as an "imperfect principle of rationality" (or a weak one). In that perspective, individuals do not make a decision using all possible information, but only all available information at the moment they are about to take that decision. Sabooglu and Villet (1992) expanded the arguments of Watkins to criticize Latsis for having made an "abusive interpretation" of the PR, since the latter attributed Popper with the hypothesis of "perfect knowledge" of the situation.[5] Hence, there are two possible situations for the individual in order to act rationally: an "objective situation" characterized by perfect knowledge of all information, and a "subjective situation" when the individual possess imperfect or limited information.[6]

Notwithstanding Popper's ambiguity in some points, he leaves no doubt regarding the above, if one is patient enough to thoroughly read his work. In *The Poverty of Historicism*, when he exposes his "zero method", he refers to the "assumption of complete rationality", he cares to clarify in brackets "the assumption of the possession of complete information" (1957: 141). Even in the very same article of 1967, one can find other places that dissolve any confusion about his intentions: "the situation, in the sense I use this term, contains already all the goals and *all feasible knowledge* that can be important, in particular the knowledge of *feasible means* to realize these goals" (1967: 144, emphasis added). Attributing to Popper a subjectivist interpretation of his PR would be accusing him erroneously of a "major logical contradiction" (Lagueux 1993b: 470). And this applies equally to a Freudian-like interpretation of his PR.[7] What is more, reading carefully the text of his conference of 1961, the case becomes crystal clear. In his analysis of the logic of social sciences (twenty-fifth thesis), not only does he quote nine times the words "objective" and "objectively" in one single paragraph to emphasize his position, but he also adds this:

> Objective "understanding" consists in realizing that the action was *objectively appropriate to the situation*. In other words, the situation is analyzed far enough for the elements which initially appeared to be psychological (such as wishes, motives, memories and associations) to be transformed into elements of the situation.
>
> (Popper 1961: 79, emphasis added)

Joseph Schumpeter, in a text that remained unpublished until 1984, gave a similar definition of "objective rationality (= applicability of a rational schema to the actor's behavior)". His reading matches perfectly with Popper's aim to set up an objectively recognized norm of behaviour as a heuristic device. Objectivity is also guaranteed by its reference to the social context:

> situational logic assumes a physical world in which we act.... Beyond this, it must also assume a social world, inhabited by other people, about whose goals we know something and, furthermore, social institutions. These social institutions determine the peculiarly social character of our social environment.
>
> (Popper 1961: 80)

This last point provided his readers the opportunity to make a comparison with Joseph Agassi's (1975) "institutional individualism", which effectively embraces in the objective situation as the individual perceives it, the social environment shaped by natural, historical and institutional constraints.[8] Individuals are the only bearers of goals and interests, while at the same time these goals and interests are socially determined.

Anti-hermeneutic individualism

A third possibility is to interpret the PR subjectively in the way that von Mises and von Hayek have understood economic behaviour. In reality, speaking of the adaptation of human acts to the situation "as we perceive it", would conceivably suggest that Popper adheres to a social explanation of an interpretative type, very popular in the German speaking world of humanities (*Verstehen*). To explain a social phenomenon, according to Hayek, is to comprehend the unique situation that an individual faces, by taking his place at the moment she decides; or in Hayek's words, "to know the situation as a result of our own subjective experience" (Hayek 1952: 31). This interpretation appears to be even more credible, in the light of the personal bonds of Popper and Hayek, which have certainly helped Popper in his conviction that historical evolution is the non-intentional by-product of individual actions (Cubeddu 1987).

However, this reading of Popper's PR, suggested by Sabooglu-Villet (1992) and Nadeau (1993), is not suitable. Not only because it would be incompatible with his anti-subjectivism, as discussed in detail above, but mainly because it would mean that Popper would be forced to accept a truly non-empirical proposition as a premise of the *explanans* of an empirical science. Further, this is in full contradiction to one of the main pillars of his "research program", his methodological monism. Popper categorically affirms that the mode of explanation and control in social sciences is fundamentally the same as that in the natural sciences: "the methods always consist in offering deductive causal explanations, and in testing them (by way of predictions)" (Popper 1957: 131; cf. 1961: 66, 1967: 142). The very section in which Popper explicitly, but very kindly, rejects Hayek's method is called "the unity of method" and therefore, it leaves no room for contradiction or incoherence (cf. Caldwell 1991:19, Hands 1991: 112, Lagueux 1993b: 470). The only problematic point about the relation of his PR to his refutability principle is the justification he gives in order to convince the reader about his choice of the behavioural principle. This will be discussed in the next section.

How Popper justifies his choice of the principle of rationality

Popper has explicitly recognized that humans do not always act rationally. Because the PR is a universal proposition that cannot be valid a priori as von Mises has suggested, and cannot be empirically proven, as is made to serve to a scientific explanation, therefore "the principle of rationality is false [*sic*]" (Popper 1967: 145). This confession, in fact, has left many of his readers astonished. Popper used conventionalist arguments to support the choice of his PR in many places of his article. He has spoken thus about a "by-product of a methodological postulate" (1967: 144), or about a "good methodological practice" (1967: 146), and even about "a good approximation of the reality, albeit recognizing that it is not true" (1967: 148, our translation).

Is it possible for Karl Popper to be as incoherent as to oppose his own philosophy of science by using conventionalist and "immunizing strata-gems" only to save his PR? In fact, many of his critics think that way. They even distinguish "two Poppers", the first called Popper$_n$ which is the philosopher of natural sciences famous for his criterion of refutability, and the second called Popper$_s$ which is the philosopher of social sciences and situational logic.[9] There are also critics such as Nadeau (1993) who find here an undeniable proof of methodological dualism in Popper, having as a point of departure Hayek's subjectivist-hermeneutic method: if the PR is understood subjectively, it is immune of any refutation since any beha-viour, no matter its irrationality, can be justified by the acting subject itself. This is, however a possibility, denied explicitly by Popper himself, as seen above, because of his faith in methodological monism.

A possible getaway would be to consider the PR as an adequate approx-imation of the truth, as seems to be suggested occasionally by Popper himself (1967: 148). Nevertheless, as Hands (1991: 113) rightly pointed out, this solution creates new complex problems related to the evasive concept of "verisimilitude". Caldwell (1991) proposes another exit to reconcile refutationism and situational logic, referring to a broader philosophical principle, namely fallibilism: the PR is a good approximation to the truth that explains many social phenomena and, because of its provisional character, it is always susceptible to revision. After all, Popper emphasizes that human knowledge constantly evolves under the fire of criticism (Boyer 1987).

At any rate, the question of choice of the particular type of rationality remains insufficiently justified, at least in a way that is not contradictory to Popperian methodology. Arguing for example, like Lagueux (2010), that the PR is an instrumental principle, would be totally unacceptable for Popper (Hands 1991). Should we accept perhaps Lallement's (1987) solution and agree that this is a pure "political choice" and that Popper was looking for a plausible behavioural principle to ground his anti-totalitarian philosophy? Although this explanation seems very attractive, we would prefer a methodological argument of the Lakatosian type to justify Popper's choice: the PR is part of the "hard core" of the Popperian research program in philosophy of social sciences that cannot be abandoned without the presence of another research program, which is empirically and theoretically more "progressive" in Lakatos' sense (cf. Latsis 1972: 240; Köertge 1979: 93; Hands 1991: 117). In spite of the above, the choice of the PR is part of a more general philosophical choice between methodological individualism and holism. Brochier (1988) has accurately called this choice one of "the grand generating myths at the heart of every scientific construction", and it is unfeasible to expel a myth from social discourse using logical or empirical proofs.

Reforming methodological individualism

Our previous analysis has revealed that methodological individualism needs to be seriously reformed to stand as a credible point of departure to social explanation. We are still far from having reached a "general agreement regarding methodological individualism as a heuristic postulate", as Blaug has concluded (1980: 46). Even if one accepts not to reduce social phenomena to their psychological or subjective dimensions, it is undeniably true that there are "social facts" not reducible to their individual components. As Alexander Rosenberg wrote, acknowledging the existence of "macromolecules", such as "the nation" or "the state", does not mean that these entities possess a metaphysical or even ontological identity, as Popper was afraid of (Rosenberg 1988: 128). As seen above, Popper has explicitly recognized the existence and the role of institutions that "determine the social character of our social environment" (1961: 80); for that reason they form an integral part of the situation an agent needs to take into account in order to make the appropriate decision (Chalmers 1985: 80).

The examples of Mill and Weber show that it is indeed possible to have an individualistic departure without underestimating the effects of socialization upon individuals and leave without explanation the influence of the institutional frame of the acting agent.[10] As Arrow (1986: 385) convincingly argued "rationality is not a quality of the individual alone, although is usually presented that way. Rather, it gathers not only its force, but also its very meaning from the social context in which it is embedded". As will be discussed in the last chapter, "institutional individualism" offers, in our view, a unique methodological approach that respects both the social environment of acting individuals as well as of their social interaction.

But this kind of methodological approach asks for a different kind of rationality. Even if one can justify Popper's choice by considering it as a quasi-metaphysical, non-refutable hypothesis, that is not enough. A much broader approach embracing the institutional frame and the effects of socialization of individuals is, at the end of the day, incompatible with strict individualistic, self-centred decision making. In Chapters 10 and 12 we will discuss some of the alternatives offered by Herbert Simon, evolutionary economics and economic sociology, attempting to build a rationality hypothesis that recognizes that individuals are both the creators and the products of society.

Notes

1 This chapter readapts an earlier version published in French in Zouboulakis (1997b).
2 Köertge, N. (1975, 1979), Latsis (1976, 1983), Chalmers (1985), Caldwell (1991), Hands (1991, 1992), Sabooglu and Villet (1992), Lagueux (1993a, 1993b), Nadeau (1993), Brochier (1994).
3 By the term "inner environment" Latsis (1976: 16) describes the information gathering, psychological and sociological characteristics that influence the decision making actors.
4 See also Popper (1957:142, 1961: 78). A propos, Boland (1982: 30–34), Boyer (1987).
5 Latsis (1983: 131–132) has moved further from his initial position of 1972, and become effectively more critical, recognizing that "Popper is not completely coherent in that case".
6 Mongin (1984: 57) thoughtfully indicates that these types of rationality are already present in the work of Max Weber, the first under the name of "accurate rationality" (*Richtigkeitsrationalität*) and the second as "subjective rationality". See also above, Chapter 4.
7 Popper (1967: 148) quotes Freudian neurotic behaviour as an example of subjectively perceived rational action. This is however not sufficient to say that Popper endorses subjectivism. Cf. Lagueux (2010: 104).
8 A propos, cf. Bouveresse (1981: 170), Boland (1982: 36), and Boyer 1987: 18). The latter calls Popper's individualism "socio-ecology in the sense that individuals

beyond society do not exist; their social 'milieu', called 'eco-nest' ['*éconiche*'] is always, at least partially, a place of social type" (our translation).

9 This distinction comes from Hands (1985, 1991, 1992); cf. O'Hear (1980: 164–165), Lallement (1987), Sabooglu and Villet (1992), Lagueux (1993a, 2010: 106).

10 Including the influence of social norms and values as suggested by North (1990), Arrow (1994), Hodgson (1997) and many others. See further, Chapter 12.

9 Probabilistic choice and strategic rationality

The idea of rational choice in uncertain conditions was elaborated in Knight's *Risk, Uncertainty and Profit* and Keynes' *Treatise on Probability*, both published in 1921. Elements of risky decision making were present in the works of Smith (1776: 120–122), Mill (1848: 407–409), Jevons (1871: 99) and Marshall (1890: 111).[1] Yet, their theories were fundamentally deterministic and none of them used probabilities as an instrument in economic theorizing (Ménard 1978: 150; 1987: 141). John von Neumann and Oskar Morgenstern (1944) introduced a rather new concept of rationality associating utility maximization with probabilistic choice in risky situations. Leonard Savage moved forward this approach, explaining uncertain prospects thanks to his "subjective expected utility" theory. John Nash (1950) made the decisive step of suggesting an equilibrium solution to a game with a finite number of players. Thus, interactive individuals participate in non-cooperative games calculating the probabilities of possible outcomes to maximize personal gains. With Nash, economics becomes a logical science where agents with imperfect knowledge about the final outcome make consistent yet interdependent choices. In this, two basic limitations of the Walrasian/Paretian model are overcome, certainty and automatic choice. In the latest versions of game theory, the idea of rational strategic behaviour has introduced an extremely important learning process in the cases of repeated and cooperative games. Rationality has turned out to be not just a process of simply drawing logical conclusions about the other player's strategies, but also a process of continuous revision of the interacting individual's strategic beliefs.

Risk, uncertainty and probabilistic behaviour

Neoclassical rationality, from Jevons and Pareto, to Hicks and Samuelson, has evolved in conditions of certainty. Thanks to Knight, economists were, without doubt, able to distinguish between risky and uncertain decisions.

In situations involving risk, agents are not certain about the prospect of their decisions but they are able to calculate its eventual risk. In that sense, to put your savings in a common bank deposit account is less risky than buying bonds, which is less risky than buying a company's shares on the stock market. On the contrary, in situations involving uncertainty there is no way to calculate the possibility of the outcome, because you simply don't know it. As Knight puts it, "the given outcome is not certain, nor even extremely probable, but only contingent" (1921: 213). A fruitful way of understanding the differences between risk and uncertainty is to associate the eventual outcome of a decision with probabilities. In situations of risk, the possible outcomes have objectively known probabilities, as in the case of a coin: it could be heads or tails with a probability of 0.5. In the case of uncertainty, the probabilities associated with the possible outcomes, "or even the range of the outcomes of actions are not known" (Hausman 1992: 22). Knight's example is very instructive: "no one would assert confidently that the chance of a particular building burning on a particular day is 'really' of any definite assigned value" (1921: 217). Risk is related to measurable randomness and should be differentiated from the notion of uncertainty, related to the unknowable. For that reason Knight gives a special role to intuition, as a source of knowledge of the uncertain. As he posits, to evaluate an uncertain prospect "we act upon estimates rather than inferences, upon 'judgement' or 'intuition', not reasoning for the most part" (1921: 223).[2] On that basis, innovative entrepreneurs take risky decisions but also uncertain ones as to the development of a new product or a new market.

Historically, there are two distinct philosophical traditions associated with the analysis of probabilistic choice, the objective and the subjective. Thinkers such as Cournot, Keynes and Carnap argue that in relation to any possible amount of knowledge or expertise, there are particular objective probabilities, independent from the decision making individual that can be deduced by strictly logical methods (Tisdell 1975: 266). In contrast, the older philosophical tradition of subjective probability goes back at least to Daniel Bernoulli who in 1738 associated the objective probability of an outcome with the individually estimated material gain resulting from it. In this Bernoullian type decision making theory, associated with the names of von Neumann, Morgenstern, Nash and Savage, choices between risky and uncertain prospects are made by calculating their expected utilities, i.e. by weighting the personal value of each prospect by the probability of its occurrence.

Let us return to the Keynesian treatment of probabilities, before examining in more detail the more influential Bernoullian tradition in economic decision theory. Keynes' main objective in 1921 was to understand the logical foundations of knowledge under conditions of uncertainty. When knowledge is obtained indirectly "by argument", the results may be "inconclusive" so scientific arguments are primarily based upon rational beliefs, which are in great part uncertain. This is how Keynes explains the necessity of studying probabilities, in order to deal with knowledge of a "lower degree of certainty" (1921: 15). For Keynes the theory of probability is anything but a theory of personal or subjective beliefs: "Probability is logical, therefore, because it is concerned with the degree of belief which it is rational to entertain in given conditions, and not merely with the actual beliefs of particular individuals, which may or may not be rational" (1921: 4).

Thus, probability is a logical relation between two sets of propositions. The probability of an event is always relative to a given ensemble of events. When an outcome is recognized as highly probable, it is relative to the total evidence. This is why Keynes was opposed to the Bernoullian design of grounding probabilities on statistical inference: "the idea that one can obtain an exact probability for the result of a statistical induction is one that Keynes ridicules" (Kyburg 1995: 27). A valid inductive argument should therefore take into account all the data, which is an impossible task due to the Humean predicament relative to the "problem of induction". Alternatively Keynes suggested "random sampling" as a means to deal with subjective probabilities "relative to the mind of the subject", in order to overcome the logical impossibility of statistical inference from individual prospects (1921: 281). Regrettably, Keynes never used these ideas in economic theory: "as was true for Cournot, there is no place in Keynes' economic model for a probabilistic approach" (Ménard 1987: 143). As an example, to analyse the behaviour of investment in the *General Theory*, which is governed by a deficiency of information, he was inclined to utilize uncertainty and convention rather than the weight of argument. Weight has usually a positive correlation with evidence, but it is independent of probability. Keynes relied more on the concept of confidence, a concept which appears to be underpinned by the weight of argument. His intention to build a general and "practical theory of the future" caused him to prefer the concepts of expectation and convention to that of probability.[3]

Non-interactive games and expected utility

According to von Neumann and Morgenstern (1944), agents have preferences represented by a utility function that possesses the expected utility property: the eventual outcome's utility is coupled with the probability of its occurrence. Conceptually, von Neumann and Morgenstern subscribe to the idea of rationality as maximization under constraint of the early marginalists with the substantial advance that agents are operating with imperfect information, i.e. without being certain about the final outcome, and choose between risky outcomes. Moreover, the restrictions imposed upon individual ordinal ranking of preferences established by the general equilibrium model, namely completeness, transitivity and continuity, are fully respected. In addition, preferences should satisfy the axiom of "independence", which implies that the addition of a new alternative outcome does not alter the individual's existing preference ordering.

Formally, if c_1, c_2,... c_k are the outcomes of a lottery and p_1, p_2,... p_k the attached probabilities, the von Neumann and Morgenstern theorem says that if the axioms of complete preordering, transitivity, continuity and independence are verified, there is a representation of the preference relation in terms of an aggregate utility function $\Sigma_i\, p_i\, U(c_i)$ that "possesses the expected utility property and is unique up to a positive linear transformation" (von Neumann and Morgenstern 1944: 23; Mongin 1998). The possibility of "linear transformation" of this theorem has its foundations on the old marginalist project of measurable utility. Obtaining measurable numerical quantities by coupling the order relation of an agent (whose preferences satisfy the above formal conditions) with the possibility to compare utility differences from outcomes, allows obtaining quantities "as measurable as temperature on the centigrade or Fahrenheit scales" (Hausman 1992: 24). During the 1950s the "measurability controversy" re-emerged once again, four decades after Pareto's "ordinalist revolution".[4] In fact, the von Neumann and Morgenstern utility function does not have the same cardinal properties as Jevons' or Edgeworth's utility function. This is because the numbers obtained through the combination of utilities and probabilities might be unrelated to the measurement of preference differences, unless further special axioms are added concerning the uniqueness of the expected utility function (Mongin 1998). As accurately remarked, "the cardinality enjoyed by von Neumann and Morgenstern's expected utility is not the outcome of a particular psychic state or ability of the decision maker, but just an analytically useful implication of the set of axioms" (Giocoli 2003: 379).

Another way of interpreting subjective probabilities was introduced by Leonard Savage and his "subjective expected utility theory". In his *Foundations of Statistics* published in 1954, Savage moves forward the von Neumann and Morgenstern axiomatic approach in order to explain, not only risky, but also uncertain prospects. Instead of coupling the eventual outcome's utility with the objective probability of its occurrence to extract the expected utility function, Savage associates the expected utility of an outcome with the agent's subjective probability, i.e. her probabilistic belief about the outcome. If, the agent believes an uncertain event has possible outcomes, c_1, c_2, ... c_k, each with a personal utility to the agent $U(c_i)$, then her choices can be explained as arising from a function in which she believes that there is a subjective probability of each outcome $p(c_i)$, and her subjective expected utility is the expected value of the utility. Hence, $\Sigma_i p(c_i) U(c_i)$ is the sum of the utility of every single outcome "discounted for the probability that it will not in fact occur" (Hollis 1994: 117). Consistency in agent's choices continues to be a crucial criterion of rationality as in von Neumann and Morgenstern's theory, yet choices are made according to a different manner: agents make their choices by following their "subjective probability distribution" i.e. their beliefs about the different likelihood of the various "states of the world" they are facing (Sugden 1991: 757). Because it was no more possible to attach an objective probability to the different outcomes, as in von Neumann and Morgenstern's case, Savage adopted a stronger independence axiom (known as "the sure thing principle") to be able to claim that the agent's subjective utility function represents her actual preferences on alternative outcomes. In Savage's framework, the sets of conceivable events and conceivable consequences are independent of one another and independent of the nature of acts out of which a person has to choose (Sugden 1991: 764).

Although both of the above approaches aimed to ground economic rationality on observable choices, nothing but introspective evidence was offered and only logical experiments were made, comparable to Pareto's imaginary experiments on indifference curves and Samuelson's "empirical" control of revealed preferences. But in contrast to indifference curves and revealed preferences that were practically untestable, von Neumann's and Savage's expected utility theories were explicitly tested and falsified by Maurice Allais (1953) and Daniel Ellsberg (1961), in their seminal papers (Hausman 1992: 212–215). Allais has logically proven that there are "rational [consistent] types of behavior which do not obey" von Neumann and Morgenstern's or Savage's axioms and that not all people share the same "pleasure of gambling" (1953: 510).[5] People's attitude in risky situations depends on their prudency, their personal fortune and the amount of money at stake, a line of criticism that will be continued by Kahneman and Tvesrky in 1979. Ellsberg has similarly contradicted the subjective expected utility theory using the old Keynesian idea of "ambiguity aversion": people are inclined to choose an option with fewer unknown elements than with many unknown elements, whatever the prize is (Ellsberg 1961).[6] Despite their genuine refutation, both theories "continued to be recognized as the undisputed characterization of rationality, while Allais' and Ellsberg's results were considered as nothing but *paradoxes*" (Giocoli 2003: 393).

Interactive games and Nash equilibrium

So far we have dealt with the simplest form of games, where a person makes a choice calculating the probability of a future event as if he or she was alone in the planet, i.e. without giving the slightest thought of what other people intend to do. These games are called "games against nature" because they are not interactive; they are, so to speak, parametric games. Von Neumann and Morgenstern (1944) dealt also with interactive games and provided full treatment and solution of a special kind of game between two rational individuals, who are antagonistic to each other, in a sense that one player's losses balance exactly the other player's gains. This is known as the "zero-sum game" and it became very popular in analysing international conflict situations during the Cold War years.[7] A game is generally described by naming its players and specifying their strategies, i.e. their complete personal plan of action. The players come with knowledge of what the possible strategies are and a probability distribution over the eventual utility outcomes. Then, for every selection of strategy by the players, each of them gets some (potentially negative) gain, called payoff.[8] Thus, in zero-sum games, the payoff-sum is zero.

In game theory it is further assumed that players share a "common knowledge": each player knows what the other knows, including her utilities and strategy and also the fact that the other player knows that she possesses this knowledge, and so on (Hausman and Macpherson 1993: 718). Common knowledge "is a precondition for predictability" in games (Bicchieri 1992: 168). This further assumption was crucial in dealing with multi-player game problems, "otherwise the model is insufficiently specified, and the analysis incoherent" (Aumann 1987: 473). John Nash (1950), in less than two pages, tried to generalize games to n-players and suggests a unique solution to the mathematical problem emanating from this situation.[9] What is universally known as the "Nash-equilibrium" describes a situation where in n-players' game situation (where n is a finite number), each player willing to maximize his expected utility under the constraint of the other players' strategies, takes an action (makes a choice) which is the best reply to the other players' actions (Sugden 1991; Hammond 1997). Nash boldly assumes that each player can predict the other player's strategies before they make their move; all players choose the best reply to one another and they also reach the equilibrium solution after "one shot" (static or simultaneous-move game). Notice that the "Nash equilibrium" represents a best reply to others, which also means that no one can benefit by playing some different strategy. This is like Walras' general equilibrium point (without an auctioneer "crying out" the potential prices to equalize demand and supply), representing as well a Pareto optimum solution, but with interactive individuals exchanging under uncertainty.

If a static game has two players only, each combination of strategies results in a pair of payoffs, one for each player (i.e. four different utility outcomes). If a game has three players and the players have two possible moves then the number of combinations or sets of strategies is eight (2^3). If the number of their moves is k, then the number of strategies is k^3. If a game has n players (a finite number) and the number of choices is k then the number of sets of strategies will be k^n. What happens if the same game is repeated many times? Obviously, every player will readjust his or her strategy in order to adapt to the other player's response. As a result, a "tit-for-tat" strategy is probably more promising than maximization: "play obligingly in the first round and then keep it up, provided that the other player does likewise" (Hollis 1994: 125). In the case of an infinite regress of conjectures "I think that she thinks that I think she thinks etc.", the prospect of a mutual destruction for both players is highly probable. If we leave aside the practical difficulties on how a player gets all the information for other players' strategies, which are eschewed thanks to the heroic assumption of "common knowledge", recent research in computer science theory has confirmed that the computational complexity for every player to predict correctly the other players' best strategy is insurmountable.[10]

One solution to escape from this situation would be to impose an assumption on these infinite conjectures and say what an agent *should* do in that case. Then, a whole tradition of separation of art from science, going back to Senior and Mill, would be broken and the normative will mix up with the positive (Bicchieri 1992). A better solution would be to cooperate as von Neumann and Morgenstern initially thought. Cooperative games are a step further towards understanding interactive behaviour for an additional important reason; they suggest a learning process in the cases of repeated and cooperative games. Robert Aumann provided a computationally less expensive solution to non-cooperative repeated games with n-players, thanks to his concept of "correlated equilibrium", with an additional restrictive condition on the players' strategy (Sugden 1991: 766–768).[11] As Thomas Schelling has demonstrated even players with conflicting interests are better off if they choose to cooperate when they are about to have a long lasting relationship.[12]

With game theory, economics became at last a logical science where agents with uncertain knowledge make consistent choices containing risk. Von Neumann and Morgenstern were perfectly clear in their intention to break, not only from the determinism of neoclassical theory, but also from a whole tradition of realistic representation of economic theory since

Ricardo's first model. Eventually, this was generated by the important shift of the physical representation, from the classical mechanistic to the modern quantum model. As accurately stated, "in game theory, as in recent physics, any one-to-one correspondence between the theory and the world had been abandoned: in the spirit of Hilbertian mathematics, the theory bore only an abstract relation to social 'reality'" (Leonard 1995: 755). As seen above, from von Neumann, to Savage and Nash, more and more restrictive assumptions were added as to the behavioural pattern of economic agents, their "common knowledge" and computational capacity. Nevertheless, one major restriction, decision making under certainty, was overcome. Despite the significant progress in game theory, especially with cooperation games, the aim of explaining how people really behave in interactive situations was never truly justified empirically, except in experimental economics using game theoretical tools.

Notes

1 Smith announces the necessity of risk premium in chapter vi, of the first book when he says that "something must be given for the profits of the undertaker of the work who hazards his stock in this adventure" (1776: 54). In chapter x he thoroughly analyses the different kinds of "chances of profit" between lotteries, insurances, sea trade, etc. Speaking of lotteries he even suggests a probabilistic argument: "there is not, however a more certain proposition in mathematics, than the more tickets you adventure upon, the more likely you are to be a loser" (1776: 121). Mill follows Smith in compensating risk as an element of profits of capital and distinguishes two sources of risk, "between different employments of capital in the same society, [and] the very different degrees of security of property in different states of society" (1848: 408). Jevons was aware of Bernoulli's work and asks his reader to take account of "the uncertainty of future events" when they estimate future interests: "we must reduce our estimate of any feeling in the ratio of the numbers expressing the probability of its occurrence" (1871: 99). Finally, Marshall refers directly to Bernoulli twice to explain that the "satisfaction which a person derives from his income" depends on his initial endowment and applies this principle to the case of calculating the premium "insurance against risk" (1890: 111 n.2).
2 Knight distinguishes thus "estimates" that are not measurable, from both a priori (objectively known in advance) and statistical (*ex post*) probabilities. See Frantz (2005: 95–110) on the role of intuition in Knight.
3 I thank Prof. Ioannis Theodosiou for making this suggestion.
4 The controversy initiated by Friedman and Savage's paper "The expected utility hypothesis and the measurability of utility", published in the *Journal of Political Economy* in 1952, included among others economists such as Allais, Arrow, Baumol, Ellsberg, Luce and Raiffa. See Mongin (1998), Giocoli (2003: 385–386).
5 Allais (Nobel Laureate in 1988) presented his test first in the "European Econometric Congress" of September 1951 and then during the "International Conference on Risk" held in Paris in May 1952. His essay was finally published in

Econometrica (in French!) and with a disclaimer from the editor (Ragnar Frisch). Marshall (1890: 693, n.ix) refers also to the "pleasure of gambling".

6 According to Keynes (1921: 53–54)

> the principle [of indifference] states that "there must be no known reason for preferring one of a set of alternatives to any other".... We have no right to say of any known difference between the two alternatives that it is "no reason" for preferring one of them, unless we have judged that a knowledge of this difference is irrelevant to the probability in question.

Ellsberg was a strategic analyst in RAND Corporation from 1959 to 1971 when he was accused for espionage and discharged from his duties because of his involvement in the "Pentagon Papers" affair. Ellsberg was politically very active during the invasion of Iraq and was repeatedly arrested for his anti-war positions (as in 2005 and 2011).

7 Two-person zero-sum games were first analysed by von Neumann in 1928 in "Zur theorie der Gesellschaftsspiele", published in *Mathematische Annalen*, 100: 295–320 (Ingrao and Israel 1990: 210). In von Neumann and Morgenstern (1944) the zero-sum games were extended to n-persons, yet without satisfactory solution provided. Prof. Iakovos Psarianos helped me in improving my knowledge in game theory.

8 Among different strategies the two more famous are the *minimax strategy*, where the player is aiming to minimize the possible loss for a worst case (maximum loss), and the *maximin strategy*, where the player tries to maximize the minimum gain. The first was analysed by von Neumann and Morgenstern in zero-sum games to denote minimizing the other player's maximum payoff. *Maximin* is on the contrary used in non-zero sum games to describe the strategy that maximizes one's own minimum payoff, as Nash has shown.

9 Nash's first two major contributions were "Equilibrium points in n-person games", published in the *Proceedings of the National Academy of Sciences* 36: 48–49, when he was a young PhD student of 21 years of age, and "Non-Cooperative Games", published in the *Annals of Mathematics*, 1951, 54: 286–295. In fact, "Nash has written very few papers on game theory: seven in all, of which three are joint works, plus a 27-page PhD dissertation" (Giocoli 2003: 299ff.).

10 See C. Daskalakis, *The Complexity of Nash Equilibria*, PhD Thesis in Computer science, University of California at Berkeley, Fall 2008.

11 Aumann (1987) postulates that every player has a unique strategy profile and will "correlate" their strategy choices before the game starts. Equilibrium occurs only when players have identical beliefs about the probabilities of all the eventual strategies, and "when for each player it is optimal given these beliefs to follow the suggested strategy" (Hammond 1997).

12 Aumann and Schelling were awarded with the Nobel Prize in Economics in 2005.

10 Herbert Simon and the concept of bounded rationality

Simon introduced the concept of "bounded rationality" (BR) as a general alternative to optimization. Against the idea of perfect rationality of neo-classical economics, it is assumed that agents have incomplete information and limited computational capacity. Thus, agents adapt to a changing environment, seeking only satisfactory solutions, according to his renowned *Satisficing Principle*. Models of BR had a variety of applications. The first application, the one at which Simon was aiming at since 1969, is behavioural economics and artificial intelligence. The second application, also initially approved by Simon himself was made in transaction costs theory. Oliver Williamson (1985), adopts a semi strong form of rationality combining BR and opportunism: agents have "limited cognitive competence and seek self-interest with guile". Some game theorists also use extensively the concept of BR. Finally, the concept of BR is applied into macroeconomic modelling as alternative behavioural assumption to maximization.

A general alternative to optimization

Neoclassical economists, since the "marginalist revolution" believed that decision making is undertaken with perfect information and full certainty, or as was said in a "perfectly unbounded manner" (Tisdell 1975: 265). With the exception of probabilistic thinking, where the outcome of the choice is uncertain, the neoclassical theory assumes that economic agents are able to access complete, instant and costless information and are capable of making all the necessary calculations to achieve the best of all outcomes. On the contrary, Simon acknowledges that human behaviour is "intendedly rational, but only limitedly so" (1957, quoted in Williamson 1985: 30). Individuals act on the basis of available information only, because they simply do not have the luxury of time and money for gathering and absorbing full information nor the computational capacity to estimate the consequences of all possible alternatives: "in situations that are complex and in which information is very incomplete (i.e. *virtually all real world situations*), the behavioral theories deny that there is any magic for producing behavior even approximating an objective maximization of profits or utilities" (Simon 1986: 223, emphasis added).

A careful reader notices that Simon speaks in the name of "the behavioral theories", referring to the theories of a particular school of thought very active in psychology since the 1920s.[1] Simon has focused on the analysis of the process of rational decision making since he was a PhD student, and his influential book *Administrative Behavior* (first edition in 1947, fourth and last in 1997),[2] contains also the idea of "procedural rationality", a concept elaborated in his other two major pieces of work: *Models of Man* (1957) and *The Sciences of the Artificial* (1969). In the latter he distinguishes between "substantive rationality", appropriate for the achievement of given goals under constraints, and "procedural rationality" appropriate for the limited knowledge and computational capacity of an individual seeking to adapt to her environment. The Hayekian influence here is openly acknowledged, yet the result is completely new.[3] Simon speaks about an "adaptive artifice" to describe the process of rational decision making in a constantly evolving, complex and uncertain environment. Also, in order to emphasize the differences with the neoclassical principle of maximization, he invents a new word to express his original concept of "satisficing", meaning a solution that satisfies sufficiently (1969: 55).

As with the concept of procedural rationality, Simon uses a specific expression which acts as latent manifestation of the development of the concept of "satisficing". In his pioneering article of 1955 published in the *Quarterly Journal of Economics* he proposes a model of rational behaviour that "requires only that the payoff exceeds some given amount" (1955: 108). He calls this payoff "satisfactory" in the sense that it is associated with the rational agent's "aspiration level", a notion imported directly from behavioural psychology. In his subsequent publications he will continue to use the notion of "aspiration level" as a measurable criterion to define a goal alternative to optimization. Mainstream economists, from the marginalists to general equilibrium theorists, have adopted this convenient position to state clearly what the rational individual seeks: simply the best; the best product, the best house, the best job, the best of what money can buy. For that reason, Simon provides a "computational mechanism" to replace the maximization process with a feasible alternative: "In a satisficing model, search terminates when the best offer exceeds an aspiration level that itself adjusts gradually to the value of the offers received so far" (1978: 10; cf. 1969: 58, 1987: 244). "So far" means that an individual can revise his or her aspiration levels in the light of his success or failure in meeting these targets over the years (Tisdell 1975: 267). "So far" does not mean a maximum according to an effectively incomplete relation, since the different target aspiration levels are never put in a comparable class to choose the "best" one (Sen 1987: 70).

To sum up, Simon discovered "satisficing" in 1956 to deal with the demanding requirements of the maximization principle; namely perfect, costless, instant information to be elaborated by hyper-rational individuals (i.e. omniscient and super-smart – "lightning calculators of pleasure and pain" according to Veblen 1898: 389), commonly known as "rational economic men". After focusing on the process of making choices, he immediately realized that people are unable to know everything and calculate the infinite consequences of it, and therefore are less than capable of achieving the best. Consequently, he invented the alternative of simply "good enough" or "at least minimally satisfactory" payoffs: "faced with a choice situation where it is impossible to optimize, or where the computational cost of doing so seems burdensome, the decision maker may look for a satisfactory, rather than an optimal alternative" (Simon 1987: 244; cf. 1955: 118). To describe the kind of behaviour that replaces perfect rationality, he introduced a new all-inclusive concept of BR.

A rational behaviour is bounded from the moment it refers to the limited knowledge of imperfect individuals who are not able to predict all the future changes, nor to possess the computational capacity of "spinning out of such consequences" (1976: 132). One could say "a real man of flesh and blood" borrowing Marshall's overused expression (1890: 22). Limits of information and computability are the two distinctive properties of BR. The first is also strongly related with interactive market conditions, where the choice of one actor depends on the choices made by the other actors (1976: 140; 1978: 9). Simon was very much aware of the contributions made by his contemporary game theorists, but criticized them for making "no concessions to computational difficulties" (1976: 133; cf. 1955: 101; 1969: 70). The second property of BR, "the search for computational efficiency", which was the permanent concern in Simon's academic career, is directly connected to the changing social conditions in which decision making takes place. This additional factor of uncertainty is a supplementary impediment to the possibility of optimization:

> Decision processes ... are subject to change with every change in what human beings know, and with every change in their means of calculation. For this reason the attempt to predict and prescribe human behavior by deductive inference from a small set of unchallengeable premises must fail and has failed.
>
> (Simon 1976: 146; cf. 1955: 101; 1969: 65; 1978: 8; 1991: 37)

The concept of BR opens this possibility of rational adaptation to the changes of the environment "through flexible decision making, or decision making rules that vary according to the circumstances and institutional setting" (Doucouliagos 1994: 881). This is why the evolutionary theory of firm growth "sympathizes" with this concept (Nelson and Winter 1982: 36).

Extensions of bounded rationality in transaction costs theory

A major theoretical concern for Simon, not discussed so far, was the study of the behaviour that takes place "inside the skins of firms". Coase's (1937) landmark paper, discussed above in Chapter 6, maintains that firms exist in order to reduce "the cost of using the price mechanism" as well to reduce the risks from uncertainty, by having a durable business organization. This ground making assertion – nowadays common knowledge to the profession – has helped greatly in the shift of attention of theoretical economists to the inner world of business organizations. This did not happen immediately, despite many other significant contributions before the Second World War.[4] Matters regarding organization theory changed dramatically in the late 1950s thanks also to Simon.[5] Economists became greatly interested in looking inside the "black box" of firms in order to study how managers, executives, employees and simple workers really behave in a contractually related hierarchical structure. In neoclassical theory all these people are assumed to behave as to maximize their own personal utility function, the sum of which is equivalent to the maximization of the firm's profit they are working for. As Simon observes, "this is an unrealistic assumption to make for a human society ... Instead, we should begin with empirically valid postulates about what motivates real people in real organizations" (1991: 30). Simon offers here the synopsis of empirical findings in the literature of organizations, which explain the four main motives governing the different actors inside the firm: authority, rewards, organizational identification and the need for coordination.

This kind of analysis has given birth to a burgeoning field of research over the past 40 years. New institutionalist economics adopted the concept of BR as a general premise of economic behaviour, and Simon explicitly approved that use at the start (1969: 72; 1978: 5), only to distance himself later on (1991: 26). Oliver Williamson used without delay the Simonian concept of BR flavoured with "subtle opportunism".[6] While he acknowledged "bounds on rationality" due to uncertainty and limited cognitive competences, in order to support the existence of transaction costs relative to information gathering and processing, he also adopted the strongest form of self-interest seeking, called opportunism, i.e. "self-interest seeking with guile" (1985: 47).[7] He was not happy with the "simple self-interest-seeking" characteristic of ordinary neoclassical men because it refers to "fully open and honest individuals". On the contrary, recognizing that economic agents have a propensity to behave opportunistically is essential for explaining the existence of a great part of transaction costs, particularly those related to the enforcement of contracts and the respect of obligations emanating from them. Because it is not reliable to take economic decisions as if people were wholly trustworthy, it is better to assume that economic agents are ready to exploit any opportunity to gain an advantage (Furubotn and Richter 1998: 5, 135). Opportunistic behaviour leaves no room for applying the principle of "satisficing" as a result of BR. Williamson (1985: 391) concludes masterfully on this point:

> As compared with orthodoxy, the human agents of transaction cost economics are both less and more calculative. They are less calculative in the capacity to receive, store, retrieve, and process information. They are more calculative in that they are given to opportunism. Taken together, that appears to correspond more closely with human nature as we know it.

In a sense, "internalizing transactions provides means for extending the domain of rationality" (Ménard 2005: 290). But in another sense, Williamson "expanded and distorted the work of the early bounded rationality theorists" (Sen 1998: 38). Simon himself, at the end of his life, was less appreciative of the new institutionalist research program (which he called "a vigorous cottage industry") because they had managed to adopt "a sort of bounded rationality" so as to allow the theory "to remain within the magical domains of utility and profit maximization" (Simon 1991: 26). Briefly, a trade-off exists between the two historic ambitions of economic theory, namely generality and realisticness. Simon emphasized the second, while Williamson was more anxious to defend the first. In either case, a general optimal solution is unattainable.

Applications of bounded rationality in game theory and macroeconomics

Because of its behaviouristic nature, Simon's concept of rationality inspired, almost immediately, some applications within a game theoretic context: oligopoly experiments, repeated games and experimental auctions.[8] Bounded rationality offers an analytical apparatus to the understanding of how players learn to modify their strategies in evolutionary games. It also helps to provide a solution to the problem of finding the restriction of available strategies by imposing constraints on information gathering and processing capacity. In any case, game theorists aimed to strengthen the neoclassical maximization theory, in opposition to Simon's own intentions (Klaes and Sent 2005: 48).

Besides, BR was of some use to macroeconomic modelling. The discipline has long suffered from its attachment to the "rational expectations hypothesis". J.F. Muth in 1961 advocated that economic agents form their expectations about the future in a particular rational way, meaning that they are aware of the laws of economic theory so their predictions of the future values of significant economic variables are generally correct and unbiased. Since "random shocks" are practically unpredictable, Muth also made the heroic assumption that expectations "tend to be distributed, for the same information set, about the prediction of the theory (or the 'objective' probability distribution of outcomes)" (Muth 1961, quoted in Tsoulfidis 2010: 327). Only statistically expected values are significant to decision making and the highest or lowest moments of predicted variables can be dismissed. Lucas, Sargent, Prescott and Wallace developed this argument in the 1970s and dominated the field for years, only to vanish in the 1980s, after their inability to explain the post-1973 recession. Sargent made a last effort to resurrect the above trend thanks to the concept of BR, which helped him to replace perfectly rational with only "adaptive expectations".[9] In this new version agents are able to learn over the years and adapt their expectations incorporating new information about past events in order to maximize their returns. As Simon comments, in the last edition of his *Sciences of the Artificial*, Sargent borrows the concept of BR without adopting the empirical methods that sustain and validate its content (1969: 71). Overall, the rational expectations theory is just another form of perfect foresight under certainty.

Malinvaud (1995: 529) had a more pragmatic view to revise the standard rationality hypothesis of macroeconomic models and suggested that one should adopt BR as a remedy to the inexactitudes of the optimization assumption. Unavoidably, this importation from behavioural sciences asks for closer cooperation between analytical modelling and direct observation of real economic behaviour, which goes in the opposite direction of the rational expectations theory (Malinvaud 1991: 137).

In his long survey, Conlisk (1996) discusses eight prominent arguments in favour of unbounded rationality, to conclude why BR is better as a departure for understanding economic phenomena. Abundant empirical evidence and "a wide range of impressive work" suggest that BR is a convincing alternative to the unworkable assumption of perfect rationality. When economists are about to explain uncertain, complex and incompletely informed decision making made by ordinary people, a wise thing to do is not to be excited like Hamlet: "what a piece of work is a man! how noble in reason! how infinite in faculty! In form and moving how express and admirable! In action how like an Angel! in apprehension how like a god!"[10]

Notes

1　Herbert Simon (1916–2001) was educated as a political scientist and economist in the University of Chicago where he received both his BA (1936) and his PhD (1943) in political science. After three years in Berkeley (1939–1942), he returned to Chicago and joined the Cowles Commission to work in different projects and seminars together with economists like Trygve Haavelmo, Jacob Marschak and Tjalling Koopmans. In 1949, he became Professor of Administration at Carnegie Tech (actually Carnegie Mellon), where he taught psychology and artificial intelligence for five decades. He received the Nobel Prize in Economics in 1978. Simon has studied psychology in depth and his *Administrative Behaviour* (1947), based on his PhD thesis, is a genuine multidisciplinary study of administrative management and decision making, with a foreword by Chester Barnard. Chapter v, entitled "Psychology of administrative decisions", contains a thorough application of behavioural methods. Behaviourism as a scientific approach in psychology was established by John Watson (1878–1958) and B.F. Skinner (1904–1990) but is rooted in the experimental psychology of E. Weber and Wundt.

2　In chapter iv, Simon distinguishes six different types of rational decisions: "objectively", "subjectively", "consciously", "deliberately", "organizationally" and "personally". The idea of "procedural rationality" was described in this book, but it was officially coined in 1969.The same applies to the concept of BR, it appears in a disguised form under the name of "limited rationality" in 1955 and 1956, and literally in 1957. Klaes and Sent (2005) trace the history of this concept, its use and institutionalization and its further diffusion in economics and other fields.

3　Simon often recognizes the influence of Hayek's ideas about uncertain knowledge and the limits of information (1969: 64), without sharing of course his antipathy to psychology.

4　Just to mention Adolph A. Berle and Gardiner C. Means (1932) *The Modern Corporation and Private Property*, New York: MacMillan; E.A.G. Robinson (1934) "The problem of management and the size of the firms", Economic Journal, 44: 240–254; Chester Barnard (1938) *The Functions of the Executive,* Cambridge, MA: Harvard University Press.

5　Other protagonists of the "organizational revolution" of the late 1950s–early 1960s include Alfred Chandler, Richard Cyert, James March and Jacob Marschak (See Ménard 1990: 4). Edith Penrose made also a significant contribution in 1959 from a different angle.

6　Klaes and Sent (2005: 45) report that Williamson was among the very first to adopt Simon's expression in his "Hierarchical control and optimum firm size", *Journal of Political Economy*, 1967.

7　The label "subtle form of opportunism" was proposed later by Williamson (1994: 81) in order to distinguish it from the "blatant form" characteristic of Machiavelli's *Prince*.

8 Cf. Aumann (1987: 478); Conlisk (1996: 681); Furubotn and Richter (1998: 194); Sent (1998, 2004: 753).
9 In his *Bounded Rationality in Macroeconomics*, Oxford: Clarendon 1993. More on Simon and Sargent, in Klaes and Sent (2005: 49).
10 Shakespeare's *Hamlet, Prince of Denmark*, Act II, Scene 2. From Conlisk (1996: 669).

11 Rationality in behavioural economics

Four decades ago, Herbert Simon announced two distinct scenarios in the future evolution of economic theorizing, both leading to a closer collaboration between economics and psychology. The first involved "the direct 'psychologizing' of economics, the explicit adoption of the program of economic behavioralism". The second scenario engaged economics with "operations research and statistical decision theory, introducing a wider and wider range of computational considerations into the models of rationality" (Simon 1976: 147). Simon in fact, wrote the first scenario to be performed by cognitive psychologists, such as Tversky, Slovic and Kahneman, only to devote himself to the development of the second scenario, when he decided to move from the psychology to the computer science department of Carnegie Mellon University. Unquestionably, Simon dismissed the neoclassical theory in favour of a behavioural approach to economic phenomena. In his contribution in the *Palgrave Dictionary* he focused on the dissident character of the field: "behavioral economics is concerned with the empirical validity of these neoclassical assumptions about human behavior and, where they proved invalid, with discovering the empirical laws that describe behavior correctly and as accurately as possible" (1987b: 221). Whether this dissident character remained a distinctive trait of the field is a matter of discussion, but the originality of the behaviourist rationality principle cannot be questioned.

Psychologists, like Daniel Kahneman and Amos Tversky, put emphasis on experimentally observed behaviour using social, cognitive and emotional factors in understanding the economic decisions of individuals and organizations when performing economic functions. The observation of consumers' and producers' behaviour under different market structures aimed at giving birth to a more realistic concept of rationality, but with extremely limited range of application. In that sense the behaviourist movement tries to reverse the fundamental shift initiated by Pareto in 1906, and one can certainly accept that it "stands out as a counterrevolution" (Bruni and Sugden 2007: 147).

Experimental economics moves further to achieve the "restoration", by trying to rescue the neoclassical rationality assumption through experimental counter-evidence.

Old and new behaviourism in economics

As seen above in Chapters 4 and 5, neoclassical economists after Pareto, were constantly anxious to demarcate their analysis from psychology considered as a source of subjectivist biases. Their main concern was to affirm that a positive science like economics should avoid any psychological insights. We have seen that this concern was not always honoured and that economists were always under the influence of some psychological principle directly (as in the case of game and expected utility theorists), or indirectly (as in the case of Robbins, Samuelson, Friedman and Becker). In fact the followers of Pareto's warning of keeping a safe distance from psychology were fewer and very dissimilar: the Austrians, the general equilibrium theorists, the Popperian situational determinists and the rational expectations macroeconomists.

Simon's contributions to organization theory together with expected utility theorists highlighted the relevance of psychology in economic decision making. George Katona in 1951, Sidney Siegel in 1961, Amos Tversky in 1969, Sarah Lichtenstein and Paul Slovic in 1971 made the first contributions to the field of economic psychology. But clearly, no real shift of microeconomic analysis to the empirical study of the psychological determinants of economic behaviour was made before Kahneman and Tversky's major contribution of 1979.[1] The expressed aim of these two professors of psychology was to challenge the validity of the assumption of rational choice "as a descriptive model of economic behavior" through experimental findings. In doing so they presented "several classes of choice problems in which preferences systematically violate the axioms of expected utility theory" (1979: 263). Most of the problems were reformulations or variants of Maurice Allais' decision making problems in risky situations. As seen above, Allais had shown in 1953 that the behavioural axioms of the expected utility theory were violated by Savage himself. Kahnenam and Tversky provided experimental evidence indicating first that people prefer lower but more certain gains, rather than greater and more uncertain ones. This runs against the expected utility principle, which says that the utilities of outcomes are weighted by their probabilities (1979: 265). Second, the two psychologists argued that in situations "where winning is possible but not probable, most people choose the prospect that offers the larger gain", violating thus the substitution principle of expected utility theory (1979: 267). Third, opposing Bernoulli's principle, they proved that decision making is independent of one's state of wealth (1979: 273). Last and most crucially, Kahneman and Tversky demonstrated that individuals treat gains and losses asymmetrically, meaning that they do not assign the same value to expected utility and disutility.

The last point is at the centre of their "prospect theory", which challenged the principle of rational choice in situations containing risk. Allais had already claimed that "the connection between monetary values and psychological values, and the dispersion of psychological values are inseparably mixed" (1953: 505). Kahneman and Tversky suggested that the subjectively perceived value differs greatly between prospective gains and prospective losses. The psychological principles of perception and judgment claim that individuals recognize more easily the value of the changes in their wealth status (in reference to their initial position) rather than the changes in their final state of wealth.[2] Evidence shows that in risky choices, the subjective valuation of strictly positive prospects and strictly negative prospects, follow different rules: "The aggravation that one experiences in losing a sum of money appears to be greater than the pleasure associated with gaining the same amount" (1979: 279). In other words, people seem to be risk-averse over gains and risk-lovers over losses (Rabin 1998:14). As a result the proposed "value function" is S-shaped:

> The value function ... is characterized by three features: (1) it is concave in the domain of gains, favoring risk aversion; (2) it is convex in the domain of losses, favoring risk seeking; (3) most important, the function is sharply kinked at the reference point, and loss-averse – steeper for losses than for gains by a factor of about 2–2.5.
>
> (Kahneman 2003: 1456)

Kahnenam and Tversky provided more experimental evidence to support the idea that "rational choice models are psychologically unrealistic" (Kahneman 2003: 1449). First, a number of experiments were put forward aiming at exploring the heuristic that individuals follow and the biases to which they are prone in decision making under uncertainty. Results from laboratory experiments have shown that individuals tend to be error prone and possibly irrational, suffering from "mindless behaviour", "insensitivity to sample size", "base rate neglect", "misconceptions of chance", "cognitive illusions", "confirmatory bias", "belief perseverance", "anchoring", etc. (Rabin 1998: 24–30; Altman 2004: 13–14). Second, a great number of experiments undertaken by Kahneman and Tversky established as a fact that decision making is shaped by "framing effects": the semantic description of possible outcomes affects greatly the individual's choice; decision makers are inclined to accept passively the formulation of different choices and are particularly influenced by the default option (Kahneman 2003: 1458–1459).[3]

Framing effects are closely related to the phenomenon of "preference reversals" discovered by Lichtenstein and Slovic in 1971. The results of experiments made by the two psychologists have shown that gamblers make inconsistent choices by reversing the order of their preferences, once the choice between two alternative lotteries is reformulated. Evidence says that the majority of people who choose the lottery with the larger probability of winning are paradoxically willing to pay more for the lottery that has a larger prospect of monetary gain, although they have a smaller probability to win. Thus, Lichtenstein and Slovic conclude that "these reversals clearly constitute inconsistent behavior and violate every existing theory of decision making" (1971: 54). The phenomenon appears to refute expected utility theory, which claims that preferences should be independent of the method of eliciting them.[4] As Daniel Hausman put it, "assuming that individuals prefer more money to less, preference reversal apparently involves gross choice inconsistency" (1992: 229).

Although these results were received with great scepticism, economists like David Grether and Charles Plott took the challenge seriously and attempted to defend the established theory by providing evidence that negates the phenomenon of preference reversals. Grether and Plott defended economic rationality as consistency, by discrediting the psychologists' work through the suggestion of different factors that had been neglected. They took into account the insufficiency of incentives of the subjects participating in the experiments and the neglect of the income effect. Thus they argued the above two factors might be sufficient to explain the reversal of preferences within the neoclassical framework.[5] To this challenge, Tversky, Slovic and Kahneman (1990) would reply offering further evidence against the rational choice theory:

> the failures of description invariance (framing effects) and procedure invariance (elicitation effects) pose a greater problem for rational choice models than the failure of specific axioms, such as independence or transitivity, and they demand descriptive models of much greater complexity.
>
> (Tversky *et al.* 1990: 215)

The debate concerning the relevance of rationality as consistency, which opposed neoclassical economists and cognitive psychologists, continued through the 1990s. More "compelling evidence" discarding the rationality assumption was put forward by psychologists, only to receive more counter-examples consistent with the rational choice model (Lagueux

2010: 64–65). Should we conclude with Sent (2004: 750) that economists prevailed over the criticism by incorporating the psychological insights "to strengthen mainstream economics"? The evolution of experimental economics seems to confirm this conclusion. But, as will be seen at the end of this chapter, the significance of intuition and emotions in decision making proves that psychologists are far from declaring defeat.

Experiments on economic behaviour to save the rationality principle

A fast expanding field in economic theory, which characterizes the greater part of current research in "experimental economics", surmounted the effort of the cognitive psychologists to explore the limits of the maximization principle by using the same laboratory techniques to provide experimental evidence in favour of this principle. Vernon Smith, although he shared the Nobel Prize with Kahneman, maintains that experimental economics "documents a growing body of evidence that is consistent with the implications of rational models ... The result is to deepen the concept of rationality and simultaneously increase consistency between the observations and the models" (Smith 1991: 878). In that sense, the variety of economic rationality that experimental economists are referring to is fundamentally the same as that of the neoclassical economics of maximization under constraint. However, there is one significant difference, as far as the empirical validity of the concept of rationality is concerned. Whereas Jevons, Marshall and even Robbins and Friedman, appeal to introspection as a unique foundation of the principle of economic behaviour, Vernon Smith and other experimental economists are using direct empirical evidence. What is most striking in their procedure is the manner in which experimental economics responds to falsifying evidence from psychology, as presented above. They are using the old "invisible hand mechanism" argument to explain social equilibrium emanating from eventually erratic and possibly irrational behaviour. Thus, Smith asks:

> Why is it that human subjects in the laboratory frequently violate the canons of rational choice when tested as isolated individuals, but in the social context of exchange institutions serve up decisions that are consistent (*as though by magic*) with predictive models based on individual rationality?
>
> (Smith 1991: 894, emphasis added)

The so-called "magic" lies in fact in learning mechanisms that help individuals to adapt to market conditions, and not accidentally Smith in his answer appeals only to Lucas and his model of "adaptive expectations" as a suggestive answer. He even recognizes that "experimental economics have no good answers to this question". Yet, Smith accuses psychologists of overstating deviations from rational behaviour and of ignoring "contrary interpretations and evidence over extended periods of time". What Smith means is that despite the frequent violations of rational behaviour experienced in the laboratory, psychologists miss the point because they consider rationality a "cognitively intensive calculating process", which can be tested directly and in isolation "from interactive experience in social and economic institutions". In fact, according to Smith, psychologists miss the "magic" element in social interaction that is responsible for market clearing processes. As he claims:

> Economic reality consists of both *the unseen and the seen* – both the indirect and direct consequences of a decision. What economics brings to the analytical table is the broader perspective that choice decisions have repercussions that actual decision makers experience but that may not be perceived.
>
> (Smith 1991: 882–883, emphasis added)

What is "unseen" in a market transaction can be illustrated by the differences between "verbal" and actual behaviour. Soliciting a verbal response to a hypothetical question is of theoretical interest only and differs greatly from what the same individual will actually do in real market conditions. In many market transactions, like in double auctions, "subjects learn in repeat play" and correct their initial offers to converge unintentionally towards an equilibrium solution. Vernon Smith (1994: 118) calls this phenomenon "unconscious optimization" and although he refers to Simon (1955), this procedure is reminiscent of Adam Smith's "invisible hand". In fact it is directly inspired from Hayek's idea of "spontaneous order". Like Hayek, Vernon Smith believes that market rationality is not the result of perfectly informed rational agents. In many cases private information can be more advantageous to competition than perfect information (Smith 1994: 119). This is what he believes: "This is best described as superrational: a better strategy than what has been deduced from rational theory, and one that clearly violates the behavioral implications of the standard impossibility theorems" (Smith 1991: 890). Unexpectedly, there are evolutionary psychologists that corroborate Smith's belief and claim that the

> human mind may often be better than rational ... it greatly outperforms the best artificial problem-solving systems that decades of

research have produced, and it solves large classes of problems that even now no human-engineered system can solve at all.

(Cosmides and Tooby 1994: 329)

In conclusion, against behavioural economists, Smith and experimental economists believe that "human decision-making is not error-prone or biased, but intelligent and subject to improvements through learning, analogous to the notion of adaptive expectations" (Altman 2004: 24). By "learning" Smith refers to the informal cognitive experience that describes how humans process and retain information in order to survive in their changing environment. "Language learning in children" is the model, for Smith: "they learn to speak in the total absence of formal instruction", only through social interaction with other people (Smith 1991: 894). We have to bear in mind that language and money were the only two social institutions that are not evolving by human design according to not only Menger and Hayek, but also according to Adam Smith and J.S. Mill.[6]

Expanding the study of economic behaviour: the roles of intuition and emotion

In the last two decades or so, economists and psychologists have continued to provide evidence for and against rational choice. Economists like Charles Plott and Ken Binmore consider deviations from rational behaviour as a result of specific causal factors that the abstract theory has neglected, and try to incorporate them into economic analysis through learning mechanisms. Briefly put, assuming that people have stable preferences, they progressively "discover" through learning by trial and error how to behave rationally (in accordance with their preferences), provided that people have adequate opportunities and incentives.[7] Many of the inconsistencies and violations of the rationality assumption vanish once individuals are correctly informed and motivated. Psychologists like Camerer, Kahneman and Lowenstein, but also economists like Starmer and Sugden have come back with alternative interpretations of the evidence suggested by Plott and Binmore. From a methodological point of view the debate is leading nowhere. Lakatos would say it constitutes a "theoretically degenerating problem shift" (1970: 118). Neoclassical experimental economists have attempted to evade falsification providing ad hoc auxiliary hypotheses (like the discovered preference hypothesis), and psychologists and non-neoclassical experimental economists have been unable to suggest a conclusive test that will convince economists to abandon their theoretical strategy, i.e. the "vision of a separate science of economics" (Hausman 1992: 240).

Nevertheless, some psychologists propose one possible exit from this imbroglio: to integrate non-rational elements in the analysis of economic behaviour. Not by coincidence, Kahneman opened his Nobel lecture paying tribute to his late colleague Amos Tversky, saying that "together, we explored the psychology of intuitive beliefs and choices and examined their bounded rationality" (2003: 1449). Among all his contributions to economics, Kahneman believed that the most significant was, as he concluded his lecture, "that intuition and reasoning are alternative ways to solve problems" (2003: 1469). Incorporating a common sense psychology of the intuitive agent is indeed a challenge not only for the neoclassicals but for economists in general, as Akerlof and Shiller have recently established (2009). The recognition of the importance of intuitive thinking in economic decision making originated long before Simon's conjecture that "we cannot, of course, rule out the possibility that the unconscious is a better decision maker than the conscious" (1955: 104). Roger Frantz's historical study claims that intuitive thinking was recognized as a source of knowledge in Adam Smith, J.S. Mill, A. Marshall, J.M. Keynes, Frank Knight, Friedrich Hayek and many others.

In fact the word "intuition" was at first used in two different ways by philosophers like Descartes and Kant as a purely intellectual vs. "transcendental" process, giving rise to two distinct modes of knowledge, analytical reasoning and intuitive perception.[8] Without reference to Descartes or Kant, Frantz argues that many great economists have made extensive use of the concept of *intuition*, meaning the "knowledge gained swiftly and immediately, and seemingly obvious, not involving the process of analysis, but giving the intuitor ... a sense of having an inside view of a thing or a relationship between or among things" (Frantz 2005: 3). Despite any objections to the impact of intuition in many thinkers (like Smith or Mill), or objections to the real meaning of it (like Knight and Hayek) the role of intuitive thinking in economic decision making has a long history.[9] Yet, in behavioural economics it was considered as an alternative mode of judgment and choice. Kahneman recognizes that most judgments and choices are made intuitively according to the rules of perception "without conscious search or computation, and without effort" (2003: 1450). Recognizing intuition as an antagonist, to rational choice, cognitive process preserves a special room for studying how "right-brained activity" influences decisions and choices.[10] Emotions like fear and hope become part of the analysis of decision making, contradicting thus the old Paretian separation of "logical" from "non-logical" actions.

Neuroeconomics and the study of the influence of emotions in decision making is today a promising field of research.[11] But emotions have always concerned economists: "Desire", "pleasure", "happiness" and "satisfaction" are emotions constantly present at the heart of economic theory, only disguised under the veil of objectivity and axiological neutrality. Thus, psychologists break away from the tradition of Pareto–Hicks–Robbins–Arrow and Debreu, only to restore the tradition of Bentham–Jevons–Edgeworth–Marshall up to Stigler and Becker, but with a stronger conceptual and technical apparatus. Neuroeconomics, as a branch of behavioural economics, aims at the direct measurement of thoughts and feelings (Camerer *et al.* 2005: 10). These findings cannot support rationality as consistency, neither of course can they establish the existence of a utility maximization function somewhere inside the brain of people. But, they can definitely help economists to assess the limits of their behavioural assumptions and realize the enormous importance of automatic and affective processes in decision making.[12] Nonetheless, the whole project of economic psychology, since its first steps in the 1860s, has faced a perpetual objection: individual action is not only a matter of atomistic behaviour emerging from a continuous interplay between neural systems, but essentially the result of social interaction with other individuals. The importance of the social nature of individual behaviour is in fact the subject matter of the next chapter.

Notes

1 Daniel Kahneman and Amos Tversky had accomplished a significant work on the field before "intruding" into economics with their publication in *Econometrica* in 1979. They had already criticized the findings of expected utility theory (in "Subjective probability: a judgment of representativeness", *Cognitive Psychology* 1972, and "On the psychology of prediction", *Psychological* Review 1973). Simon quotes these publications approvingly in his 1976 book chapter in order to criticize the relevance of probabilistic behaviour (1976: 134). As known, Tversky died prematurely and missed the opportunity to win the Nobel Prize in Economics, awarded to Kahneman jointly with Vernon Smith in 2002.

2 "Our perceptual apparatus is attuned to the evaluation of changes or differences rather than to the evaluation of absolute magnitudes" (1979: 277).

3 Kahneman (2003: 1458) gives an example of opposite choices made only by altering the relative salience of different aspects of the same problem. Two alternative programs to combat an Asian disease expected to kill 600 persons are proposed; if program A is adopted 200 people will be saved and if program B is adopted, there is 0.33 probability that 600 people will be saved and 0.67 probability that no one will be saved. The same problem can be described differently: if A is adopted, 400 people will die and if B is adopted there is 0.33 probability that nobody dies and 0.67 probability that 600 people will die. In the first description of the same problem the program A is preferred while in the second, the majority prefers the program B. In the first case respondents demonstrate a risk-averse attitude, while in the second they favour the risk seeking option.

4 The requirement of "procedure invariance" asserts that different measurements of preferences should give rise to the same preferential ordering. See Tversky *et al.* (1990: 204); Hausman (1992: 240); Rabin (1998: 37–38).

5 Hausman (1992: 230–236) presents analytically the debate between economists and psychologists on that point; cf. Lagueux (2010: 63–65).

6 While both money and language were intentionally created to facilitate exchange and communication, their historical evolution was not "consciously designed". As Popper would say (1957: 65), it has "just grown as the undesigned result of human action". This is exactly how Smith (1776, book i, chap. 4) and Mill (1848, book iii, chap. 7) explained the creation and evolution of money and language. Just as language is an institution created to fulfil the needs for communication inside a social group, money was created "as a common language" to make the comparison of values easier. On Menger's ideas see Hodgson (1993: 109–120).

7 See Plott, C. (1996). "Rational individual behavior in markets and social choice processes: the discovered preference hypothesis", in Arrow, K.J. *et al.*, eds. (1996) *The Rational Foundations of Economic Behavior*, London: MacMillan, pp. 225–50; Binmore, K. (1999) "Why experiment in economics?", *Economic Journal*, 109: F16–24. For a critical survey of the "discovered preference hypothesis" see Bruni and Sugden (2007: 162–171).

8 Descartes employed the word intuition to mean

> not the uncertain evidence of the senses or the false judgment of the imagination that constructs rapidly its subject, but the conception realized by a pure and attentive spirit, that is so simple and clear so that it leaves no doubt about what it is meant.
>
> (*Regulae ad directionem ingenii*, Third Rule, 1628, our translation)

Kant on the contrary meant by "intuition" the "direct and immediate view of an object of thought that is actually present in the spirit and may be fully conceived in its individual reality" (*Critique of Pure Reason*, 1787).

9 Not everyone would agree with Frantz, who argues that sympathy is experienced instantaneously and without any previous knowledge, so "sympathy is an intuitive experience". Mill was a notorious anti-intuitionist. As an empiricist philosopher and utilitarian social reformer, Mill was opposed to the idea of natural, innate qualities of human nature that are impossible to experience objectively. Knight and Hayek strictly rejected behaviourism as a method of study of economic decision making in general.

10 Neuroscience asserts that the centre of emotions is situated in the right hemisphere of the brain, where the overall world view of the environment is generated. In the left hemisphere is situated the centre of reasoning, calculating and analytical thinking. See Camerer *et al.* (2005: 17ff.).

11 Kirman *et al.* (2010) present the research agenda of the impact of emotions on rationality.

12

> [Neuroeconomic findings] raise questions about the usefulness of some of the most common constructs that economists commonly use, such as risk aversion, time preference, and altruism. Second, [they show] how the existence of specialized systems challenges standard assumptions about human information processing and suggest that intelligence and its opposite – bounded rationality – are likely to be highly domain specific. Third,

brain-scans conducted while people win or lose money suggest that money activates similar reward areas as do other "primary reinforcers" like food and drugs, which implies that money confers *direct* utility, rather than simply being valued only for what it can buy. Fourth, [they] show that research on the motivational and pleasure systems of the brain human challenges the assumed connection between motivation and pleasure.

Camerer *et al.* (2005: 31–32)

12 The rationality of embedded individuals

The separation of economic from other social considerations was the result of the redefinition of the field of economic analysis by the marginalists at the end of nineteenth century. In classical political economy the social field was provisionally dissected by means of abstraction, to reveal the essential causes that explain economic phenomena. Economic rationality evolved in a durable system of social relations. Recently, this theoretical practice has been re-established. Evolutionary institutionalists (like North and Hodgson) believe that economic activity is always institutionally embedded. Institutions, both formal and informal, guarantee regularity and consistency of economic behaviour over time. Therefore, decision makers reach different outcomes if they operate within different institutional settings. In that sense rationality is historically specific, and this is a point of view very close to Smith and Mill. Economic sociologists (Granovetter, Smelser, Swedberg and others) also believe that economic behaviour is socially embedded. The actor is connected with other actors and is part of social groups and social context. Rationality becomes again a variable, not a parameter, of economic explanation. At the end, the idea of social embeddedness calls for a reconsideration of the boundaries of economics, and other social disciplines as was required in classical political economy.

Social consciousness in Marx

Marx's view of the individual and individual behaviour is the result of his general theory of history called "historical materialism". According to the materialist view of history, individuals are members of a social class and their identity is determined by their position in the capitalist mode of production. In a famous passage of his preface to the *Contribution to the Critique of Political Economy* (1859), Marx explains the idea of social (or class) consciousness: "the mode of production of material life conditions the general process of social, political and intellectual life. It is not the consciousness of men that determines their existence, but their social existence that determines their consciousness" (Marx 1859: 273).[1] In order to understand the capitalist mode of production, Marx suggests a holistic analysis according to which "the social whole takes precedence over its individual elements" (Milonakis and Fine 2009: 37). The analysis of the capitalist process cannot be made except in terms of social classes, which constitute its very essence. Any attempt to neglect or to obscure the role of social classes means "to rob economic theory of its social content" (Schumpeter 1954: 551).

All the same, Marx uses the classical principle of profit seeking behaviour ("a greater gain is preferred to a smaller in all cases") as an assumption in order to explain economic phenomena such as price formation through the market mechanism (1847: 19), capital movement towards the most profitable industries (1849: 208), competition among capitalists (1867: 853), capital accumulation (1867: 1096), etc. The nature of capitalist behaviour is better portrayed when Marx explains the struggle that the capitalists stage against the tendency of the falling rate of profit (1865: 1001–1015). Competition forces capitalists to increase investment in constant capital in order to obtain individually a greater share of the total mass of surplus value. Inevitably, the rise of global accumulation leads to the continuous fall in the rate of profit. This fundamental characteristic of the system is simply the unintended result of the individual hunt for profit and competition among capitalists. This holistic conception leaves no room for individual differentiation or even individual choice. It postulates homogeneity within social classes and unmistakable class consciousness among its members, which act accordingly (Mingat *et al.* 1985: 360).[2] Briefly put, holistic conception refers to a society devoid of individuals.

In Chapters 3, 4, 5 and 8 above, we have examined at length the methodologically opposite view, which argues that individuals live alone in a pre-social state of society and act in isolation with other human beings. However, there is a midway position between the holistic view of a society with no individuals and the atomistic view of isolated individuals, which recognizes both the individuality of acting persons as well as their interaction with their social environment. This embedded individual approach "emphasizes individuals as active beings able to act upon and change social frameworks" (Davis 2003: 108). In fact, there are at least two distinct traditions within the embedded individual approach, which are of a particular interest regarding their impact upon economic rationality, the evolutionary-institutionalist and the economic sociology tradition.

Evolutionary institutionalism and the social nature of rationality

Institutionalism is often accused of having too many holistic affinities. Thorstein Veblen and John Commons were indeed both influenced by the organicist analogy without ever espousing the extreme positions of Herbert Spencer (Hodgson 1993: 127). Thus Veblen was a fervent critic of "the hedonistic conception of man ... who oscillates like a homogeneous globule of desire of happiness under the impulse of stimuli that shift him about the area, but leave him intact" (1898: 389). Nevertheless, he also dismissed the idea that individual actions can be explained in terms of social circumstances exclusively, as his idea of "machine-induced rationality" indicates (Tilman 2004: 157). So with Commons (1931) who defined an institution as a "collective action in control, liberation and expansion of individual action". Veblen and Commons espoused the midway position according to which "humans mould their circumstances, just as they are moulded by them" (Hodgson 2001: 141). This view corresponds to what Agassi named as "institutional individualism" (1975). While it admits that individual action is the starting point for every social explanation, institutional individualism denies other forms of individualism based on psychological or subjectivist sources. Psychological individualism is denied because it is impossible to explain social phenomena in psychological terms and besides many social phenomena are often the result of "unintended individual actions": individuals pursuing their own aims but also influencing the social system. Subjectivism is denied too, not only because social wholes do exist and shape individual plans, still without having any distinct aims and interests of their own, but also because causal explanations are, indeed possible in social sciences.

New institutionalists, such as Coase and Williamson, have limited the significance of the interaction between the individual and its social environment, on its consequences on the internal organization of firms. Douglass North is exceptional. He has progressively shifted his views towards understanding institutional change as an interactive process between individuals and their context.[3] In his early work, which attempted to explain the formation and evolution of institutions, North started with a rational choice analytical framework. He initially held that institutions originate from the attempt of individuals to find optimum solutions to their economic problems and as a response to changes in relative prices (or more generally costs) that the individuals face (North 1981). Because the neoclassical efficiency argument proved to be inadequate to explain the persistence of inefficient institutions, as North himself recognized (1990: 7; 2005: 7), he abandoned the neoclassical point of view, focusing on the way that property rights are distributed by the rulers in order to understand the historical evolution from the agricultural to the industrial revolution.[4]

To explain inefficiency and underdevelopment, as well as to find an answer to the free rider problem, North used at first a loose notion of the "ideology of the ruled people". In his post 1990 work he put greater emphasis on informal constraints, such as myths, dogmas, prejudices and taboos, to understand how all these constraints shape individual decision making and interact with institution building. Ideology gained a pivotal role; it is defined as "the subjective perceptions (models, theories) all people possess to explain the world around them" (North 1990: 23, fn.7). Thus he completely modified the neoclassical behavioural assumption:

> If our understanding of motivation is very incomplete, we can still take an important forward step by taking explicit account of the way institutions alter the price paid for one's convictions and hence play a critical role in *the extent to which nonwealth-maximizing motivations influence choices.*
>
> (North 1990: 26, emphasis added)

In North's latest work individuals are neither *de novo* creators in an institution-free social condition, nor the pure by-products of their social and physical environment. Hence, on the one hand, institutional change is the result of individual action: "the agent of change is the individual entrepreneur responding to the incentives embodied in the framework" (North 1990: 83). Change can also be the unintended consequence of individual action. But, on the other hand, formal institutions, such as labour unions, governments or central banks, influence the process of change by intentionally designing the path of change. North has produced a notable work in explaining the way that formal and informal institutions create incentives that sustain economic growth. His recent book focuses on the process of economic change and particularly on the importance of culture as a factor of change or inertia. "Culture consists of the intergenerational transfer of norms, values and ideas" and together with the formal institutional framework it provides the incentives that dictate the path of growth (2005: 59). Therefore, North has been rightly characterized as an institutional individualist since "on the one hand the individual is constrained by the existing institutional structure, whereas on the other hand, he or she is capable of changing that structure according to his or her preferences" (Groenewegen *et al.* 1995). As a result of this position, the representation of the individual is context specific and the continuous interaction of beliefs, institutions and organizations explains the evolution path of societies (2005: 52).

Geoffrey Hodgson reaches North from a very different direction, moving from Marxism to evolutionary institutionalism, and his development remains original.[5] A prolific writer,[6] Hodgson has also contributed to the issue of the social nature of economic rationality in three ways: (*i*) by delineating the limits of methodological individualism; (*ii*) by criticizing the flaws of maximization from an evolutionary point view; and, (*iii*) by demonstrating the importance and efficacy of habits and rules in decision making.

Hodgson's fundamental objection to individualism as a point of departure for analysing social phenomena in general lies in his antithesis to the program of reductionism in science. Although he recognizes that "science cannot proceed without some dissection and some analysis of parts" (1993: 235), Hodgson questions the possibility of reducing every phenomenon to its elementary units. To explain social phenomena "only in terms of individuals is untenable, if individuals themselves are then to be explained in terms other than individuals alone" (Hodgson 2001: 146). There is an infinite regress problem that requires to end the analysis somewhere. Why should the analysis be simply reduced only to the level of the individual? Why not extend the analysis "to the most elementary sub-atomic particles presently known to science", like genes and molecules? (Hodgson 1993: 235) As seen above, Mill and Weber gave their own convincing answers to stop the chain of regress employing the ideas of the socially embedded individuality and the ideal-type of social action respectively. Hodgson adopts the same methodological approach trying to enrich the analysis of individual intentionality with institutionalistic elements and to explain the evolution of institutions through individual action. This double causation movement upwards (to explain how institutions are created by individuals) and downwards (to explain how institutions both constrain and enable individual behaviour) constitutes Hodgson's version of institutional individualism: "institutions simultaneously depend upon the activities of individuals and constrain and mould them" (2001: 296).[7]

Hodgson also contributed to the critical understanding of optimization and efficiency from an evolutionary point view. After Alchian (1950), Friedman (1953) and Hayek (1952), mainstream economists attempted to justify the maximization assumption thanks to a "natural selection" argument: maximizing behaviours that are selected in a competitive evolutionary process are superior and more efficient. This argument is based on the false idea that competition acts like an evolutionary process favouring the fittest. Furthermore, this argument perpetuates a distorted view of the evolutionary process of promoting the more efficient organisms, equating the fittest with the superior, in the normative sense. Hodgson (1993), together with many other evolutionary economists (Vanberg, Witt, Winter *et al.*)

dismissed this false idea, which has influenced many economists to infer efficiency from the "natural" selection process of competition. Hodgson convincingly argued that the survival of the firms does not coincide with their economic performance, nor with the tendency to cooperate or not. As with technological innovations, products as well as firms may survive based on suboptimal solutions linked with the phenomenon of path-dependency.[8]

Finally, Hodgson has re-established why habits and rules are important in decision making. In accordance with Nelson and Winter (1982) and North (1990, 2005), Hodgson included among institutions, not only formal rules and organizations but also informal constraints and their enforcement characteristics such as routines, habits, rules and ethical values, which involve human interaction and exchange (Hodgson 1998: 179). Informal institutions and arrangements encompass a whole matrix of social norms and moral values, rules, habits and routines that constrain and also induce economic behaviour. *Rules* are "conditional or unconditional patterns of thought or behavior which can be adopted either consciously or unconsciously by agents" (Hodgson 1997: 664). Rules differ from norms "by virtue of the different ways they enforce task to individuals" (Hodsgon 2006: 4). *Habits* are impersonal rules followed unconsciously, and describe a general tendency to engage in a repetitive form of action (Hodgson 1993: 226; 2001: 289). *Routines* are also based on past experience, but they differ from habits in the sense that they always involve a social unit and explain "all regular and predictable behavioral pattern of firms" (Nelson and Winter 1982: 14). Rules, habits and routines may take the form of a custom to explain regularity in social behaviour, as seen above in Smith and Mill.[9] Finally, *values* are ethical convictions about what is right and wrong (Weber 1904). Values like trustworthiness, honesty, loyalty, confidence, commitment and reputation, although they are considered as necessary conditions to every economic transaction, are in a way antagonistic to the strict economic calculation of the maximizing opportunistic behaviour (Arrow 1974: 23; Akerlof 1980; Hodgson 1998: 250; Sen 2005).

As with formal institutions, rules, habits and routines do matter greatly to economists because they guarantee regularity and consistency of economic behaviour over time.[10] Eventually they enhance optimization "when the choice set is known and it is possible to employ [rule] procedures" (Hodgson 1997: 665). Rules, habits and routines reduce complexity and uncertainty, limit the problem of information extensiveness and provide solutions to the individual agent's cognitive limitations. Furthermore, following Veblen, Hodgson considers that these informal institutions "play a role similar to that of the gene in the natural world" (1993: 253). Routines also possess this quality by helping the firm to retain skills and other forms of intra-firm knowledge and also the capacity to replicate through imitation and personal mobility (Nelson and Winter 1982: 134). For that reason they are responsible for the endurance of institutions through time: "Habits are the constitutive material of institutions, providing them with enhanced durability, power and normative authority" (Hodgson 2001: 296). In other words, economic behaviour evolves within a durable system of institutionally embedded social rules, and economic analysis should take it into account.

Economic sociology and the requirement for a non-separate science of economics

As seen at length above, rational choice, and other individualistic explanations since the marginalists, presuppose, as a general rule, the institutional setting without explaining it: initial endowments, property rights and distribution of wealth in general, preferences, social norms and habits, culture and ideology are all taken for granted and are somehow internalized in every individual's pattern of behaviour. Joseph Schumpeter (1954: 21) made a significant point by comparing the two subject matters, the neoclassical economist's and the economic sociologist's: "economic analysis deals with the question *how people behave* at any time and what the economic effects are they produce [*sic*] by so behaving; economic sociology deals with the question *how they came to behave as they do*" (emphasis added). He even considered economic sociology so important as to consider it as "the fourth fundamental field" of economic knowledge, after economic history, statistics and economic theory.

In fact, the roots of economic sociology lie in the so-called younger German Historical School of Georg Simmel, Werner Sombart and Max Weber (Trigilia 1998: 61).[11] All these German sociologists have focused their analysis on the cultural and institutional factors favourable to the capitalist development, as well as on the social transformation of western societies emanating from the spread of capitalism.[12] Weber contributed greatly to the genesis of the discipline and named it "Social Economics" (Weber 1904) and later "Sociology of Economics" (Weber 1917: 430; cf. Schumpeter 1954: 21 fn.1). We have seen above (Chapter 4) how Weber, following Smith and Mill, wanted to explain the nature of economic phenomena in terms of socialized individuals who have internalized in their plans the values and norms of their social environment. His ideal-type constructions aimed to understand historical phenomena, such as the genesis of capitalism, from the viewpoint of their cultural foundations. His concept of "instrumental rationality" idealizes the goal-oriented (profit maximization) rational behaviour that captures the "spirit of capitalism" and explains one necessary condition to the rise of the entrepreneurial culture in northwestern Europe.

Among the "sociological categories of economic action" Weber included (*i*) the private appropriation of the means of production, (*ii*) free market competition, (*iii*) available and free to move labour force, (*iv*) sufficient production technology, (*v*) an advanced system of commercial economy including credit tools, banks, legally established business firms etc. and (*vi*) an advanced legal system to secure and enforce transactions between firms and individuals (Weber 1922: chap. 2). According to Swedberg (2011) this is *the* "central text of economic sociology". If one reads the recent work of economic sociologists (such as Mark Granovetter, Neil Smelser, Richard Swedberg, Carlo Trigilia, Viviana Zelizer *et al.*) one finds comparable considerations about the institutional conditions of economic life. Most crucially for our purpose is the concept of the actor and the explanation of social action. Although there are differences as to the significance of holistic elements that shape individual action between Smelser (more holistic) and Granovetter (more individualistic), it is generally agreed that every individual actor is "influenced by other actors and is part of groups and society" (Smelser and Swedberg 1994: 4). Granovetter (1985: 483) has significantly emphasized this tension between the "oversocialized conception of man" in sociology where people follow the norms of the society they belong to, and the "undersocialized conception of man", which corresponds to the standard neoclassical economic view of "atomized utilitarianism". While Granovetter's amalgamation of classical and neoclassical economics is altogether unacceptable for an historian of economic thought, his middle range analysis is completely convincing:

> Actors do not behave or decide as atoms outside a social context, not do they adhere slavishly to a script written for them by the particular intersection of social categories that they happen to occupy. Their attempts at purposive action are instead embedded in concrete, ongoing systems of social relations.
>
> (Granovetter 1985: 487)

Polanyi's (1944) strong concept of embeddedness in non-market societies is adapted to express a lower level of embeddedness in modern capitalist societies. Examples of how this idea of socially embedded action works in practice concern the impact of ethnic trading networks in capitalist economies (Landa 1994; Granovetter 2000); the significance of the system of rotating credit association in developing countries (Granovetter 2000); the weight of non-material motives in economic transactions (Henrich *et al.* 2001); the role of informal arrangements and cooperation between industrial firms (Zouboulakis and Kamarianos 2002); the meaning of credit and commercial circuits among family members and other personal connections (Zelizer 2006).[13] All these findings stress the danger of narrowness of analysis if significant elements of social structure are left outside the study of economic phenomena.[14]

In reality, the social embeddedness approach, as well as the evolutionary institutionalist approach examined above, introduces once again the old classical request for a non-separate science of economics. In his important book, Daniel Hausman (1992) has rightly suggested that the commitment of economists as a separate science dealing with economic phenomena as they were independent from their social substratum is the source of their inability to capture the entire economic "realm" in modern societies. But he accuses Mill of inspiring this separatist commitment of economists from their fellow social scientists. In fact, as it was argued at length above (Chapter 2) and elsewhere (Zouboulakis 2000), this was neither Mill's nor Ricardo's intention, but Jevons' and Walras', despite their willingness to a provisional pure theory of economics. Mill never defended a separate science of political economy. On the contrary he delineated a limited and partial science of economic phenomena. His intentions were clear as he confessed in his autobiography:

> Political Economy, in truth, has never pretended to give advice to mankind with lights but his own; though people who knew nothing *but* political economy (and therefore knew that ill) have taken upon themselves to advise, and could only by such lights as they had.
>
> (Mill 1873: 179, original italics)

Ricardo's genius idea to construct an abstract explanatory model of how the economy works in theory was misused, leading to the description of an imaginary reality, free from social consideration. As said above, a rational reconstruction of economic reality holds insofar as it reveals the real causes of economic phenomena and goes beyond the occasional and the accidental. Economists until Mill and beyond (like Cairnes and Neville Keynes) were fully aware of the provisional character of their abstract theories and asked for a correction "by making proper allowance for the effects of any impulses of a different description, which can be shown to interfere with the result in any particular case" (Mill 1843: 903). This was the basis of a fundamental unity of social sciences which was definitely broken into independent, not to say autarkic, sub-fields in the neoclassical era. Needless to point out that the idea of expanding the "economic approach" *à la* Becker (1976) to other social disciplines is a characteristic case of misapplication, in the sense of misappropriation of a neighbouring field without any invitation.[15]

Since the establishment of neoclassical economics a number of non-heterodox economists have also supported the idea of a non-autarkic economic analysis for the sake of the economic analysis itself. Papandreou remarked as early as 1950, "the only way out of the impasse, the only way for arriving at an empirically relevant science is to the [psychological and sociological] commitments ... by utilizing the findings of the other social sciences" (1950: 721). From a different standpoint, Simon (1978: 15) called for more intense communication between various fields that study human behaviour. Even the celebrated return of psychology in economics, discussed in the previous chapter, goes in the same direction as Simon's call. Finally, Arrow has also underlined the need for a broader investigation of the social context, recognizing "the ineradicable social element in the economy" (Arrow 1994: 2). Taking the above into consideration North's suggestion comes naturally: "our analytical frameworks must integrate insights derived from these artificially separate disciplines if we are to understand the process of change" (2005: 11).

Notes

1 Pages refer to the French variorum edition of Marx's *Oeuvres Completes*, edited by Maximilien Rubel in 1965 and 1968. Besides the *Contribution to the Critique of Political Economy* published in 1859, we refer to *The Misery of Philosophy* (1847), the essay *Wage, Labour and Capital* (1849), *Capital* vol. i (1867) and *Capital* vol. iii (1865), published posthumously.

2 The term "holism" was coined by Jan Smuts in 1926 and was further known as "Methodological Collectivism" by Karl Popper in 1945. As a methodological practice it goes back to Auguste Comte (if not back to Plato), although it was Emile Durkheim who, in 1892, explicitly justified the existence of "total social facts". On Comte and Durkheim see Gordon (1991: 292, 442). On the multiple meanings of "holism" see Mäki (1993: 27). In Marx, not only the economic basis but also ideology and politics are included in a holistic norm, influencing, opposing and interacting each other.

3 For a more detailed analysis of North's evolutionism, see Zouboulakis (2005b), from which the next two pages draw.

4 North has formally recognized that it is correct to "separate the path chosen by Oliver Williamson ... from the path I [North] have chosen which seeks to discover how institutions evolve through time" (North 1993, 12). Similarly, he acknowledged that his last book is "a very substantial extension of the new institutional economics" (2005: preface).

5 Hodgson (2006) distinguishes himself from the post-1990 North on the matter of the definition of organizations vs. institutions and formal rules vs. informal constraints. On these definitions see below.

6 According to his personal webpage, Hodgson (born in 1946) is "the author of over 15 books, over 130 articles and over 80 articles in academic books". Since his first book (*Socialism and Parliamentary Democracy* 1977) he has been persistently interested in the role of institutions but focused on the impact of evolutionary ideas in economics in the last 20 years.

7 Davis (2003: 119) examines the implications of this interactive causation to the explanation of individual learning that takes place inside an institution.

8 The concept of path-dependency suggests that decisions taken in the past (right or wrong ones) continue to affect any future development against other potential choices that were eventually more efficient. This process is characterized by inertia, in the sense that once an outcome begins to stabilize, it becomes progressively locked to attractors that are not always optimal, and by "non ergodicity": historical "small events" are not averaged away and "forgotten" by the dynamics of the evolution of the economy. Brian Arthur and Paul David introduced this concept in economics after 1985.

9 An amazing way of explaining stability and regularity of behaviour is to consider that people's tastes remain forever stable, as Stigler and Becker (1977: 82) suggested, opposing explicitly to Mill.

10 Biggart and Beamish (2003: 453) treat economic conventions as an alternative to custom and routine behaviour since they also enhance stability and coordination in the economic sphere.

11 Contrary to Max Weber, who produced a colossal work, Georg Simmel (1858–1918) is essentially known for his *Philosophy of Money* (Philosophie des Geldes) first published in 1900 with a new edition in 1907. Analogously, Werner Sombart (1863–1941) is best known for one significant work, *The Modern Capitalism* published in 1902, and again in 1916 and 1928. Sombart studied economics and sociology under Gustav Schmoller and became a Professor in Economics and Sociology in Berlin. He was one of the PhD supervisors of Wassily Leontief in Berlin in 1928. Talcott Parsons (1902–1979), one the founders of American Sociology, accomplished his PhD studies in Heidelberg in 1927 and his thesis focused on the ideas of Sombart and Weber about the development of capitalism.

12 J.J. Gislain and P. Steiner (1996) also include Emile Durkheim and Francois Simiand among the fathers of economic sociology. Smelser and Swedberg (1994) include Marx, Durkheim, Schumpeter, Polanyi and Parsons. Trigilia (1998) agrees with them with the exception of Marx.

13 However, Biggart and Beamish (2003: 450) consider that the social "embeddedness approach continues to be a partial explanation" in the sense that it "treats markets as structurally determined and implicitly outside the realm of meaning, interpretation and individual agency". On the contrary, the School of the "Economy of Conventions" offers the real middle-range theory which explains market order.

14 Evidence shows that "well designed public policies can harness self-interest for the common good", while policies assuming that citizens act always as knaves induce people to behave more egoistically (Bowles 2008).

15 In their outstanding critical presentation of Becker's "economic imperialism", Fine and Milonakis (2009: 78–92) extend their critique not only to new institutionalist economics, which is excessive, but also to evolutionary economics and new economic sociology, which is unfair, as suggested here. Ingham (1996) agrees with Fine and Milonakis against the new-economic sociologists but is more receptive vis-à-vis the evolutionary institutionalists. For an interesting positive reappraisal of the "Chicago School" theory of rational choice see Foka-Kavalieraki and Hatzis (2011).

Conclusion
What is rational after all?

> What difference does it make that humans fall short of substantively rational behavior, which would entail full knowledge of all possible contingencies, exhaustive exploration of the decision tree, and a correct mapping between actions, events and outcomes? The short answer is that it makes a lot of difference. Economic history is a depressing tale of miscalculation leading to famine, starvation, defeat in warfare, death, economic stagnation and decline, and indeed the disappearance of entire civilizations. And even the most casual inspection of today's news suggests that this tale is not a purely a historical phenomenon.
>
> (North 2005: 7)

The study of the evolution of the concept of rationality has revealed 12 different meanings in the way economists represent people's behaviour during their economic transactions, as consumers or producers, investors or bankers. Adam Smith described the moral conduct of people moved by antithetic sentiments such as love of the self and sympathy for other fellow beings. Despite its universalistic flavour this behaviour was historically specific since individuals produce and exchange according to a rule of conduct that is the by-product of culture and education, i.e. the outcome of informal and formal institutions. As in many philosophical traditions, this rule of moral conduct was only grounded on introspection and was open to criticisms of unreliability and subjectivity.

John Stuart Mill shared Smith's socially embedded view of rationality and its subsequent historically specific character, but diverged from him significantly as far as the method of justification is concerned. As an empiricist philosopher he asked for empirical proofs to ground the PR on firm psychological observation. But, Mill's methodology of social sciences condemned psychology to the low level of empirical science, subordinate to the medium level science of human character or ethology and to the upper level deductive science of political economy.

William Stanley Jevons belongs to a different epoch in the development of the economic discipline. Although he was neither the first (Cournot and Dupuit came first), nor the greatest mathematical economist (Walras and Marshall were better equipped), Jevons succeeded in presenting a complete theoretical model in which the concept of utility maximization under constraint was the *premium mobile* of every transaction. To justify this principle Jevons used mainly introspective evidence, but his followers, such as Edgeworth, attempted to incorporate the new findings of experimental psychology into economics. So, just as the psychological foundations of the rationality principle were clear according to this view, so was the willingness to assert its universal character and applicability due to its mathematical nature.

Vilfredo Pareto inaugurates a fourth concept of rationality, away from utilitarianism and its rudimentary psychology basis, in order to build an empirical science of economics based on the observation of external manifestations of the acts of rational choice. This concept of instrumental rationality shares with the marginalists the claim of universalism, only insofar as economic (or "logical") actions are concerned. But it also shares the assumptions of free and unlimited knowledge and computational capacity. This was only insinuated by Jevons, Marshall and Edgeworth, to be stated openly by Walras and Pareto, and became an essential element in general equilibrium theory. Beyond his detachment from psychology, Pareto's other major difference with the marginalists was his conviction that economic knowledge explains only a small part of social phenomena, those which are the result of the rational choice of means to serve a given objective. The greatest part was left to sociology.

Pareto's theory of choice paved the way to two distinct movements within the neoclassical research program, the Hicks–Allen–Arrow–Hahn–Debreu tradition of general equilibrium and the Robbins–Samuelson–Stigler–Becker tradition of microeconomic analysis. The presence of psychological foundations is the characteristic trait that distinguishes these two movements and suggests two distinct concepts of rationality. While both movements continue within the rationality as consistency approach inaugurated by Pareto, they differ insofar as they request or not some kind of psychological motive grounded on introspection. Robbins run the half distance away from psychology in order to expel the utilitarian inheritance from economic theory. To justify the economizing behaviour under scarcity conditions he utilizes introspective arguments, just like Samuelson does after him. Despite Samuelson's intentions to "drop off the last vestiges of utilitarianism" his latent behaviourist revealed preference analysis was closer to psychology than the one he criticized, the MRS analysis of Hicks and Allen. However, what is common to both movements is their universalistic claim to explain every act of rational choice (very aggressively in the case of Becker and Stigler) and their faith in the human capacity to gather and manipulate all available information.

This is precisely Friedrich Hayek's strongest disagreement with the entire neoclassical program, the rejection of the "pretence of knowledge": humans have limited access to information and restricted computational skills. To pretend that consumers and producers know everything about present and future needs and prices and are able to calculate all the consequences emanating from their choices is unforgivable according to Hayek. So, he suggests the abandonment of the spectre of the omniscient individual together with the endless search for optimality. But, Hayek distinguishes himself also from every other tradition in economics regarding the nature and scope of the rationality principle. His anti-naturalistic positions forced him to deny any possibility of a causal explanation of human motives and actions. Against the scientific explanations of psychology, he proposed his subjectivist-hermeneutic method. Similarly, his strong anti-holistic commitment prevented him from accepting any kind of social embeddedness of individual actions. In brief, Hayek had his own original concept of rationality with no social references, forcefully anti-psychologistic and with limited capacities of agents in processing available information in their decision making.

His fellow Austrian colleague in the LSE, Karl Popper shared with him many common elements concerning the rationality principle. Popper was equally anti-collectivistic in his methodological starting point of analysis of social phenomena, as he was opposed to the idea of explaining individual actions through psychological motives. One of the main reasons was that social phenomena are often the "non-intentional" results of individual actions, like in Hayek. Yet, Popper suggested an eighth kind of rationality, which distinguishes him from Hayek. His principle of complete rationality suggests that individuals act appropriately to their situation "making the optimal use of all available information" (Popper 1957: 140). This was Popper's conventionalist argument to save the "animating principle of rationality" from refutation. In line with Machlup, Samuelson and Friedman, Popper used the same methodological strategy to defend rationality, as against Hutchison's methodological disapproval, Hayek's theoretical challenge and the empirical criticism of the late 1930s. So, the neoclassical rationality principle as consistency (in its various forms) has been continuously refuted while the older utilitarian principle of maximization is irrefutable, because no evidence can ever refute a proposition that agents seek to maximize an elusive entity such as utility (Sen 1977; Boland 1981; cf. Hodgson 2012). Popper's suggestion was to keep it alive as "a good approximation" that cannot be abandoned without abandoning the neoclassical program altogether.

After the Second World War, four different meanings of rationality were suggested to try to solve the epistemological problems of the standard neoclassical principle. Von Neumann and Morgenstern introduced the concept of strategic rationality, which associates utility maximization with probabilistic choice. The restrictive conditions of certainty and perfect knowledge were abandoned. To solve the problem of the indeterminacy of the maximization process, first "expected utility" and then "subjective expected utility" were proposed. Thus, elementary psychology introspectively based reappeared, although the solutions suggested by von Neumann, Morgenstern and Savage were full of paradoxes. Thanks to Nash, the realistic process of market interaction was theoretically resolved. While rationality was still based on the consistency of preferences, choices were made by interactive individuals and were dependent on the choices of others. But, while one problem was solved, two others emerged, like in the old Greek myth of Heracles struggling against the "Lernaean Hydra": interactive players had to share a common knowledge about everyone's strategy and possess infinite computational skills to predict correctly the other players' moves.

Herbert Simon provided a convincing answer to the problem of maximization indeterminacy and to those of limited information and computational skills. His original concept of BR helped economists to deal with uncertain, complex and incompletely informed decision making. But the loss of theoretical meaning was significant: abandoning maximization as a goal is equivalent of quitting the search for a social optimum solution, a search that goes back to Adam Smith. Furthermore, Simon's behaviourism lacks empirical evidence. There are no empirical or experimental findings confirming "satisficing" behaviour and some critics have wrongly concluded that satisficing behaviour leads agents to apply "rules of thumb" (Vriend 1996: 278) or to sub-optimal solutions (Lagueux 2010: 47). To deal with these additional problems Williamson extended Simon's concept of BR to the research agenda of transaction costs theory. Whilst a general optimum solution was not feasible, the concept of opportunism permitted the return of self-interest seeking agents with an important addition. Behaving opportunistically in business transactions became an integral part of the scope economic analysis.

The last two kinds of rationality originate from outsiders: the neighbouring fields of psychology and sociology and the heterodox trend of evolutionary institutionalism. Cognitive psychologists have done great service to economists, providing decisive empirical tests that refute the assumption of rationality as consistency. Instead, psychological evidence suggests that individuals tend to be error prone and possibly irrational, acting inconsistently because of framing effects and preference reversals.

The prospect theory, established by Kahneman and Tversky offers an alternative description of human behaviour in situations involving risk. Despite all the counterevidence suggested by experimental economists, the rationality as consistency principle proved to be no longer defensible. To foster an alternative rationality principle capable of explaining economic decision making under uncertainty and also to integrate non-rational elements in the analysis of economic behaviour, psychologists and economists collaborate to explore experimentally the role of intuition and emotions. Nevertheless, this new research project faces an insurmountable objection: individual behaviour is more than a matter of atomistic impulse and willingness; it is fundamentally the result of social interaction.

The last kind of rationality reconciles with the classical tradition, which conceived individual action as being embedded in an evolving system of values, habits and social relations. What is new about evolutionary institutionalists and economic sociologists is their distinct view of the embedded individual. Both traditions focus on the social prerequisites of social action. But, while evolutionary economists insist on the role of formal and informal institutions in framing individual decision making in order to explain economic performance through time, sociologists focus on the impact of social embeddedness upon economic relations. Their common ground lies in their willingness to reconsider the separation between different branches with the purpose to explain fully economic rationality.

A schematic presentation of the 12 different kinds of economic rationality is attempted in the following figure. The most important authors are classified according to three criteria: (*i*) the significance of social embeddedness of individual actions; (*ii*) the importance of psychological foundations in explaining economic behaviour; (*iii*) the presence of the requirement for unlimited knowledge and computational capacity in order to act properly.

Looking at the figure, one finds authors classified according to one single criterion only, like Smith, North, Hodgson, Granovetter and Swedberg. These social thinkers believe that economic rationality is the result of the social embeddedness of individuals within a particular social and cultural context. To explain how economic agents behave, there is no need to refer to any psychological motive. Furthermore, there is no need to assume unlimited knowledge and exceptional computational skills, because embedded individuals are assisted in their economic decisions by the rules, habits, routines and other formal institutions of the society they belong to. Similarly, the authors who emphasize the role of psychology as the main foundation of motives behind economic decisions are classified under this criterion only. Simon, Kahneman and Tversky, but also von Neumann, Morgenstern and Savage share in common the psychological

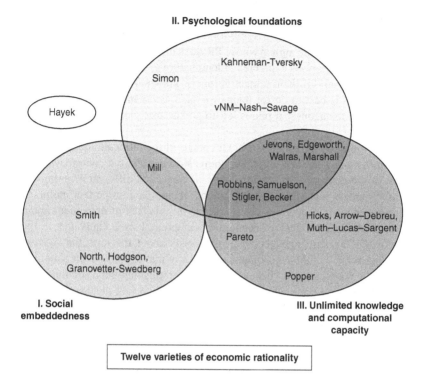

II. Psychological foundations

Kahneman-Tversky

Simon

Hayek

vNM–Nash–Savage

Jevons, Edgeworth, Walras, Marshall

Mill

Robbins, Samuelson, Stigler, Becker

Smith

Hicks, Arrow–Debreu, Muth–Lucas–Sargent

Pareto

North, Hodgson, Granovetter-Swedberg

Popper

I. Social embeddedness

III. Unlimited knowledge and computational capacity

Twelve varieties of economic rationality

means of explaining economic behaviour. They all decline to recognize any significant role played by sociological factors. Because they value so much the role of psychology, they obviously acknowledge the lack of perfect knowledge of individuals as well as their limited computational capacity. Precisely because authors like Pareto, Hicks, Arrow, Debreu but also Muth, Lucas and Sargent, as well as Popper, reject any assistance from psychological or sociological factors to explain individual decision making, they absolutely need to resort to a hyper-rationality assumption. In a nutshell: "I know everything, and I can calculate every possible consequence of it; therefore, I can take optimum decisions".

In so far as an author shares two criteria, he is classified in the intersection of two ellipses. As is Mill, who believes in the psychological origin of getting more wealth but his explanations suggest that the action of the desire of wealth is shaped by the historical frame. The same is true about the marginalists and the neoclassicals: Jevons, Walras, Edgeworth and Marshall on the one side; Robbins, Samuelson (of the WARP theory), Stigler and Becker on the other side, they all use a rudimentary psychology, based on introspection to justify the origin of maximizing behaviour. Because of the weakness of the psychological foundations, they also need assistance from the hyper-rationality assumption to secure the attainment of optimality. Still, there is one author whose PR does not fit any proposed criterion: Hayek, for the reasons explained at length above, suggests that individuals act appropriately to their subjective plans, knowing better than any third person what is best to do for their own sake, and somehow a social order emerges spontaneously if one is left to pursue freely one's own individual interest.

Our journey through the different epochs of the rationality principle has taught us many lessons. First, economists do not share a common definition of the concept of rationality over the ages, and different meanings of this "slippery concept" coexist among them. One important point of disagreement in economics has its origins in this lack of agreement about the "founding postulate" of economic behaviour. This is equivalent to the lacking of an agreement between physicists about the laws that govern the "behaviour" of the fundamental elements of matter, or between biologists about the way that cells "behave" when accomplishing the basic functions of life. Every social scientist is now aware of the fact that particles and cells do not really "behave", because they lack intentionality. But, this was not so in the age of Jevons and Walras, or even of Samuelson and Friedman when they constantly and deliberately assimilated the economic with the physical processes. Therefore, abandoning forever the icon of physics will not harm our understanding of the real economic processes, quite the opposite. It will liberate us from the naturalistic fallacy of the so-called mechanisms of the market.

Second, the rationality of the actor should not be confused with the rationality of the economic system itself. Assuming that I am acting rationally and that you are rational too, and they are also equally rational, does not prevent us from making a foolish action altogether. As is asserted in North's opening quotation above, "economic history is a depressing tale of miscalculation leading to famine, starvation, defeat in warfare, death, economic stagnation and decline". Yet, from Cournot to Debreu, and from Hayek to Vernon Smith, many exceptional minds firmly believed that social order is the natural outcome of non-coordinated rational behaviours. The survival of the system is independent of the rationality of its actors.

Third and last, it should be definitely recognized as a fact that one quintessential characteristic of humans is that they live embedded within a common system of moral values and social habits that give them a sense of social existence and identity. Succinctly put, human "intelligence is not simply 'in the mind': it is situated and contextual" (Hodgson 2001: 290). This fact questions both the limits of methodological individualism as well as the legitimacy of separating economics from other human disciplines. We have seen that it is indeed possible to have an individualistic departure that acknowledges both the social environment of acting individuals, as well as their social interaction. As Weber wrote, "the economic activity of an individual is social only if it takes account of the behavior of someone else" (1922: 22). This is a laconic reply against disciplinary isolation. This is also far away from celebrating that "there is only one social science" and that it is economics that "really constitutes the universal grammar of social science", as Jack Hirshleifer once wrote (1985: 53). Though, the converse position is also objectionable: we cannot abandon partial economic theory for the sake of a loose sociological description of the economy. Amartya Sen put it quite perfectly:

> The conclusion I come to is the need for a simultaneous recognition of the conditional importance of investigations of significantly identified partial pictures and of the absolute necessity to understand that they cannot be the endpoint of economics, not even of economic theory.
>
> (Sen 2008: 620)

References

Agassi, J. (1975) "Institutional individualism", *British Journal of Sociology*, 26: 144–155.

Akerlof, G. (1980) "A theory of social custom of which unemployment may be one consequence", *Quarterly Journal of Economics*, 94: 749–775.

Akerlof, G. (1987) "Rational models of irrational behavior", *American Economic Review*, 77: 137–142.

Akerlof, G. and Shiller, R. (2009) *Animal Spirits: How Human Psychology drives the Economy, and why it Matters for Global Capitalism*, Princeton, NJ: Princeton University Press.

Allais, M. (1953) "Le comportement de l'homme rationnel devant le risque: critiques des postulats et axiomes de l'école américaine", *Econometrica*, 21: 503–546.

Altman, M. (2004) "The Nobel Prize in behavioral and experimental economics: a contextual and critical appraisal of the contributions of Daniel Kahneman and Vernon Smith", *Review of Political Economy*, 16: 3–41.

Aron, R. (1967) *Les étapes de la pensée sociologique*, Paris: Gallimard.

Arrow, K.J. (1950) "A difficulty in the concept of social welfare", *Journal of Political Economy*, 58 (4): 328–346.

Arrow, K.J. (1974) *The Limits of Organization*, New York: Norton.

Arrow, K.J. (1986) "Economic theory and the hypothesis of rationality", *Journal of Business*, 59 (4): 385–399.

Arrow, K.J. (1994) "Methodological individualism and social knowledge", *American Economic Review*, 84: 1–9.

Ashley, W. (1891) "The rehabilitation of Ricardo", *Economic Journal*, 1: 474–489.

Ashraf, N., Camerer, C. and Lowenstein, G. (2005) "Adam Smith, behavioural economist", *Journal of Economic Perspectives*, 19 (3): 131–145.

Aspers, P. (2001) "Crossing the boundaries of economics and sociology: the case of Vilfredo Pareto", *American Journal of Economics and Sociology*, 60 (2): 519–545.

Aumann, R. (1987) "Game theory", in J. Eatwell, M. Milgate and P. Newman, *The New Palgrave Dictionary of Political Economy*, London: MacMillan, vol. 2, pp. 460–482.

Backhouse, R.E. (2002) *The Penguin History of Economics*, Greek translation, Athens: Kritiki 2009.

Backhouse, R.E. (2006) "Sidgwick, Marshall and the Cambridge School of Economics", *History of Political Economy*, 38: 15–44.

Backhouse, R.E. and Medema, S. (2009) "Robbins' essay and the axiomatization of economics", *Journal of the History of Economic Thought*, 31: 485–499.

Baumol, W.J. (2007) "Generalist's generalissimo", *American Economist*, 51 (2): 22–24.

Becker, G.S. (1962) "Irrational behavior and economic theory", *Journal of Political Economy*, 70: 1–13.

Becker, G.S. (1976) *The Economic Approach to Human Behavior*, Chicago: University of Chicago Press.

Becker, G.S. (1993) "The economic way of looking at behavior", *Journal of Political Economy*, 101: 385–409.

Beraud, A. (1992) "La contribution fondatrice. Origine et développement de la pensée économique d'Adam Smith", in A. Beraud, G. Faccarello, *Nouvelle histoire de la pensée économique*, Paris: La Découverte.

Bicchieri, C. (1992) "Two kinds of rationality", in N. DeMarchi (ed.), *Post-Popperian Methodology of Economics*, Dordrecht: Kluwer Academic Press, pp. 155–188.

Biggart, N.W. and Beamish, T.D. (2003) "The economic sociology of conventions: habit, custom, practice and routine in market order", *Annual Review of Sociology*, 29: 443–464.

Birken, L. (1988) "From macroeconomics to microeconomics: the marginalist revolution in sociocultural perspective", *History of Political Economy*, 20: 251–264.

Blaug, M. (1961) *Economic Theory in Retrospect*, 4th edn, Cambridge, UK: Cambridge University Press, 1985.

Blaug, M. (1976) "Kuhn vs. Lakatos or Paradigms vs. Research Programs in the history of economics", in S.J. Latsis (ed.) *Method and Appraisal in Economics*, Cambridge, UK: Cambridge University Press, pp. 149–180.

Blaug, M. (1980) *The Methodology of Economics*, French transl. Paris: Economica, 1982.

Blaug, M. (2009) "A symposium on *The Nature and Significance of Economic Science* by Lionel Robbins", *Journal of the History of Economic Thought*, 31: 417–517.

Böhm-Bawerk, E. von (1890) "The historical vs. the deductive method in political economy", *Annals of the American Academy of Political and Social Science*, 1: 244–271.

Boland, L. (1979) "A critic of Friedman's critics", *Journal of Economic Literature*, 17: 503–522.

Boland, L. (1981) "On the futility of criticizing the neoclassical maximization hypothesis", *American Economic Review*, 71: 1031–1036.

Boland, L. (1982) *The Foundations of Economic Method*, London: Allen & Unwin.

Boland, L. (1989) *The Methodology of Economic Model Building. Methodology after Samuelson*, London: Routledge.

Boumans, M. and Davis, J.B. (2010), *Economic Methodology*, Basingstoke: Palgrave-Macmillan.

Bouveresse, R. (1981) *Karl Popper*, Paris: Vrin, 2nd edn. 1986.

Boyer, A. (1987) "Karl Popper face aux sciences sociales", *Economies et Sociétés, Série PE, Oeconomia*, 8: 5–24.

Bowles, S. (1998) "Endogenous preferences: the cultural consequences of markets and other economic institutions", *Journal of Economic Literature*, 36 (1): 75–111.

Bowles, S. (2008) "Policies designed for self-interested citizens may undermine 'the moral sentiments': evidence from economic experiments", *Science*, 320: 1605–1609.

Bowles, S. and Gintis, H. (1993) "The revenge of Homo Economicus: contested exchange and the revival of political economy", *Journal of Economic Perspectives*, 7, (1), pp. 83–102.

Brochier, H. (1981) "Rationalité économique", in *Encyclopaedia Universalis*, Paris, vol. xiii, pp. 997–999.

Brochier, H. (1988) "Fondements idéologiques et visée scientifique en Economie", *Economies et Sociétés, Série PE, Oeconomia*, 10: 169–188.

Brochier, H. (1994) "A propos de l'individualisme méthodologique: l'ouverture d'un débat", *Revue d'Economie Politique*, 104: 25–52.

Bruni, L. (2002) *Vilfredo Pareto and the Birth of Modern Microeconomics*, Cheltenham: E. Elgar.

Bruni, L. and Guala, F. (2001) "Pareto and the epistemological foundations of choice theory", *History of Political Economy*, 33: 21–49.

Bruni, L. and Sugden, R. (2000) "Moral canals: trust and social capital in the work of Hume, Smith and Genovesi", *Economics and Philosophy*, 16 (1): 21–45.

Bruni, L. and Sugden, R. (2007) "How psychology was removed from economics and how it might be brought back", *Economic Journal*, 117: 146–173.

Bruni, L. and Sugden, R. (2008) "Fraternity: why the market need not be a morally free zone", *Economics and Philosophy*, 24: 35–64.

Cairnes, J.E. (1857) *The Character and Logical Method of Political Economy*, 2nd edn. 1875, Ontario: Batoche Books, 2001.

Caldwell, B. (1982) *Beyond Positivism: Economic Methodology in the 20th Century*, London: Allen & Unwin.

Caldwell, B. (1983) "The neoclassical maximization hypothesis: a comment", *American Economic Review*, 73 (4): 824–830.

Caldwell, B. (1991a) "Clarifying Popper", *Journal of Economic Literature*, 29: 1–33.

Caldwell, B. (1991b) "The methodology of scientific research programs in economics: criticisms and conjectures", in G. Shaw (ed.), *Economics, Culture and Education: Essays in Honor of Mark Blaug*, Aldershot: E. Elgar, pp. 95–107.

Camerer, C., Lowenstein, G. and Prelec, D. (2005) "Neuroeconomics: how neuroscience can inform economics", *Journal of Economic Literature*, 43: 9–64.

Canguilhem, G. (1968) *Etudes d'histoire et de philosophie des sciences*, 4th edn. Paris: Vrin, 1979.

Carnap, R. (1935) *Philosophy and Logical Syntax*, Thessaloniki: Egnatia 1975 (English/Greek bilingual edn).

Cartwright, N. (1994) "Mill and Menger: ideal elements and stable tendencies", *Poznan Studies in the Philosophy of Science and the Humanities*, 38: 171–188.

Casson, M. (1993) "Cultural determinants of economic performance", *Journal of Comparative Economics*, 17: 418–442.

Chalmers, A.F. (1976) *What is Thing called Science?* St. Lucia: University of Queensland Press, 2nd edn. 1982.

Chalmers, A.F. (1985) "Methodological individualism: an incongruity in Popper's philosophy", in G. Currie and A. Musgrave (eds), *Popper and the Human Sciences*, Dordrecht: Martinus Nijhoff, pp. 73–87.

Chipman, J.S. and Lenfant, J.S. (2002) "Slutsky's article: how it came to be found and interpreted", *History of Political Economy*, 34: 553–597.

Christodoulides, P. (1979) *Explanation in Science and the Concept of Model*, Thessaloniki: Egnatia (in Greek).

Clower, R. (1994) "Economics as an inductive science", *Southern Economic Journal*, 60: 805–14.

Coase, R. (1937) "The nature of the firm", *Economica*, 4: 386–405.

Coase, R. (1975) "Marshall on method", *Journal of Law and Economics*, 18: 25–31.

Coase, R. (1992) "The institutional structure of production", *American Economic Review*, 82: 713–719.

Coats, A.W. (1972) "The economic and social context of the Marginal Revolution of the 1870s", *History of Political Economy*, 4: 303–324.

Coats, A.W. (1976) "Economics and psychology: death and resurrection of a research programme", in S. Latsis (ed.) *Method and Appraisal in Economics*, Cambridge, UK: Cambridge University Press, pp. 43–64.

Colander, D. (2007) "Edgeworth's Hedonimeter and the quest to measure utility", *Journal of Economic Perspectives*, 21: 215–225.

Colander, D. (2009) "What was 'it' that Robbins was defining?", *Journal of the History of Economic Thought*, 31: 437–448.

Commons, J.R. (1931) "Institutional economics", *American Economic Review*, 21: 648–657.

Conlisk, J. (1996) "Why bounded rationality?", *Journal of Economic Literature*, 34: 669–700.

Cosmides, L. and Tooby, J. (1994) "Better than rational: evolutionary psychology and the invisible hand", *American Economic Review*, 84 (2): 327–332.

Creedy, J. (1984) "Edgeworth: utilitarianism and arbitration", *History of Political Economy*, 16: 609–618.

Cremaschi, S. (2010) "Adam Smith without Homo Economicus", *Bulletin PCRC*, 3: 23–35.

Cubeddu, R. (1987) "Popper et l'école autrichienne", *Economies et Sociétés, Série PE, Oeconomia*, N°8: 41–62.

Dalziel, P. and Higgins, J. (2006) "Pareto, Parsons and the boundary between economics and sociology", *American Journal of Economics and Sociology*, 65 (1): 109–126.

Davis, J. (2003) *The Theory of the Individual in Economics: Identity and Value*, London: Routledge.

Deane, P. (1978) *The Evolution of Economic Ideas*, Cambridge, UK: Cambridge University Press.

DeMarchi, N.B. (1972) "Mill and Cairnes and the emergence of marginalism in England", *History of Political Economy*, 4: 344–363.

DeMarchi, N.B. (1986) "Mill's unrevised philosophy of economics", *Philosophy of Science*, 53: 89–100.

Diaye, M. and Lapidus, A. (2005) "A Humean theory of choice of which rationality may be one consequence", *European Journal of the History of Economic Thought*, 12: 89–111.

Diaye, M. and Lapidus, A. (2012) "Pleasure and belief in Hume's decision process", *European Journal of the History of Economic Thought*, 19 (3): 355–384.

Doucouliagos, N. (1994) "A note on the evolution of Homo Oeconomicus", *Journal of Economic Issues*, 28: 877–883.

Drakopoulos, S. (1994) "Economics and the new physics: some methodological implications", *South-African Journal of Economics*, 62: 333–353.

Drakopoulos, S. (2011) "Wicksteed, Robbins and the emergence of mainstream economic methodology", *Review of Political Economy*, 23: 461–470.

Drakopoulos, S. and Karayiannis A.D. (1999) "Mainstream consumer theory: delay, acceptance and history of economic thought texts", *History of Economics Review*, 30: 68–81.

Duncan, G. (1978) *Marx and Mill: Two Views of Social Conflict and Social Harmony*. Cambridge, UK: Cambridge University Press.

Dupuy, J.P. (1992) *Introduction aux sciences sociales*, Paris: Editions Marketing.

Edgeworth, F.Y. (1879) "The hedonical calculus", *Mind*, 4: 394–408.

Edgeworth, F.Y. (1881) *Mathematical Psychics: An Essay on the Application of Mathematics to the Moral Sciences*, London: C. Kegan Paul & Co.

Eidlin, F. (1990) "Ideal types and the problem of reification", unpublished typescript presented at the *XIIth World Congress of Sociology*, Madrid, 9–13 July 1990.

Ekelund, R.B. and Olsen, E.S. (1973) "Comte, Mill, Cairnes: the positivist empiricist interlude in late classical economics", *Journal of Economic Issues*, 7 (3): 383–416.

Ellsberg, D. (1961) "Risk, ambiguity, and the savage axioms", *Quarterly Journal of Economics*, 5: 643–669.

Elsner, W. (1989) "Adam Smith model of the origins and emergence of institutions", *Journal of Economic Issues*, 23 (1): 189–213.

Elster, J. (1985) "The nature and scope of rational-choice explanation", in E. LePore and B.P. McLaughlin (eds) *Actions and Events: Perspectives on the Philosophy of Donald Davidson*, Oxford: Blackwell, pp. 60–72.

Elster, J. (1989a) *Nuts and Bolts for the Social Sciences*, Cambridge, UK: Cambridge University Press.

Elster, J. (1989b) "Social norms and economic theory", *Journal of Economic Perspectives*, 3 (4): 99–117.

Etzioni, A. (1986) "The case for a multiple utility conception", *Economics and Philosophy*, 2: 159–183.

Evensky, J. (1992) "Ethics and the classical liberal tradition in economics", *History of Political Economy*, 24: 61–77.

Evensky, J. (2001) "Adam Smith's lost legacy", *Southern Economic Journal*, 67 (3): 497–517.

Fernandez-Grela, M. (2006) "Disaggregating the components of the Hicks–Allen composite commodity", in P. Mirowski and D.W. Hands (eds) *Agreement on Demand: Consumer Theory in the Twentieth Century*, Durham, NC: Duke University Press, pp. 32–47.

Fine, B. and Milonakis, D. (2009) *From Economics Imperialism to Freakonomics: The Shifting Boundaries between Economics and other Social Sciences*, London: Routledge.

Foka-Kavalieraki, Y. and Hatzis, A. (2011) "Rational after all: toward an improved model of rationality in economics", *Revue de Philosophie Economique/Review of Economic Philosophy*, 12.

Fontaine, P. (1997) "Turgot's 'institutional individualism'", *History of Political Economy*, 29: 1–20.

Frantz, R. (2005) *Two Minds: Intuition and Analysis in the History of Economic Thought*, Berlin: Springer.

Freund, J. (1965) "Introduction", in Max Weber *Essais sur la Théorie de la Science*. Paris: Pocket, 1992.

Friedman, M. (1953) "The methodology of positive economics", in *Essays in Positive Economics*, Chicago: University of Chicago Press, pp. 3–43.

Furubotn, E.G. and Richter, R. (1998) *Institutions and Economic Theory*, Ann Arbor: University of Michigan Press, 2nd edn. 2005.

Galbraith, J.K. (2007) "Paul Samuelson on his 90th birthday", *American Economist*, 51 (2): 39.

Garegnani, P. (1984) "Value and distribution in the classical economists and Marx", *Oxford Economic Papers*, 36: 291–325.

Giocoli, N. (2003) *Modeling Rational Agents*, Cheltenham: E. Elgar.

Gislain, J.J. and Steiner, P. (1995) *La sociologie économique 1890–1920*, Paris: Presses Universitaires de France.

Gordon, S. (1991) *The History and Philosophy of Social Science*, London: Routledge.

Gottesman, A.A., Ramrattan, L. and Szenberg, M. (2005) "Samuelson's economics: the continuing legacy", *Quarterly Journal of Austrian Economics*, 8 (2): 95–104.

Granovetter, M. (1985) "Economic action and social structure: the problem of embeddedness", *American Journal of Sociology*, 91: 481–510.

Granovetter, M. (2000) "The economic sociology of firms and entrepreneurs", in R. Swedberg (ed.) *Entrepreneurship: The Social Science View*, Oxford: Oxford University Press.

Groenewegen, P.D. (1995) *A Soaring Eagle: Alfred Marshall 1842–1924*, Aldershot: E. Elgar.

Groenewegen, J., Kerstholt, F. and Nagelkerke, A. (1995) "On integrating new and old institutionalism: Douglass North building bridges", *Journal of Economic Issues*, 29: 467–475.

Gross, M. and Tarascio, V. (1998) "Pareto's theory of choice", *History of Political Economy*, 30: 169–187.

Hall, R.L. and Hitch, C.J. (1939) "Price theory and business behavior", *Oxford Economic Papers*, 2: 12–45.

Hamilton, G.G. (1994) "Civilizations and the organization of economics", in N.J. Smelser and R. Swedberg (eds) *Handbook of Economic Sociology*. Princeton: Princeton University Press.

Hammond, P. (1997) "Rationality in economics", *Rivista internazionale di Scienze sociali* CV: 247–288.

Hands, D.W. (1985) "Karl Popper and economic methodology", *Economics and Philosophy*, 1: 83–99.

Hands, D.W. (1991) "Popper, the rationality principle and economic explanation", in G.K. Shaw (ed.) *Economics, Culture and Education: Essays in Honor of Mark Blaug*, Cheltenham: E. Elgar, pp. 108–119.

Hands, D.W. (1992) "Falsification, situational analysis and scientific research programs: the Popperian tradition in economic methodology", in N. DeMarchi (ed.) *Post-Popperian Methodology of Economics*, Dordrecht: Kluwer Academic Press, pp. 19–53.

Hands, D.W. (2006) "Integrability, rationalizability and path-dependency", in P. Mirowski and D.W. Hands (eds) *Agreement on Demand: Consumer Theory in the Twentieth Century*, Durham, NC: Duke University Press, pp. 153–185.

Hands, D.W. (2009) "Effective tension in Robbins' economic methodology", *Economica*, 76: 831–844.

Hart, J. (2002) "A conversation with Terence Hutchison", *Journal of Economic Methodology*, 9: 359–377.

Hart, J. (2010) "Terence Hutchison and Frank Knight: a reappraisal of their 1940–1941 exchange", *Journal of Economic Methodology*, 17: 359–373.

Hausman, D. (1981) "John Stuart Mill's philosophy of economics", *Philosophy of Science*, 48: 348–365.

Hausman, D. (1988a) "An appraisal of Popperian methodology", in N. DeMarchi (ed.) *The Popperian Legacy in Economics*, Cambridge, UK: Cambridge University Press, pp. 65–85.

Hausman, D. (1988b) "Economic methodology and philosophy of science", in G.C. Winton and R.F. Teichgraeber III, *The Boundaries of Economics*, Cambridge, UK: Cambridge University Press, pp. 88–116.

Hausman, D. (1989) "Economic methodology in a nutshell", *Journal of Economic Perspectives*, 3: 115–127.

Hausman, D. (1992) *The Inexact and Separate Science of Economics*, Cambridge, UK: Cambridge University Press.

Hausman, D. (1998) "Problems with realism in economics", *Economics and Philosophy*, 14: 185–213.

Hausman, D. and McPherson, M. (1993) "Taking ethics seriously: economics and contemporary moral philosophy", *Journal of Economic Literature*, 31 (2): 671–731.

Hausman, D. and Mongin, P. (1998) "Economist's responses to anomalies: full-cost pricing versus preference reversals", in J. Davis (ed.) *New Economics and its History*, Durham, NC: Duke University Press, pp. 255–272.

Hayek, F. von (1937) "Economics and knowledge", *Economica*, 4: 33–54.

Hayek, F. von (1952) *The Counter-revolution of Science*, French translation *Scientisme et sciences sociales*, Paris: Plon, 1986.

Henrich, J., Boyd, R., Bowles, S., Camerer, C., Fehr, E., Gintis, H. and McElreath, R. (2001) "In search of Homo Oeconomicus: behavioural experiments in 15 small-scale societies", *American Economic Review*, 91 (2): 73–78.

Hicks, J.R. (1939) *Value and Capital*, Oxford: Oxford University Press.

Hicks, J.R. and Allen, R.G.D. (1934) "A reconsideration of the theory of value", *Economica*, 1: 52–76.

Hirsch, A. (1980) "The assumption controversy in historical perspective", *Journal of Economic Issues*, 14: 99–118.

Hirsch, A. (1992) "J.S. Mill on verification and the business of science", *History of Political Economy*, 24: 843–866.

Hirsch, A. (2000) "Reply to Hollander and Peart's 'John Stuart Mill's method' ", *Journal of the History of Economic Thought*, 22: 349–360.

Hirschman, A. (1976) *The Passions and the Interests*, Princeton: Princeton University Press.

Hirshleifer, J. (1985) "The expanding domain of economics", *American Economic Review*, 75 (6): 53–68.

Hodgson, G.M. (1986) "Behind methodological individualism", *Cambridge Journal of Economics*, 10: 211–229.

Hodgson, G.M. (1993) *Economics and Evolution*, Ann Arbor: The University of Michigan Press.

Hodgson, G.M. (1997) "The ubiquity of habits and rules", *Cambridge Journal of Economics*, 21: 663–684.

Hodgson, G.M. (1998) "The approach of institutional economics", *Journal of Economic Literature*, 36: 166–192.

Hodgson, G.M. (2001) *How Economics forgot History: The Problem of Historical Specificity in Social Science*, London: Routledge.

Hodgson, G.M. (2006) "What are institutions?", *Journal of Economic Issues*, 40: 1–25.

Hodgson, G.M. (2012) "On the limits of rational choice", *Economic Thought*, 1: 94–108.

Hollander, S. (1983) "William Whewell and John Stuart Mill on the methodology of political economy", *Studies in the History and Philosophy of Science*, 14: 127–168.

Hollander, S. (1985) *The Economics of John Stuart Mill*, London: Blackwell.

Hollander, S. (1986) "The relevance of John Stuart Mill: some implications for modern economics", in R.D.C. Black (ed.) *Ideas in Economics*, London: Macmillan Press pp. 129–159.

Hollander, S. and Peart S. (1999) "John Stuart Mill's method in principle and practice: A review of the evidence", *Journal of the History of Economic Thought*, 21: 369–397.

Hollis, M. (1994) *The Philosophy of Social Science*, Cambridge, UK: Cambridge University Press.

Hollis, M. and Nell, E. (1975) *Rational Economic Man*, Cambridge, UK: Cambridge University Press.

Howson, S. (2004) "The origins of Lionel Robbins' *Essay on the Nature and Significance of Economic Science*", *History of Political Economy*, 36: 413–443.

Hume, D. (1748 [1739]) *A Treatise of Human Nature*, Bowen Island, BC: Jonathan Bennett, 2010.

Hutchison, T.W. (1938) *The Significance and Basic Postulates of Economic Theory*, 2nd edn. New York: A. Kelley, 1960.

Hutchison, T.W. (1941) "The significance and basic postulates of economic theory: a reply to Prof. Knight", *Journal of Political Economy*, 49 (5): 732–750.

Hutchison, T.W. (1956) "Professor Machlup on verification in economics", *Southern Economic Journal*, 22: 476–483.

Hutchison, T.W. (1972) "The Marginal Revolution and the decline and fall of English classical political economy", *History of Political Economy*, 4: 442–468.

Hutchison, T.W. (1982) "The politics and philosophy in Jevons's political economy", *Manchester School of Economics and Social Studies Review*, 50: 366–378.

Hutchison, T.W. (2009) "A formative decade: methodological controversy in the 1930s", *Journal of Economic Methodology*, 16: 297–314.

Ingham, G. (1996) "Some recent changes in the relationship between economics and sociology", *Cambridge Journal of Sociology*, 20: 243–275.

Ingrao, B. and Israel, G. (1990) *The Invisible Hand: Economic Equilibrium in the History of Science*, Cambridge, MA: MIT Press.

Jalladeau, J. (1978) "Research program vs. Paradigm in the development of Economics", *Journal of Economic Issues*, 12: 583–608.

Jehle, G.A. and Reny, P.J. (2001) *Advanced Microeconomic Theory*, Boston: Addison Wesley.

Jensen, H. (1996) "John Stuart Mill. a herald of social economics", in E.J. O'Boyle (ed.) *Social Economics: Premises, Findings and Policies*, London: Routledge.

Jensen, H. (2001) "John Stuart Mill's theories of wealth and income distribution", *Review of Social Economy*, 59(4): 491–507.

Jevons, W.S. (1876) "The future of political economy", *Fortnightly Review*, 20: 617–631. Reprinted in *The Principles of Economics*, (1905), New York: Kelley, 1965.

Jevons, W.S. (1879 [1871]) *The Theory of Political Economy*, Harmondsworth: Penguin Books 1970.

Jevons, W.S. (1892 [1874]) *The Principles of Science*, London: MacMillan, 2nd edn.

Kahneman, D. (2003) "Maps of bounded rationality: psychology for behavioral economics", *American Economic Review*, 93: 1449–1475.

Kahneman, D. and Tversky, A. (1979) "Prospect theory: and analysis of decision under risk", *Econometrica*, 47: 263–291.

Karantonis, I. (1980) *Economics Viewed from the Point of Modern Epistemology*, Thessaloniki: Kyriakidis (in Greek).

Karayiannis, A.D. (2001a) *Economic Methodology. An Historic Analysis*, Athens: Kritiki (in Greek).

Karayiannis, A.D. (2001b) "Behavioural assumptions in Nassau Senior's economics", *Contributions to Political Economy*, 20: 17–29.

Kennedy, G. (2005) *Adam Smith's Lost Legacy*, Basingstoke: Palgrave-Macmillan.

Keynes, J.M. (1921) *A Treatise on Probability*, London: MacMillan.

Keynes, J.M. (1936) *The General Theory of Employment, Interest and Money*, London MacMillan, 1973.

Keynes, J.M. (1937) "The general theory of employment", *Quarterly Journal of Economics*, 51: 209–223.

Keynes, J.N. (1891) *The Scope and Method of Political Economy*, New York, Kelley & Millman, 1955.

Kim, J. (1995) "Jevons versus Cairnes on exact economic laws", in I. Rima (ed.) *Measurement Quantifications and Economic Analysis*, London and New York: Routledge, pp. 140–156.

Kincaid, H. (1996) *Philosophical Foundations of the Social Sciences*, Cambridge, UK: Cambridge University Press.

Kirman, A., Livet, P. and Teschl, M. (2010) "Rationality and emotions", *Philosophical Transactions of the Royal Society B* 365: 215–219.

Klaes, M. and Sent, E.M. (2005) "A conceptual history of the emergence of bounded rationality", *History of Political Economy*, 37: 27–59.

Klant, J. (1988) "The natural order", in N.B. DeMarchi (ed.) *The Popperian Legacy in Economics.* Cambridge, UK: Cambridge University Press, pp. 87–117.

Knight, F.H. (1921) *Risk, Uncertainty and Profit*, New York: A.M. Kelley, 1964.

Knight, F.H. (1940) "What is truth in economics?", *Journal of Political Economy*, 48 (1): 1–32.

Knight, F.H. (1941) "The significance and basic postulates of economic theory: a rejoinder", *Journal of Political Economy*, 49 (5): 750–758.

Köertge, N. (1975) "Popper's metaphysical research program for the human sciences", *Inquiry*, 19: 437–462.

Köertge, N. (1979) "The methodological status of Popper's rationality principle", *Theory and Decision*, 10: 83–95.

Kolm, S.C. (1986) *Philosophie de l'Economie*, Paris: Seuil.

Koniavitis, T. (1993) *Pluralism in Sociology: A Methodological Approach*, Athens: Odisseas (in Greek).

Koopmans, T. (1957) *Three Essays on the State of Economic Science*, New York: McGraw Hill.

Kyburg, H.E. (1995) "Keynes as a philosopher", in A.F. Cottrell and M.S. Lawlor (eds) *New Perspectives on Keynes*, Durham, NC: Duke University Press, pp. 7–32.

Lagueux, M. (1993a) "Analyse économique et principe de rationalité", *Revue de Synthèse*, 64: 9–31.

Lagueux, M. (1993b) "Popper and the rationality principle", *Philosophy of the Social Sciences*, 23: 468–480.

Lagueux, M. (2010) *Rationality and Explanation in Economics*, London: Routledge.

Lakatos, I. (1970) "Falsificationism and the methodology of scientific research programmes", in I. Lakatos and A. Musgrave (eds) *Criticism and the Growth of Knowledge*, Cambridge, UK: Cambridge University Press, pp. 91–196.

Lallement, J. (1987) "Popper et le principe de rationalité", *Economies et Sociétés, Série PE, Oeconomia*, N°8: 25–40.

Landa, J.T. (1994) *Trust, Ethnicity and Identity*, Ann Arbor: University of Michigan Press.

Latsis, S. (1972) "Situational determinism in economics", *British Journal for the Philosophy of Science*, 8: 207–245.

Latsis, S. (1976) "A research program in economics", in S. Latsis (ed.) *Method and Appraisal in Economics*, Cambridge, UK: Cambridge University Press, pp. 1–41.

Latsis, S. (1983) "The role and status of the rationality principle in the social sciences", in R. Cohen and M. Wartowsky (eds), *Epistemology, Methodology and the Social Sciences*, Dordrecht: Reidel, pp. 123–151.

Lee, F.S. (1984) "The marginalist controversy and the demise of full-cost pricing", *Journal of Economic Issues*, 18: 1107–1132.

Legris, A. and Ragni, L. (2005) "Théorie de l'action, rationalité et conception de l'individu chez Pareto", *Cahiers d'Economie Politique*, 49: 103–126.

Leonard, R.J. (1995) "From parlor games to social science: von Neumann, Morgenstern and the creation of game theory, 1928–1944", *Journal of Economic Literature*, 33: 730–761.

Lester, R.A. (1946) "Shortcomings of marginal analysis for wage-employment problems", *American Economic Review*, 36: 63–82.

Lichtenstein, S. and Slovic, P. (1971) "Reversals of preference between bids and choices in gambling decisions", *Journal of Experimental Psychology*, 89: 46–55.

Longuet, S. (1998) *Hayek et l'école autrichienne*, Paris: Nathan.

Losee, J. (1980) *A Historical Introduction to the Philosophy of Science*, Oxford University Press.

Maas, H. (2005) *William Stanley Jevons and the Making of Modern Economics*, Cambridge, UK: Cambridge University Press.

Maas, H. (2009) "Disciplining boundaries: Lionel Robbins, Max Weber and the borderlands of economics, history and psychology", *Journal of the History of Economic Thought*, 31 (4): 500–517.

Machlup, F. (1946) "Marginal analysis and empirical research", in F. Machlup *Essays in Economic Semantics*, New York: WW Norton, 1967, pp. 147–190.

Machlup, F. (1955) "The problem of verification in economics", *Southern Economic Journal*, 22: 1–21.

Machlup, F. (1956) "Rejoinder to a reluctant ultra-empiricist", *Southern Economic Journal*, 22: 483–493.

Machlup, F. (1964) "Prof. Samuelson on theory and realism", *American Economic Review*, 54: 733–736.

Machlup, F. (1967) "L'homo oeconomicus et ses collègues", in E. Claassen (ed.) *Fondements philosophiques des systèmes économiques*, Paris: Payot, pp. 117–130.

MacLennan, B. (1972) "Jevons's philosophy of science", *Manchester School of Economics and Social Studies Review*, 40: 53–71.

Maitre, P. (2000) "L'hypothèse de la sympathie: Une perspective historique", *Economies et Sociétés, PE*, 30: 39–67.

Mäki, U. (1989) "On the problem of realism in economics", *Ricerche Economiche*, 43: 176–198.

Mäki, U. (1993) "Economics with institutions: agenda for methodological enquiry", in U. Mäki, Bo Gustaffson and C. Knudsen (eds) *Rationality, Institutions and Economic Methodology*, London: Routledge.

Malinvaud, E. (1991) *Voies de la recherche macroéconomique*, Paris: Odile Jacob-Points Seuil.

Malinvaud, E. (1995) "Sur l'hypothèse de rationalité en théorie macro-économique", *Revue Economique*, 46: 523–536.

Marchionatti, R. and Gambino, E. (1997) "Pareto and political economy as a science: methodological revolution and analytical advances in economic theory in the 1890s", *Journal of Political Economy*, 105: 1322–1348.

Mariyani-Squire, E. (2009) "Methodological conflict: Simon, Samuelson and Friedman", in K. Puttaswamaiah, *Milton Friedman, Nobel Monetary Economist: A Review of Theories and Policies*, Enfield, NH: Isle Publ. Co.

Marshall, A. (1881) "Review of F.Y. Edgeworth's *Mathematical Psychics*", *Academy*, June 18: 457.

Marshall, A. (1885) *Present Position of Political Economy*, London: Macmillan Press.

Marshall, A. (1897) "The old generation of economists and the new", *Quarterly Journal of Economics*, 11 (2): 115–135.

Marshall, A. (1920 [1890]) *Principles of Economics*, 8th edn., London: Macmillan Press, 1985.

Marx, K. (1965) *Oeuvres. Economie I*, édition établie et annotée par Maximilien Rubel, Paris: NRF La Pléiade.

Marx, K. (1968) *Oeuvres. Economie II*, édition établie et annotée par Maximilien Rubel, Paris: NRF La Pléiade.

Mayer, T. (1995) *Doing Economic Research*, Aldershot: E. Elgar.

Mays, W. (1962) "Jevons's conception of economic method", *Manchester School of Economics and Social Studies Review*, 30: 223–249.

Meardon, S.J. and Ortmann, A. (1996) "Self-command in Adam Smith's *Theory of Moral Sentiments*: a game-theoretic interpretation", *Rationality and Society*, 8: 57–80.

Meidinger, C. (1994) *La science économique, questions de méthode*, Paris: Vuibert.

Ménard, C. (1978) *La formation d'une rationalité économique: A.A. Cournot*, Paris: Flammarion.

Ménard, C. (1987) "Why was there no probabilistic revolution in economic thought", in L. Kruger, G. Gigerenzer, and M.S. Morgan (eds) *The Probabilistic Revolution*, Cambridge, MA: MIT Press, vol. 2, pp. 139–146.

Ménard, C. (1990) *L'économie des organisations*, Paris: La Découverte, 3rd edn., 2012

Ménard, C. (1993) "Thinking analogically: economics as an 'as if' science", communication at the *XIX International Congress of History of Science*, Zaragoza, Spain.

Ménard, C. (1994) "Organizations as coordinating devices", *Metroeconomica*, 45 (3): 224–247.

Ménard, C. (1995) "Markets as institutions versus organizations as markets. Disentangling some fundamental concepts", *Journal of Economic Behavior and Organization*, 28: 161–182.

Ménard, C. (2005) "A new institutional approach to organization", in C. Ménard and M. Shirley (eds) *Handbook of New Institutional Economic*, Dordrecht: Springer, pp. 281–318.

Menger, C. (1883) *Problems of Economics and Sociology*, Urbana: University of Illinois Press, 1963.

Mill, J.S. (1836) "On the definition of political economy and on the method of investigation proper to it", in *Collected Works*, vol. iv, pp. 309–339, J.M. Robson (ed.) Toronto: Toronto University Press, 1967.

Mill, J.S. (1843) *A System of Logic Ratiocinative and Inductive*, in *Collected Works* vol. vii-viii, J.M. Robson (ed.) Toronto: Toronto University Press, 1973.

Mill, J.S. (1848) *Principles of Political Economy with some of their Applications to Social Philosophy*, William J. Ashley (ed.), 1909, New York: A. Kelley, 1973.

Mill, J.S. (1873) *Autobiography*, Harmondsworth: Penguin Books, 1989.

Milonakis, D. and Fine, B. (2009) *From Political Economy to Economics: Method, the Social and the Historical in the Evolution of Economic Theory*, London: Routledge.

Mingat, A., Salmon P. and Wolfelsperger, A. (1985) *Methodologie Economique*, Paris: Presses Universitaires de France.

Mirowski, P. (1984) "Physics and the 'Marginalist Revolution'", *Cambridge Journal of Economics*, 8: 361–379.

Mirowski, P. (1989) *More Heat than Light: Economics as Social Physics, Physics as Nature's Economics*, Cambridge, UK: Cambridge University Press.

Mises, L. von (1960) *Epistemological Problems of Economics*, transl. by George Reisman, L. von Mises Institute: Auburn Alabama, 3rd edn, 2003

Mongin, P. (1984) "Modèle rationnel ou modèle économique de rationalité?", *Revue Economique*, 35: 9–63.

Mongin, P. (1986) "La controverse sur l'entreprise (1940–1950) et la formation de l'irréalisme méthodologique", *Economies et Sociétés, Oeconomia*, 5: 95–151.

Mongin, P. (1988) "Le réalisme des hypothèses et la 'partial interpretation view'", *Philosophy of the Social Sciences*, 8: 281–325.

Mongin, P. (1994) "L'optimisation est-elle un critère de rationalité individuelle?", *Dialogue*, 33: 191–222.

Mongin, P. (1998) "Expected utility theory", in J. Davis, D.W. Hands and U. Mäki (eds) *The Handbook of Economic Methodology*, Cheltenham: E. Elgar.

Mongin, P. (2000) "Les préférences révélées et la formation de la théorie du consommateur", *Revue Economique*, 51: 1125–1152.

Mosselmans, B. (1999) "Reproduction and scarcity: the population mechanism in classicism and in the 'Jevonian Revolution'", *European Journal of the History of Economic Thought*, 6: 34–57.

Mosselmans, B. (2007) *William Stanley Jevons and the Cutting Edge of Economics*, London: Routledge.

Musgrave, A. (1981) "Unreal assumption in economic theory: the F-twist untwisted", *Kyklos*, 34: 377–387.

Nadeau, R. (1993) "Confuting Popper on the rationality principle", *Philosophy of the Social Sciences*, 23: 446–467.

Nagel, E. (1963) "Assumptions in economic theory", *American Economic Review*, 53: 211–219.

Nelson, R. and Winter, S.G. (1982) *An Evolutionary Theory of Economic Change*, Cambridge, MA: Harvard University Press.

North, D.C. (1981) *Structure and Change in Economic History*, New York: W. Norton & Co.

North, D.C. (1990) *Institutions, Institutional Change and Economic Performance*, Cambridge, UK: Cambridge University Press.

North, D.C. (1993) "Institutions and credible commitment", *Journal of Institutional and Theoretical Economics*, 149: 11–23.

North, D.C. (2005) *Understanding the Process of Economic Change*, Princeton: Princeton University Press.

Neumann, J. von and Morgenstern, O. (1944) *Theory of Games and Economic Behavior*, Princeton: Princeton University Press, 1994.

O'Hear, A. (1980) *Karl Popper*, London: Routledge & Kegan Paul.

Papandreou, A.G. (1950) "Economics and the social sciences", *Economic Journal*, 60: 715–723.

Papandreou, A.G. (1958) *Economics as a Science*, Chicago: J.P. Lippincott Co.

Papandreou, A.G. (1959) "Explanation and prediction in economics", *Science*, 129: 1096–1100.

Papandreou, A.G. (1963) "Theory construction and empirical meaning in economics", *American Economic Review*, 53: 205–210.

Pareto, V. (1897) "The new theories of economics", *Journal of Political Economy*, 5: 485–502.

Pareto, V. (1909) *Manuel d'Economie Politique, Œuvres complètes*, vol. 7, Genève: Librairie Droz, 1981.

Pareto, V. (1917) *Traité de Sociologie générale, Œuvres complètes*, vol. 12, Genève: Librairie Droz, 1968.

Pearce, K.A. and Hoover, K.D. (1995) "After the revolution: Paul Samuelson and the textbook Keynesian model", in A.F. Cottrell and M.S. Lawlor, *New Perspectives on Keynes*, Durham, NC: Duke University Press, pp. 183–216.

Peart, S. (1995a) "'Disturbing causes', 'noxious errors', and the theory-practice distinction in the economics of J.S. Mill and W.S. Jevons", *Canadian Journal of Economics*, 28: 1194–1211.

Peart, S. (1995b) "Measurement in utility calculations: the utilitarian perspective", in I. Rima (ed.) *Measurement Quantifications and Economic Analysis*, London and New York: Routledge, pp. 63–84.

Peart, S. (1996) *The Economics of W.S. Jevons*, London: Routledge.

Peil, J. (1999) *Adam Smith and Economic Science*, Aldershot: E. Elgar.

Persky, J. (1995) "The ethology of homo oeconomicus", *Journal of Economic Perspectives*, 9: 221–231.

Polanyi, K. (1944) *The Great Transformation*, Boston: Beacon Press, 1957.

Popper, K. (1945) *The Open Society and its Enemies*, 5th edn., London: Routledge & Kegan Paul, 1966.

Popper, K. (1957) *The Poverty of Historicism*, London: Routledge, 1991.

Popper, K. (1961) "The logic of the social sciences", in K. Popper, *In a Search of a Better World*, London: Routledge, 1992.

Popper, K. (1967) "La rationalité et le statut du principe de rationalité", in E. Claassen (ed.) *Fondements philosophiques des systèmes économiques*, Paris: Payot, pp. 142–150.

Popper, K. (1974) *La quête inachevée. Autobiographie intellectuelle*, Paris: Presses Pocket, 1989.

Prasch, R. (1991) "The ethics of growth in Adam Smith's *Wealth of Nations*", *History of Political Economy*, 23: 337–351.

Quinton, A. (1989) *Utilitarian Ethics*, London: Duckworth.

Rabin, M. (1998) "Psychology and economics", *Journal of Economic Literature*, 36: 11–46.

Raffaelli, T., Becattini, G. and Dardi, M. eds. (2006) *The Elgar Companion to Alfred Marshall*, Cheltenham: E. Elgar.

Redman, D. (1997) *The Rise of Political Economy as a Science*, Cambridge, MA: MIT Press.

Ricardo, D. (1951) *Principles of Political Economy*, in *The Collected Works of David Ricardo*, P. Sraffa (ed.), Cambridge, UK: Cambridge University Press, vol. 1.

Robbins, L. (1932) *An Essay on the Nature and Significance of Economic Science*, London: MacMillan, 3rd edn, 1987.

Rosenberg, A. (1988) *Philosophy of Social Science*, Boulder, CO: Westview Press.

Rowthorn, R. and Sethi, R. (2008) "Procedural rationality and equilibrium trust", *Economic Journal*, 118: 889–905.

Ryan, A. (1970) *The Philosophy of John Stuart Mill*, Atlantic Highlands, NJ: Humanities Press Int., 1990.

Sabooglu, M. and Villet, M. (1992) "Déterminisme situationnel et rationalité", *Economies et Sociétés, Série PE, Oeconomia*, °17: 5–31.

Samuelson, P. (1938) "A note on the pure theory of consumer's behavior", *Economica*, 5 (17): 61–71.

Samuelson, P. (1947) *Foundations of Economic Analysis*, Cambridge, MA: Harvard University Press.

Samuelson, P. (1952) "Economic theory and mathematics: an appraisal", *American Economic Review*, 42 (2): 56–66.

Samuelson, P. (1963) "Problems of methodology: discussion", *American Economic Review*, 53: 231–236.

Samuelson, P. (1964) "Theory and realism: a reply", *American Economic Review*, 54: 736–739.

Samuelson, P. (1965) "Professor Samuelson on theory and realism: reply", *American Economic Review*, 55: 1164–1172.

Samuelson, P. (2001) "On just how great 'great books are'", *European Journal of the History of Economic Thought*, 8 (3): 305–308.

Schabas, M. (1985) "Some reactions to Jevons' mathematical program: the case of Cairnes and Mill", *History of Political Economy*, 17: 337–353.

Schabas, M. (1990) *A World Ruled by Number: W.S. Jevons and the Rise of Mathematical Economics*, Princeton: Princeton University Press.

Schmidt, C. (1985) *La sémantique économique en question*, Paris: Calmann-Levy.

Schumpeter, J.A. (1954) *History of Economic Analysis*, London: Allen & Unwin.

Schumpeter, J.A. (1984) "The meaning of rationality in the social sciences", *Journal of Institutional and Theoretical Economics*, 140 (4): 577–593.

Screpanti, E. and Zamagni, S. (1993) *An Outline of the History of Economic Thought*, Oxford: Oxford University Press.

Sen, A. (1977) "Rational fools: a critique of the behavioural foundations of economic theory", *Philosophy and Public Affairs*, 6 (4): 317–344.

Sen, A. (1987a) *On Ethics and Economics*, Oxford: Blackwell.

Sen, A. (1987b) "Rational behavior", in J. Eatwell et al., *The New Palgrave Dictionary of Political Economy*, London: MacMillan, vol. 4, pp. 68–76.

Sen, A. (2005) "Why exactly is commitment important for rationality?", *Economics and Philosophy*, 21: 5–13.

Sen, A. (2008) "The discipline of economics", *Economica*, 75: 617–628.

Senior, N.W. (1836) *An Outline of the Science of Political Economy*, repr. of original 6th edn. of 1872, New York: Allen & Unwin, 1965.

Sent, E.M. (1998) "Bounded rationality", in J. Davis, D.W. Hands and U. Mäki (eds) *The Handbook of Economic Methodology*, Cheltenham: E. Elgar.

Sent, E.M. (2004) "Behavioural economics: how psychology made its (limited) way back into economics", *History of Political Economy*, 36: 735–767.

Simon, H. (1955) "A behavioural model of rational choice", *Quarterly Journal of Economics*, 69: 99–118.

Simon, H. (1963) "Problems of methodology: discussion", *American Economic Review*, 53: 229–231.

Simon, H. (1996 [1969]) *The Sciences of the Artificial*, MIT Press, 3rd edn., Greek transl. Athens: Synalma, 1999.

Simon, H. (1976) "From substantive to procedural rationality", in S. Latsis (ed.) *Method and Appraisal in Economics*, Cambridge, UK: Cambridge University Press, pp. 129–148.

Simon, H. (1978) "Rationality as process and as product of thought", *American Economic Review*, 68: 1–16.

Simon, H. (1986) "Rationality in psychology and economics", *Journal of Business*, 59 (4): 209–224.

Simon, H. (1987) "Satisficing", in J. Eatwell *et al.* (eds) *The New Palgrave Dictionary of Political Economy*, London: Macmillan, vol. 4, pp. 243–244.

Simon, H. (1991) "Organizations and markets", *Journal of Economic Perspectives*, 5 (2): 25–44.

Skinner, A. (1987) "Smith, Adam", in J. Eatwell *et al.* (eds) *The New Palgrave Dictionary of Political Economy*, London: Macmillan, vol. 4, pp. 357–375.

Smelser, N.J and Swedberg, R. (1994) "The sociological perspective on the economy", in N.J Smelser and R. Swedberg (eds) *The Handbook of Economic Sociology*, Princeton: Princeton University Press, pp. 3–26.

Smith, A. (1759) *The Theory of Moral Sentiments*, Oxford: Clarendon Press, 1976.

Smith, A. (1776) *An Inquiry into the Causes and Nature of the Wealth of Nations*, Chicago: University of Chicago Press, 1976.

Smith, C. (1973) *J.S. Mill, ou la realité des sensations*, Paris: Seghers.

Smith, V. (1991) "Rational choice: the contrast between economics and psychology", *Journal of Political Economy*, 99: 877–897.

Smith, V. (1994) "Economics in the laboratory", *Journal of Economic Perspectives*, 8: 113–131.

Sobel, J. (2005) "Interdependent preferences and reciprocity", *Journal of Economic Literature*, 43: 392–436.

Song, H. (1995) "Adam Smith as an early pioneer of institutional individualism", *History of Political Economy*, 27: 425–448.

Steiner, P. (1998) *Sociologie de la connaissance économique*, Paris: Presses Universitaires de France

Steiner, P. (1999a) *La sociologie économique*, Paris: La Découverte.

Steiner, P. (1999b) "Sociologie et Economie: la théorie paretienne de l'action économique", in C. Mallandrino and R. Marchionatti (eds) *Economia, sociologia e politica nel pensiero et nell'opera di Vilfredo Pareto*, Genève: Olschi.

Steiner, P. (2003) "Pareto et Weber: action logique, rationnelle et incertitude", in M. Cherkaoui (ed.) *Mélanges en l'honneur de Giovanni Busino*, Genève: Librairie Droz.

Stigler, G.J. (1950) "The development of utility theory", in G. Stigler *Essays in the History of Economics*, Chicago: University of Chicago Press, 1965, pp. 66–155.

Stigler, G.J. and Becker, G. (1977) "De Gustibus Non Est Disputandum", *American Economic Review*, 67: 76–90.

Sugden, R. (1991) "Rational choice: a survey of contributions from economics and philosophy", *Economic Journal*, 101: 751–785.

Suzumura, K. (2005) "An interview with Paul Samuelson: Welfare Economics, 'old' and 'new', and social choice theory", *Social Choice and Welfare*, 25: 327–356.

Swedberg, R. (2000) "The social science view of entrepreneurship: introduction and practical applications", in R. Swedberg (ed.), *Entrepreneurship: The Social Science View*, Oxford: Oxford University Press.

Swedberg, R. (2011) "Max Weber's central text in economic sociology", in M. Granovetter and R. Swedberg (eds) *The Sociology of Economic Life*, Boulder, CO: West View Press, pp. 62–77.

Szenberg, M., Gottesman, A.A. and Ramrattan, L. (2005) "Paul Samuelson: philosopher and theorist", *International Journal of Social Economics*, 32 (4): 325–338.

Terlexis, P. (1999) *Max Weber*, Athens: Papazissis, 3 vols (in Greek).

Tilman, R. (2004) "Karl Manheim, Max Weber and the problem of social rationality in Thorsten Veblen", *Journal of Economic Issues*, 38: 155–172.

Tisdell, C. (1975) "Concepts of rationality in economics", *Philosophy of the Social Sciences*, 5: 259–272.

Trigilia, C. (1998) *Economic Sociology: state, market and society in modern capitalism*, Greek translation Athens: Papazisis, 2004.

Tsoulfidis, L. (2010) *Competing Schools of Economic Thought*, Berlin: Springer.

Tversky, A., Slovic P. and Kahneman D. (1990) "The causes of preference reversal", *American Economic Review*, 80: 204–217.

Varian, H. (2006) "Revealed preference", in M. Szenberg, L. Ramrattan and A.A. Gottesman (eds) *Samuelsonian Economics and the 21st century*, Oxford: University Press, pp. 99–114.

Veblen, T. (1898) "Why is economics not an evolutionary science?", *Quarterly Journal of Economics*, 13: 371–397.

Velupillai, V. (1996) "The computable alternative in the formalization of economics: a counterfactual essay", *Kyklos*, 49: 251–272.

Voisin, M.J. (1987) *Fondements psychologiques et formalisation de la théorie marginaliste de l'échange: Jevons et Edgeworth*, PhD Thesis, Université de Paris 1 (unpublished).

Vriend, N.J. (1996) "Rational behavior and economic theory", *Journal of Economic Behaviour and Organization*, 29 (2): 263–285.

Wallerstein, I. (1996) "Social science and contemporary society: the vanishing guarantees of rationality", *International Sociology*, 11 (1): 7–25.

Walras, L. (1874) *Eléments d'économie politique pure*, édition comparée de 1926, Paris: Economica, 1988.

Watkins, J.W.N. (1970) "Imperfect rationality", in R. Borger and R. Cioffi (eds) *Explanation in the Behavioral Sciences* Cambridge, UK: Cambridge University Press, pp. 167–217.

Weber, C. (2001) "Pareto and the 53 percent ordinal theory of utility", *History of Political Economy*, 33: 541–576.

Weber, M. (1904) "Objectivity in social science and social policy", reprinted in M. Weber *The Methodology of Social Sciences*, Glencoe Illinois: The Free Press, 1949.

Weber, M. (1905) *L'éthique protestante et l'esprit du capitalisme.* Paris: Plon, 1967.

Weber, M. (1917) "Le sens de la neutralité axiologique en sciences économiques et Sociologiques", in *Essais sur la théorie de la science*, Paris: Pocket, 1992.

Weber, M. (1922) *Economy and Society*, vol. I, Berkeley: University of California Press, 1978.

Weintraub, E.R. (1983) "On the existence of competitive equilibrium: 1930–1954", *Journal of Economic Literature*, 21: 1–39.

Weintraub, E.R. (1998) "Axiomatisches Mißverständnis", *Economic Journal*, 108: 1837–47.

Weintraub, E.R. (2002) *How Economics became a Mathematical Science*, Durham, NC: Duke University Press.

West, E.G. (1996) "Adam Smith on the cultural effects of specialization: Splenetics versus Economics", *History of Political Economy*, 28: 83–106.

Whitaker, J.K. (1975) "John Stuart Mill's methodology", *Journal of Political Economy*, 83: 1033–1050.

Whitaker, J.K. (2006) "The early economic writings", in T. Raffaelli, G. Beccatini and M. Dardi, *The Elgar Companion to Alfred Marshall*, Cheltenham, UK: E. Elgar.

White, M. (1989) "Why are there no supply and demand curves in Jevons?", *History of Political Economy*, 21: 425–456.

White, M. (1991) "Jevons 'blunder' concerning value and distribution: an explanation", *Cambridge Journal of Economics*, 15: 149–160.

White, M. (1994) "The moment of Richard Jennings: the production of Jevons's marginalist economic agent", in P. Mirowski (ed.) *Natural Images in Economic Thought*, Cambridge, UK: Cambridge University Press, pp. 197–230.

White, M. (2004) "In the lobby of the Energy Hotel: Jevons' formulation of the postclassical 'economic problem'", *History of Political Economy*, 36: 227–271.

Wicksteed, P.H. (1910) *The Common Sense of Political Economy, Including a Study of the Human Basis of Economic Law*, London: Macmillan.

Williamson, O.E. (1985) *The Economic Institutions of Capitalism*, New York: The Free Press.

Williamson, O.E. (1993) "Calculativeness, trust and economic organization", *Journal of Law and Economics*, 36: 453–86.

Williamson, O.E. (1994) "Transaction costs economics and organization theory". In N.J. Smelser and R. Swedberg, *Handbook of Economic Sociology.* Princeton: Princeton University Press, pp. 77–107.

Winch, D. (1970) "Introduction", in J.S. Mill *Principles of Political Economy*, Harmondsworth: Penguin Books, 1985.

Winch, D. (1972) "Marginalism and the boundaries of economic science", *History of Political Economy*, 4: 325–345.

Winch, D. (1996) *Riches and Poverty. An Intellectual History of Political Economy in England 1750–1834*, Cambridge, UK: Cambridge University Press.

Winch, P. (1958) *The Idea of a Social Science and its Relation to Philosophy*, 2nd edn. London: Routledge, 1990.

Wong, S. (1973) "The 'F-twist' and the methodology of Paul Samuelson", *American Economic Review*, 63 (3): 312–325.

Wong, S. (1978) *The Foundations of Paul Samuelson's Revealed Preference Theory*, London: Routledge.

Zafirowski, M. (2001) "Max Weber's analysis of marginal utility theory and psychology revisited: latent propositions in economic sociology and the sociology of economics", *History of Political Economy*, 33: 437–458.

Zafirowski, M. (2008) "Classical and neoclassical conceptions of rationality: findings of an exploratory survey", *Journal of Socio-Economics*, 37: 789–820.

Zelizer, V. (2006) "Circuits in economic life", *Economic Sociology: The European Electronic Newsletter*, 8 (1): 30–35.

Zouboulakis, M.S. (1993) *La science économique à la recherche de ses fondements. La tradition épistémologique ricardienne, 1826–1891*, Paris: Presses Universitaires de France.

Zouboulakis, M.S. (1995) "Le débat sur le réalisme des hypothèses dans les années 1870", *Revue Economique*, 46: 973–981.

Zouboulakis, M.S. (1997a) "Mill and Jevons: two concepts of economic rationality", *History of Economic Ideas*, 5: 7–25.

Zouboulakis, M.S. (1997b) "L'individualisme méthodologique de Popper est-il défendable?" *Social Science Information*, 36, 3: 493–505.

Zouboulakis, M.S. (2000) "Une critique de la schizophrénie méthodologique", *Economies et Sociétés*, Série PE, N°30: 121–132.

Zouboulakis, M.S. (2001) "From Mill to Weber: the meaning of the concept of economic rationality", *European Journal of the History of Economic Thought*, 8 (1): 42–57.

Zouboulakis, M.S. (2002) "John Stuart Mill's institutional individualism", *History of Economic Ideas*, 10 (3): 29–45.

Zouboulakis, M.S. (2005a) "On the social nature of rationality in Adam Smith and John Stuart Mill", *Cahiers d'Economie Politique*, 49: 51–63.

Zouboulakis, M. (2005b) "On the evolutionary character of North's idea of institutional change", *Journal of Institutional Economics*, 1 (2): 145–158.

Zouboulakis, M.S. (2007) *Problems of Method in Economics*, Volos: University of Thessaly Press (in Greek).

Zouboulakis, M.S. (2010a) "Samuelson's economic methodology", in K. Loizos (ed.) *Paul Anthony Samuelson (1915–2009)*, Athens: Metamesonykties Ekdoseis (in Greek).

Zouboulakis, M.S. (2010b) "Trustworthiness as a moral determinant of economic activity: lessons from the classics", *Forum for Social Economics*, 39 (3): 209–221.

Zouboulakis, M.S. and Kamarianos, J. (2002) "Rationality and cooperation between firms: testing habitual behavior in Greek industries", *Revista d'Economia Institucional*, 7 (Dec): 98–113 (in Spanish).

Index

Page numbers in **bold** denote figures.

Printed in the United States
by Baker & Taylor Publisher Services